Redeveloping Brownfields

• LANDSCAPE ARCHITECTS • PLANNERS • DEVELOPERS

Thomas H. Russ, ASLA, REM

McGraw-Hill

New York   San Francisco   Washington, D.C.   Auckland   Bogotá
Caracas   Lisbon   London   Madrid   Mexico City   Milan
Montreal   New Delhi   San Juan   Singapore
Sydney   Tokyo   Toronto

Cataloging-in-Publication Data for this title is on file with the Library of Congress.

McGraw-Hill

A Division of The McGraw·Hill Companies

1 2 3 4 5 6 7 8 9 0   DOC/DOC   9 0 4 3 2 1 0 9

P/N 0-07-135729-7
ISBN 0-07-135311-9

The sponsoring editor for this book was Wendy Lochner, the editing supervisor was Steven Melvin, and the production supervisor was Pamela Pelton. It was set in Matt Antique by Joanne Morbit of McGraw-Hill's Hightstown, NJ, Professional Book Group composition unit.

Printed and bound by R. R. Donnelley & Sons Company.

 This book is printed on acid-free paper.

Contents

Introduction

Planning and Redeveloping Brownfields has been written to meet the needs of landscape architects, engineers, and site planners familiar with site design issues but unfamiliar with the issues encountered on contaminated or previously developed properties. From this book, the site design professional may become familiar with the environmental site assessment process and protocols and able to incorporate the work of the environmental professional into his or her own work. The book will also help the site designer understand and communicate the environmental issues to others in the role as lead project professional.

Brownfields are defined as properties that are underutilized or abandoned because of the presence or perception of environmental contamination. In the past, site designers could assume when they began their work that a site was clean or would be when construction began. Environmental contamination was a condition that would be addressed by other professionals and need not be a significant consideration in the new site design. Brownfield redevelopment is an emerging area of practice, and as such, there are opportunities as the body of knowledge and state of the practice are defined. There are few organized specific resources available for site designers working on brownfield sites; thus the purpose of this book is to begin to respond to that need and to begin the conversation about what works. And what doesn't.

It has been my experience that there are substantial advantages to be gained by incorporating the environmental issues into the site planning on many brownfield sites. It has also been my experience that the environmental work and site design processes are usually performed in nearly complete isolation from one another.

Changes in public policy, concern about suburban sprawl, and urban undercrowding have led to new opportunities for site design professionals in cities of all sizes. The redevelopment of contaminated sites is an emerging area of practice that will require landscape architects and site engineers to work closer with environmental professionals than has been the case in the past. Unlike the environmental professional, the site design professional has historically taken the lead in the development of land and, as such, can embrace the requirements of the practice of brownfield redevelopment more immediately than the environmental professional can learn land planning. The incorporation of the issues of stakeholders has been a routine part of the site professional's practice. With some notable exceptions, the methods used on brownfield sites are more often modifications of familiar land development practices than entirely new technology. Even new technologies such as phytoremediation employ some knowledge and techniques familiar to site designers. Site designers need to acquire the language of site redevelopment and gain an understanding of the methods of the environmental professional to be effective project leaders on redevelopment projects.

The policies and laws that comprise the history of the brownfield issue and the state of current policy and law that influence the practice of redevelopment are summarized in Chapter 1. The history of brownfields is in part a history of environmental law in the United States. The major pieces of legislation are discussed as well as more recent federal and state policy tends. The importance of the public policy to the site designer is in the principles of environmental law and regulations that continue to shape the use of impacted sites even after redevelopment in some cases. A working knowledge of these principles is critical if the design professional is to represent the client's interests in this arena and communicate effectively with environmental professionals and to understand how changes in public policy may affect one's practice.

The methods employed by environmental professionals have their own well-defined nomenclature and principles. To fully appreciate and assess the work of the environmental professional, the site professional will also need to acquire a working knowledge of the methods and nomenclature. Chapter 2 outlines the environmental site assessment process from the Phase I through to the planning and implementation of the Phase II. The limits and scope of the environmental site assessment are important elements of the early work the site designer must incorporate into the site design. Understanding the limits of a site assessment is critically important when evaluating the risk assessment data for a site. There are a number of site assessment methods and protocols, but the most widely used standard is the standard published by the American Society of Testing and Materials (ASTM). Chapter 2 gives an overview of the ASTM key site assessment guidance documents including discussion of key terms and underlying assumptions built into the standards. Other standards are mentioned to provide the reader with a glimpse into the variety of methods and practices relied upon by the environmental professional. Chapter 2 also provides an introduction into the planning and methods employed in environmental sampling. The design professional should have an understanding of these methods and the associated terms in order to better communicate and understand the work of other professionals.

Once a site assessment is completed, it is the site designer who must work the data into the proposed site redevelopment program. The reader is introduced to the concept of risk assessment and risk-based decision making. Guidelines to the communication process are included in a section on risk communication. Finally, Chapter 2 lists and describes the major or most common contaminants and briefly describes the sources and health effects. The chapter provides the site professional with an introduction to the language of the environmental site assessment process.

Chapter 3 focuses on the broad range of planning issues facing the site planner. Chief among these concerns is interaction with the various stakeholders or parties with an interest in a given project. Stakeholders range from landowners and developers, to lenders and regulatory agencies, to public officials and neighbors. Most site planners have experience in addressing the concerns of stakeholders and are familiar with preparing for and conducting public hearings and meetings. Brownfield projects differ from these projects primarily because of the issues of contamination associated with the site. Site professionals must become adept at discussing the environmental and health risks associated with their projects and relating these risks to the design proposal. Chapter 3 expands the discussion of risk assessment introduced in Chapter 2 and explores the concept of environmental risk. The relationship between risk and exposure and the differences between lifestyle risks and environmental risks are discussed. The use of contaminated material in the design and construction of the redeveloped site is also discussed in the contexts of material handling and the general engineering properties of soils.

Chapter 3 outlines the range of possible redevelopment strategies available for brownfield projects. The discussion on redevelopment includes a description of the advantages and disadvantages of the strategies as well as some of the cost implications. Remediation technology is also outlined in this chapter to provide the design professional with a grounding in the terms and types of technology used most often on brownfield sites. Introductory discussions of bioremediation and phytoremediation are included. Finally Chapter 3 outlines the concept of life cycle assessment, which is of concern to the brownfield site designer. The nature of contaminated sites may require designers to rethink concepts of design life and project costs. The question of the costs of obsolescence may be a new consideration for designers and developers but may be extremely important on some projects.

Managing storm water on the redevelopment site is a critical element in site design and a particular challenge to designers. While there are often issues of contamination, many brownfield sites were originally developed without storm water controls or facilities and are located in urban settings that offer precious little extra space to develop new facilities. Chapter 4 addresses many of the challenges designers may face on such difficult sites. Strategies for sites with impermeable caps are discussed as well as infiltration systems and the treatment characteristics of each system. The adaptation of best management practices to fit site constraints is discussed. The anticipated impact of the NPDES Phase II rules due to be enforced in the year 2000 is also addressed. Different types of impermeable and permeable caps used on brownfield sites are described, and storm water management strategies for each are discussed. The chapter focuses on the use of infiltration as the first-choice approach but recognizes that conditions on some brownfield sites are such that infiltration is to be discouraged. The design of storm water facilities with the greatest capability for improving water quality is of particular importance on brownfield sites, and a variety of methods and their relative capabilities are presented in Chapter 4.

Chapter 5 is concerned with the use of plants on the brownfield site. In many cases it is considered that the presence of the cap precludes the use of significant vegetation on these sites; in other cases the levels of contamination may inhibit plant vigor. These and other conditions common to brownfields are discussed, and suggested design solutions are offered for the reader's consideration. Particular attention is paid to improving soil quality and saving existing vegetation as well as suggesting plants with tolerances that may make them suitable to brownfield sites. A discussion of phytoremediation includes the advantages and disadvantages of phytoremediation. The use of genetically engineered materials is also discussed.

The site design must include a consideration of the conditions on the site during construction, and Chapter 6 outlines some areas of concern. While site professionals are familiar with the design of erosion and sediment controls, brownfield sites include the added element of potentially contaminated sediment. The integrity of the erosion and sediment control plan is a critical everyday concern on the disturbed brownfield site. The principles of erosion and sediment control are described in the context of brownfield site issues. The discussion includes issues of site management that may fall beyond the design professional's responsibilities but that should be built into the site design and erosion and sediment control planning. The development and use of a preparedness, prevention, and contingency plan as described in the NPDES nonpoint source program regulations is also described to provide the designer preparing the erosion plan on a brownfield with a description of the additional elements that could be anticipated.

The impact of expanding a professional practice to include brownfield work is the subject of Chapter 7. The pollution exclusion contained in most professional errors and omissions insurance and how it might affect the practice is addressed early in the chapter. The risks to the firm in expanding their relationship or in taking an equity position on a brownfield project are also described. Much of Chapter 7 is concerned with the development of health and safety plans for the design staff and the communication of risk to staff and readers of the final plans. The aspects of a health and safety plan are included in the text. Finally, the chapter discusses the hiring and managing of the design professional as a subcontractor and evaluating the work of the environmental professional.

The appendix lists the current *risk-based concentrations* (RBC) prepared by the EPA, Region 3. This RBC list provides the reader with an easy reference with which to compare environmental reports. Also included is a glossary of terms used throughout the book.

Redeveloping Brownfields offers a broad view of the state of the practice as it is today. As we continue to learn more and as the redevelopment of impacted sites becomes more common, we may expect new methods and innovative approaches to develop as more design professionals are faced with the problems of brownfields. We should expect more collaborations with environmental professionals, expanding to include biotechnology professionals, as landscape architects and site engineers begin to include the considerations of remediation and the functions of microflora and microfauna in their designs.

Thomas H. Russ

Acknowledgments

This book would not have been possible without the support of many people. The process of professional maturation is an education over time, with many teachers. I owe much to the teachers, mentors, and colleagues who have taught me the important lessons of life and my profession. Tom Mudra, Dale Buck, Dr. Richard Jarvis, Robert B. Ludgate, PE, PLS, Richard Stauffer, ASLA, Edward Black, RLA, Gary Cupples, PLS, and Dr. Jack Treadway. William W. Montley, CHMM, Robert Ludgate, PE, PLS, and Dr. Frank Pine were instrumental in the critical review of the initial ideas and proposal. Thank you to Charles Lee, PE, for his support during the preparation of this book. William Carroll, PLS, prepared all of the construction details and line drawings. Thank you to Ira Whitman, PE, for permitting the use of his comparison of remedial action methods. This book was completed with the support and important criticism of William W. Montley, CHMM. The best of this work is a reflection of their knowledge and professionalism. Finally, a special thank you to Karla Baccene for her patience, important and valued criticism, enthusiasm, support, encouragement, and love throughout this process.

CHAPTER 1

Legal Environment of Brownfields

Brownfields are generally defined as abandoned and underutilized industrial properties that are known or suspected to be contaminated. Various researchers estimate that from 25,000 to 400,000 sites across the United States may be considered brownfields. While these properties are generally considered a legacy of the urban-industrial past, brownfields are also found in small towns and rural areas throughout the United States. Increasing competition and global economic forces have been largely responsible for the redistribution of industrial resources, and the attendant devaluation of environmentally suspect industrial and commercial property. The existing large inventory of such properties has been the unintended consequence of environmental public policy and real estate market responses. Thus brownfields stand as both an opportunity for recovering urban land and as a reminder of the harmful and wasteful practices of the past.

Brownfields

Brownfields have come to present a major challenge to communities across the United States, representing simultaneously the vestige of former industrial employers, lost tax revenues, and costly environmental problems. A study of the brownfields in 200 cities with populations greater than 30,000 was conducted by the U.S. Conference of Mayors in January 1996. The 39 cities that responded said they did have brownfields; in fact, together they reported that there were more than 20,000 such properties. The impacted area from 36 of these cities totaled more than 43,000 acres. The estimates of total annual tax losses among 33 of these cities ranged from $121 million to $386 million. The study found that city size was not a relevant factor in predicting where brownfields were located: Half of all cities responding to the study had a population under 100,000. The mayors used this study to leverage awareness of the scale and impact of the brownfield issue in urban areas already struggling with lowered revenues and resources.

Until the 1990s the challenge to redevelop contaminated properties was restrained by problematic public policy, reluctant lenders, and significant financial risks. Since then, however, the opportunities for redevelopment have improved dramatically. Currently 35 states have some type of voluntary cleanup program, and the federal and state governments have enabled a variety of incentives to encourage redevelopment by the public sector. The purpose of these voluntary cleanup programs is to make redevelopment of these sites attractive to private investors so that they will assume all or part of the burden of stabilizing or mitigating the environmental problems on the sites. While these changes are encouraging, the redevelopment of environmentally impacted or contaminated properties is still very much an emerging area of professional practice for landscape architects and site designers.

Brownfields may present a designer with a wide range of unfamiliar site restrictions and conditions. Foremost among these is the realization that the site is contaminated to some degree. Site designs must account for the mitigation of contamination to protect the users and the environment. Normal practices of landscape planting and storm water management may be severely restricted on such sites. On the other hand, landscape architects may find on such sites the opportunity to design landscapes that actually improve the environmental conditions. These sites require new combinations of design and plant materials, which may require designers to work closely with other professionals and scientists.

Site designers in the past have had the luxury of presuming that a site was "clean" unless otherwise informed. In the event of redevelopment of an impacted site, the designer was usually not involved in the remedial action design; sites were cleaned up, and then the redevelopment occurred as if on a clean site. As private money is attracted into the redevelopment of impacted sites, the opportunities and need for creative solutions emerge. As in any emerging area of practice, there are innumerable circumstances for innovation. Each situation advances the individual practice as well as the scope of the profession. To be effective participants in a brownfield project, landscape architects and site engineers should consult an environmental professional who understands the value and limitations of the site assessment process. This collaboration will ensure that the most up-to-date and innovative site remediation technologies are utilized.

Historical Approach to Land Use and Planning

The history of land use in the United States reflects the social and political history of the country. During colonial times, land use was governed by the principles of common law and the founding fathers' belief that property rights are "natural rights," or rights intrinsic to the individual. The framers of the Constitution believed that certain rights are natural—that is, they are neither derived from nor given by government. Representative government is based on the premise that the state's rights are not greater than the individual's rights. Property rights are a natural right. When the activities of government or of individuals encroach upon the rights of an individual, the individual has a right to compensation. Furthermore, the return on the encroachment, or taking, must be greater than the cost to the individual. Thus, in the colonial period, efforts to control the use of land as private property were unpopular and rarely successful—after all, the country was young, and there was a seemingly limitless supply of land. The mood of the times was better described by the concept of Manifest Destiny than by local zoning regulations.

Innovation in land use and land planning was accepted slowly. Incremental changes in people's expectations and values evolved over time, with experience. As towns grew and industry developed, popular opinion began to favor some types of controls, and the Supreme Court reflected this attitudinal change when it agreed in 1924 that private property is subject to control. In *Euclid v. Ambler Realty,* the Supreme Court decided that local government had the right to regulate land use in districts and to direct growth within their districts. This decision essentially extended the power of government to an important role beyond the existing common law controls. The decision still favored landowners to the extent that the burden of proof was on a municipality to show why a regulation should be enforced. If challenged, the municipality would have to demonstrate specific harm that would be mitigated by the regulation. In cases after *Euclid,* governments were given wider authority and power to regulate and control land use and development.

Eventually, however, it was successfully demonstrated to the courts that many exclusionary zoning practices in force were economically or socially discriminatory.

The power to regulate land use has evolved since *Euclid* with subsequent cases tried before the Supreme Court, and more recent cases have defined the limits of local land use controls. In the latest round of land use decisions by the courts, governments have been restricted in their power and have been shown to have a duty to not discriminate in zoning practices. Home rule has been placed under requirements, and democratization has been injected into the local planning process. Since the 1960s popular opinion has shifted to support regulations that protect human and environmental health. More recently the public has recognized in a general sense that land use regulatory practices are not sustainable and that a new round of changes may be necessary. There is a growing realization that to have a healthy environment, we must find ways to make cities work environmentally, economically, and socially.

The Emergence of Brownfields

In the 1970s and 1980s federal legislation was passed to regulate the cleanup of polluted industrial sites. This legislation established the "Superfund" and laws governing the cleanup of contaminated places. The legislation required that a buyer might have to assume the liability to clean up environmental contamination from past activities conducted on a particular site, without regard for actual fault. An effect of the federal and state Superfund laws was to create an extremely risk sensitive commercial and industrial real estate marketplace. Buyers were reluctant to assume the risk of the often-exorbitant costs of environmental liability, and sellers were reluctant to be listed in the chain of title because it would render them potentially liable for any pollution discovered on the site.

In the early 1990s many of the cities in the former Rust Belt found their industrial land and infrastructure undervalued and underutilized. Although environmental public policy was only one of a number of contributing factors, it was one factor that could be changed. The history of Superfund cleanups on both the federal and state levels had been dismal: At one point the few successful federal cleanups had averaged more than $32 million each. Although these sites were clearly the worst of the worst, more than 25,000 other sites were listed on the Environmental Protection Agency's Comprehensive Environmental Response, Compensation and Liability Act (CERCLA) National Priority List, with no realistic prospect of resolution. The number of sites in state programs exceeded even this. As a result, in historically industrial areas of cities, property values and conditions declined as risk-averse buyers looked to new, presumably uncontaminated, sites.

The law provided several means by which a landowner might defend herself or himself from claims of liability. The most common of these was the *Innocent Landowner Defense,* which required a landowner to make an appropriate inquiry into the historic use and current condition of land prior to purchase and be able to demonstrate that, as a result of this inquiry, there was no knowledge or reason to know of environmental contamination. The stipulation to include the environmental condition of a property in the buyer's normal prepurchase due diligence has led to a demand for entirely new types of environmental services.

Federal Laws Impacting Brownfields

National Environmental Policy Act

Many environmental protection laws were passed prior to 1970, but they accomplished very little in relation to the fast-growing pollution problems plaguing cities and towns.

Increasingly the American people were becoming dissatisfied with empty programs and toothless legislation. To address the growing concern, the first meaningful public policy regarding the environment was developed.

The National Environmental Policy Act (NEPA) was passed in 1969 and signed into law by President Nixon on New Year's Day, 1970. Although the NEPA regulates only those activities of the federal government, it has had far-reaching impacts in the private sector because all federal facilities and permits must pass an NEPA impact inquiry. The NEPA is important because it is a strong and enforceable law. Most important, though, the NEPA articulates a national environmental policy with specific goals. The Supreme Court has held that the NEPA did not create new enforceable "rights." Nevertheless, the law does stipulate administrative procedures that must be followed.

The NEPA was a small, but incredibly significant first step toward environmental regulation of land use. Historically, the enforcement elements of the NEPA were, and still are, an uncommon act of Congress. It is generally believed that most of the congressional lawmakers did not understand the enforcement power of the law or grossly underestimated it (Orloff and Brooks 1980). At the time, Congress was in a rush to adjourn for the Christmas holidays, and most wanted to show their constituents some legislative progress on environmental issues. Congressional historians believe that most of the members of Congress who voted for the bill believed it to be merely a statement of policy with no enforcement elements. Over time, however, the NEPA has proven to be quite powerful. It was also the first of a series of important and meaningful environmental protection laws.

The power in the NEPA is found in Title I, Sec. 102(c), which requires the government to "report on proposals for legislation and other major Federal actions significantly affecting the quality of the human environment, a detailed statement by the responsible official on—(i) the environmental impact of the proposed action, (ii) and adverse environmental effects which cannot be avoided should the proposal be implemented, [and] (iii) alternatives to the action...." This statement is the basis for the involved environmental impact statements to obtain the NEPA permits required for all government-funded projects.

The NEPA has had profound effects on the way the government and private sectors conduct business. The implementation of the NEPA is also a useful example of how societal change occurs incrementally and often very slowly. Its passage is also an example of change that evolves first at the grassroots level; the NEPA was passed largely in an attempt to mollify the public.

Superfund

In 1980, after the outcry over Love Canal and the recognition of many similar kinds of problems in other places, Congress enacted the Comprehensive Environmental Response, Compensation and Liability Act (CERCLA), also known as the "Superfund act." The act mandated the cleanup of contaminated sites and established a system of ranking them. Suspect sites were placed on a list known as the Comprehensive Environmental Response Compensation and Liability System, or CERCLIS, list. Each site was visited and evaluated, and those that ranked the highest were put on the National Priority List (NPL). Sites on the NPL were considered the worst of the worst and were slated for action by the EPA. Those named on only the CERCLIS list were simply left there, although some might have been ranked on an individual state equivalent of the NPL. In any case there was no effective mechanism for removing a site from the CERCLIS list, and few people had an interest in becoming involved with properties known to be CERCLIS sites. As part of the move in the 1990s to encourage state activities in brownfield redevelopment, the EPA delisted 25,000 sites by designating them as *no further remedial action planned* (NFRAP) *sites.*

The law defines who is responsible for the cleanup. Responsible parties are current owners and operators, any prior owner or operator who owned or operated the site when hazardous substances were diagnosed, the generators of the hazardous substances, and the transporters that brought the material to the site. *Responsible parties* (RPs) are liable for the cleanup costs incurred by the government and/or other persons, damage to the environment, and costs of health assessments. The average cleanup cost of a Superfund site has been about $30 million. Possible defenses to avoid liability include an act of God, an act of war, and an innocent landowner.

The law also states that responsible parties are to be strictly liable as well as joint and severally liable. *Strict liability* refers to liability without fault—that is, a person may be held liable simply by owning a property regardless of whether he or she has contributed to the contamination. *Joint and several liability* means that liability may not be proportional—that is, even if a party is responsible for only a small portion of the contamination, he or she could be held liable for the entire cost of a cleanup. The justifiable concern over acquiring the liability for environmental cleanups chilled the industrial real estate market. An unanticipated consequence of the CERCLA was reduced sales of existing industrial properties. Bankers elected to not fund projects for fear of liability. Buyers opted for lower-risk, undeveloped sites rather than former industrial sites.

The CERCLA requires that a buyer make an appropriate inquiry into the history of a site, especially its ownership and use. An *innocent landowner* is a property owner who can demonstrate that he or she acquired the property by no action of his or her own (for example, if he or she inherited the property) or that, at the time of purchase, he or she exercised "good commercial or customary practice" in investigating the property before purchase. A person that acquires a property after hazardous material has been disposed of on the property may not be liable if, at the time of acquiring the property, that person made a commercially reasonable investigation and, as a result of that investigation, had no reason to believe the land was contaminated. When judging a person's investigation, a court is supposed to consider whether the defendant had any specialized knowledge or experience, the relationship of the purchase price to the uncontaminated value of the property, and whether it was reasonable for a person to know of or to detect contamination on the property. Clearly, real estate and design professionals would be held to a higher standard due to their specialized knowledge and site evaluation training.

Since the passage of the CERCLA and the beginning of formal *environmental site assessments* (ESAs), the professional practice has changed as information has become more accessible, new disclosure laws have been passed, and standards have been established by professional groups and lenders. The completion of an ESA requires adhering to standards of professional practice that are, in turn, based on a knowledge of science, business-industrial processes, and laws and regulations.

Resource Conservation and Recovery Act

The Resource Conservation and Recovery Act (RCRA) regulates the generators, transporters, and treaters of hazardous wastes. It was the RCRA that articulated the cradle-to-grave concept in federal law and the statute that defines *hazardous wastes*. The act was first passed in 1970 as the Resource Recovery Act, an amended form of the 1965 Solid Waste Disposal Act. It was amended in 1976 and passed as the Resource Conservation and Recovery Act. The 1984 amendments are known as the "Hazardous and Solid Waste Amendments." The RCRA establishes that a solid waste is a hazardous waste if it:

1. Exhibits the characteristics of a hazardous waste (ignitability, corrosivity, toxicity, and reactivity)

2. Has been specifically named and is listed

3. Is not specifically excluded

Table 1.1 explains the criteria in greater detail.

Table 1.1   Identifying Hazardous Wastes

Materials are wastes only if they are discarded, abandoned, or disposed of. Materials stored indefinitely (90 days) may be considered wastes. A waste may be considered as hazardous according to the following criteria:

1. It is ignitable if it is a liquid, unless it contains less than 24% alcohol, it has a flash point of less than 60°C (140°F) or is a nonliquid capable under normal conditions of spontaneous combustion, it is an ignitable compressed gas, or it is an oxidized per DOT.
2. It is corrosive if it is a liquid with a pH less than or equal to 2 or greater than 12.5, or it can corrode steel at a rate greater than $1/4$ inch per year at 55°C (130°F).
3. It is normally unstable and reacts violently with water, it reacts violently without detonating, generates fumes, gases, or vapors when mixed with water, it contains cyanide or sulfide and generates vapors between 2 and 12.5 pH, or it is capable of detonation under normal pressure and temperature.
4. It has the capacity to leach hazardous constituents at concentrations listed in the regulations. The toxicity of a substance is determined by the *toxicity characteristics leaching procedure* (TCLP).
5. It is a listed hazardous waste on one of RCRA three lists of hazardous waste.

A material is not a hazardous waste if it has been identified as exempt. These wastes include but are not limited to the following:

6. A household waste.
7. A waste from agricultural operations that is used as a fertilizer.
8. Mining overburden that is reused at the mine site.
9. Wastes from burning coal by utilities.
10. Drilling wastes from oil and natural gas drilling.
11. Wastes generated in the extraction, benefaction, and processing of natural resource ores.
12. Cement kiln waste dusts.
13. Arsenic-treated wood waste generated by end users.
14. Certain chromium-bearing wastes.

Hazardous waste generators, transporters, and treaters are required to keep detailed records. There are specific storage requirements for spill containment and the length of time a waste can be stored before a facility's designation is changed from a "hazardous waste generator" to a "storage facility." Allowances for small-quantity generators are less stringent than they are for large-quantity generators.

Clean Water Act

The Clean Water Act was passed in 1972 as the Federal Water Pollution Control Act. It was amended and renamed in 1977. The law is concerned primarily with the control of toxic water pollutants. In 1987 and 1996 Congress passed extensive amendments to improve water quality in areas where compliance with minimum discharge standards was insufficient to meet water quality goals. The Clean Water Act has five main elements:

1. A system of national effluent standards for each type of business

2. Water quality standards

3. A National Pollution Discharge Elimination System (NPDES), which is a discharge permit program

4. Provisions for special problems such as oil spills

5. A construction loan fund for *publicly owned treatment works* (POTWs)

NPDES AND NONPOINT SOURCE RUNOFF PROGRAMS

Of these, it is the NPDES program that has the greatest impact on site development. The NPDES regulations are concerned with both point source and nonpoint source pollution. It is a permitting program that requires dischargers to disclose the nature and quantity of their discharges. The Clean Water Act gives the EPA the authority to specify pollution limits. *Point sources* are discrete effluent points such as pipes and are most often linked to industries or POTWs. Point-source operators have been required to have NPDES permits for more than 10 years. These permits require keeping detailed records for 3 years. The EPA further requires that all nonpermit events be reported within 24 hours and that written confirmation be supplied within 5 days.

Regulating nonpoint sources has been more difficult. *Nonpoint sources* refers to water pollution that cannot be attributed to a discrete process or point of discharge but that derives instead from, for example, storm water runoff. Implementation of the Nonpoint Source Program was delayed until 1992, at which time the states were required to implement the Phase I rules. Phase I rules dealt with larger cities and certain industries, including the construction industry. The need to plan and direct the use of land and land-based activities to protect the quality of surface and groundwater is a generally accepted principle of planning. The NPDES was created to address both point sources and nonpoint sources of pollution. The NPDES permit process is directed toward individual political subdivisions, landowners, and discrete points of discharge. This approach has achieved important results in reducing the quantity and toxic impacts of industrial and public sewage pollution discharges. The nonpoint Source (NPS) Phase I Program has undertaken the regulation of storm water runoff from industrial and larger construction sites as well as municipalities with storm water collection systems serving more than 100,000 people (see Table 1.2).

During Phase II, additional areas will be governed by NPS regulations, including commercial, retail, institutional, and smaller construction sites, as well as municipalities with storm water systems serving fewer than 100,000 people. Much of this regulation will affect previously unregulated facilities built without allowances for storm water

Table 1.2   Nonpoint Source Pollutants

Pollutant	Source	Impacts
Sediment	Construction and agriculture	Destruction of aquatic habitat
Nutrients	Agriculture and suburban lawns	Contributes to eutrophication of surface waters; destruction of aquatic habitat; health threats to infants
Human and animal wastes	Domestic animal wastes, farm wastes, wastewater treatment, septic systems	Source of nutrients, disease; contributes to eutrophication of surface waters, destruction of aquatic habitat
Pesticides	Agriculture and suburban use	Damage to aquatic vegetation and animals; bioaccumulation
Hydrocarbons	Fuel stations, parking lots	Poison to aquatic life, birds; damage to vegetation

quality control. In many instances affected facilities would previously have been built without any on-site storm water management systems. The NPS regulations may require local agencies to rethink traditional strategies for meeting water quality regulations and storm water management objectives.

Pressure and conflicts at the local level will increase in frequency and fervor as the scope of NPS regulations begins to narrow and shift away from "institutional polluters." To date the impacts have fallen primarily on industry, government, and business. The Phase II regulations will continue to focus on these constituent groups; however, the scope will involve smaller businesses, small local governments, schools, and institutions. As the issues of NPS pollution and storm water management are impressed on smaller groups, the challenge to develop effective regulatory programs, educate the public, and administer the programs will become more acute. Public officials and agencies will have to seek new approaches for involvement and participation in the design of these policies and programs if they are to succeed.

Until recently, runoff was regulated only in particular industries. In 1988 the scope of regulation expanded to include a broader range of industries, including construction sites over 5 acres and municipalities with separate storm sewers serving more than 100,000 people. In 1995, the Phase II NPDES NPS rules were promulgated, and they require permitting of commercial, retail, light industrial, and institutional sites, construction sites of less than 5 acres, and cities with storm sewers serving fewer than 100,000 people.

Other Laws

SAFE DRINKING WATER ACT

The Safe Drinking Water Act was first passed in 1974 and has been amended several times. Where the Clean Water Act established the permit programs for water discharges, the Safe Drinking Water Act regulates drinking water quality. It does this through the imposition of water quality standards called *maximum contaminant levels,* or MCLs. The Safe Drinking Water Act is important to those engaged in brownfield redevelopment because it is the statutory basis for the MCLs that are sometimes used as a default cleanup standard in remediation projects. The MCLs present a very difficult cleanup standard for a project.

TOXIC SUBSTANCES CONTROL ACT

The passage of the Toxic Substances Control Act (TSCA) in 1976 gave the EPA the responsibility for protecting human health and the environment from toxic chemicals used in commerce. The law serves to regulate substances not adequately covered by the RCRA and the CERCLA. Among the activities regulated by the TSCA are PCBs, dioxins, and asbestos. The law also regulates other toxic substances and the introduction of new toxic substances used in commerce.

SUPERFUND AMENDMENTS AND REAUTHORIZATION ACT

In 1986 Congress responded to needed changes in the CER-CLA by passing the Superfund Amendments and Reauthorization Act (SARA). The law included an administrative element to provide additional funding for Superfund cleanups, but, from a practical standpoint in terms of brownfield development, the law is most important for the Worker Right-to-Know (Title II) and Emergency Planning and Community Right-to-Know (Title III). The Worker Right-to-Know required the development of standards for the protection of workers employed in site or spill cleanups. The result was the OSHA 40-hour program for hazardous waste workers.

Although passed as Title III of SARA, the Emergency Planning and Community Right-to-Know Act (EPCRA) stands alone in most discussions of applicable laws and regulations. This law has its origin in the 1984 chemical disaster in Bhopal, India, in which approximately 2500 people were killed and tens of thousands were injured when methyl isocyanate gas was released from a chemical plant. Soon after the Bhopal incident, the American public became concerned when a chemical release occurred in West Virginia. Although the West Virginia event was not on the scale of Bhopal, it served to raise serious concerns among the American public. Congress responded to the public concern: "Can it happen here?" The EPCRA requires each state to establish an emergency response commission to work with local officials to prepare emergency response plans that address the concerns of the specific community. Facilities with the characteristics that are identified in the law are required to provide the *local emergency planning committee* (LEPC) and local fire and emergency services with the information that would be required to assure public safety in the event of an emergency. Typical information includes the location of hazardous materials, tanks, pressurized equipment, fire protection facilities, and the identification of responsible facility personnel.

INTERMODAL SURFACE TRANSPORTATION ACT

The Intermodal Surface Transportation and Energy Act (ISTEA) was hailed as a landmark in transportation legislation because it required transportation planning to consider social, economic, community, and environmental factors. Among the ISTEA requirements is that transportation plans be consistent with federal, state, and local energy programs. The law also requires that plans need to relieve congestion and to prevent congestion as well as take a long-term view to land use and development.

AMERICANS WITH DISABILITIES ACT

The Americans with Disabilities Act (ADA) was passed to protect disabled people from discrimination in the workplace and in public facilities. Title III of ADA requires public buildings to meet minimum standards and make reasonable accommodations for disabled people. Occasionally, the age and original purposes of buildings on brownfield sites may present design professionals with challenges to meet these requirements.

Brownfield Initiatives

The regulatory structure that had effectively stalled the real estate market for existing industrial properties eventually came under scrutiny by cities and states: Neither developers nor lenders were prepared to become involved with any but the cleanest of sites, and the number of abandoned or underutilized sites continued to grow. While the obstacles to the redevelopment of impacted properties were and still are significant, the impacts of these properties had accumulated to the point where various local and state governments began to take the initiative in the early 1990s to develop programs to encourage redevelopment in various urban centers. The focus of these programs ranged from straightforward urban renewal projects to efforts to capitalize on growing stocks of industrial properties acquired by cities for back taxes and projects concerned with the environmental cleanup of sites impacting neighborhoods. The criticism of these early programs from private sources was primarily focused on the inability of local and state governments to shield private developers from the liability risks of the Superfund law and to provide predictable cleanup standards. Cities and states witnessed the abandonment of former industrial properties as industries were consolidated into new facilities. Industries elected to build new facilities in sprawling suburban greenfields, taking jobs and tax revenue out of cities.

As a result of these unexpected effects of policies implemented in the 1970s, attempts were made in various states to encourage reuse of abandoned industrial sites by removing the regulatory barriers at the local level. Early successes in Minnesota, Michigan, and other states served to encourage "brownfield" legislation and voluntary cleanup programs in more than 29 states. As these programs have gradually evolved, a set of commonalities has emerged. The most common elements of voluntary cleanup programs are the following:

- The relief from environmental liability for the actions of others
- Predictable cleanup standards
- Protection for lenders
- Public participation in the review process
- Protection from third-party lawsuits
- Reopeners

Cleanup standards commonly include allowances for performance-based criteria allowing for the consideration of risks associated with exposure and the proposed use of the site. Methods for calculating risks associated with exposures to specific chemicals and exposure pathways are gaining increased importance as they are used in conjunction with land development projects. Risk-based corrective actions are becoming the most common method of determining remedial strategies.

The recent public policy trends at the federal and state levels are creating new opportunities for landscape architects in the redevelopment process; however, the design of these postindustrial urban landscapes presents significant new challenges. Landscape architects are faced with the challenges to balance widely diverse redevelopment issues such as the reuse of nonhazardous waste materials, severely degraded soils, and retained and on-site controlled contamination, as well as issues of environmental justice, along with sustainable development and defensible space considerations. Traditional site analysis techniques must be adapted to include the results of environmental site assessments, corrective action, and mitigation strategies in the design synthesis. A variety of voluntary cleanup programs have been established across the country, and while there are many differences among the various programs there are also many commonalities (see Table 1.3).

Under the voluntary cleanup programs, some states agree to provide owners and developers with assurance that they will be protected from liability for events and contamination that occurred in the past. These assurances are provided usually in exchange for the mitigation or remediation of existing known conditions or the demonstration that no conditions of concern exist. Assurances are provided in the form of a *letter of no further action required* or a *remediation completion certification* in which the state acknowledges the

Table 1.3   Comparison of State Brownfield Programs

State	Cleanup Standards	Liability Releases	Lender Protection	Comments
Arizona	Risk based or state Superfund	Joint and several liability repealed		
Arkansas	Site specific	Certificate of completion		
California		Certificate of completion and no further action letters	Limited liability for lenders	
Colorado		No further action determination allowed, but no liability release permitted		
Connecticut	Groundwater standards, deed restrictions	Public absorbs liability for sites in program		
Delaware		Liability protection		Tax abatement to offset cost of cleanup
Florida		Land use based or site specific covenant not to sue		
Idaho		Certificate of completion, covenant not to sue	Lender liability limit	
Illinois	Risk based	No further action letter; joint and several liability repealed		
Indiana	Background or risk based			
Louisiana				
Maine	Site specific	No further action letters	Public funding available	
Maryland	Background, site specific, statewide health based	Certificate of completion, no further action letter	Liability protection	
Massachusetts				
Michigan			Limits for lenders	
Minnesota		Certificate of completion, close-out letter, covenant not to sue		
Missouri		No further action letter		

Table 1.3   Comparison of State Brownfield Programs (*Continued*)

State	Cleanup Standards	Liability Releases	Lender Protection	Comments
Montana		Liability release for voluntary cleanup, letter of completion, no further action letter		
Nebraska		No liability release		1994
New Hampshire				1996
New Jersey	Site specific, based on groundwater and soil cleanup standards			1996
New York				
North Carolina		Limited		1994
Ohio	Numeric standard or site specific			1994
Oregon	Numeric standard	No further action but no liability release		1995
Pennsylvania	Site specific, health based	With reopeners	Lender liability release	1994
Rhode Island		Letter of completion		1995
Tennessee		Letter of completion but no liability release		1995
Texas		Background or site specific		1995
Vermont				
Virginia		Certificate of completion		1995
Washington		No liability release		1996
West Virginia		Liability release		1996
Wisconsin	Background or groundwater standards	Certificate of completion, close-out letter		1994

SOURCE: Adapted from Rogoff 1997.

acceptability of conditions found on the site. In most cases this letter informs the developer that if other, previously unknown, contamination is found, the state will be liable for the cleanup or will stand between the developer and a third party.

These programs often provide for significant protections for lenders as well. In the absence of such protection, lenders are reluctant to become involved in an impacted site. The lender has a historical basis for concern in actions by the federal courts where lenders, under specific conditions, were found to be liable for the cleanup of properties in which they held a primary interest. In general, lenders are protected from liability as long as they can demonstrate that any actions or involvement with the site was strictly in the interest of protecting their financial investment but did not extend to participating in the management or ownership of the site or facility. In practice, however, this has not always been a bright line that could be demonstrated to the satisfaction of the courts. Furthermore, impacted properties are often devalued at least to the extent of the cost of cleanup or the practical costs of limitations of use. It is a common practice for the sale price of an impacted property to be reduced at least by the cost of the anticipated cleanup activities. Limitations on the use of the site may further limit its value at the time of sale or the opportunity for profitable use after development.

State voluntary cleanup programs usually include a method of determining cleanup standards for impact sites. Prior to these laws most states did not have practical standards that could be used for the cleanup of contaminated properties. Very often the state laws did not empower regulatory agencies to negotiate or agree to a cleanup standard less onerous than a predeveloped condition, which for many sites is physically and economically impractical. Without relief from such cleanup requirements, developers simply went elsewhere. As the voluntary cleanup programs have become more common, the practice in the more recent laws is to allow developers a menu of choices for determining cleanup standards. The menu may include the following:

- Safe Drinking Water Act Maximum Contaminant Levels (MCLs)

- Other published standards such as HUD or EPA screening levels

- State standards

- Published health-based risk standards

- The development of a site-specific standard, often based on health risks and the proposed use of the site

Many states have also entered into Memoranda of Agreement with the U.S. EPA, which acknowledge that the state program is acceptable to the EPA and that the EPA will accept the findings of the state program. This agreement provides some assurance to program participants that the program they develop with the state in exchange for liability protection and cleanup standards will be honored by the federal agency.

The redevelopment of environmentally impacted sites is rarely undertaken with the expressed purpose of effecting an environmental cleanup. Environmental issues are of concern in the project only to the extent that they limit or impact the development program either physically or financially. Brownfield projects generally are either publicly funded or are financed through private sources. Publicly funded projects may use a different measure to determine the viability of a project. For example, an increase in local employment or tax revenue may outweigh other cost consideration. In privately financed projects, brownfields are first and foremost real estate development projects, and secondarily environmental projects. In practice, the financial issues of a brownfield redevelopment project are more difficult to solve than the environmental or site design issues. In addition to the additional costs of assessment, design, and construction, which are expected, impacted properties have increased financial risks and liabilities associated primarily with unknown risks of third-party lawsuits and the discovery of previously unknown contamination of site conditions. The degree to which these risks can be quantified or mitigated is often the determining factor in whether the project is initiated.

Conditions and Reopeners

The liability relief provided by state programs is a significant protection and incentive for developers. In various programs the state either agrees to step into the liability chain to protect the developer or agrees to bypass the developer should future action be deemed necessary. These concessions have conditions or limitations, also called *reopeners,* that may allow the state to rescind its protection. These reopeners include the discovery of fraud on the part of the developer, failure on the part of the developer to complete a cleanup according to the agreement, failure to maintain remediation processes or engineering controls, failure to honor the site use restrictions, or any actions on the part of the developer that exacerbate existing contamination.

Environmental Insurance

Environmental insurance is available from a variety of sources and provides a great deal of flexibility in providing coverage to prospective purchasers, owners, and lenders. The Environmental Protection Agency has prepared an overview of environmental insurance. In this document they identify three categories of environmental risk:

- Remediation-based risks
- Property value impairment risks
- Personal injury risks

The EPA suggests that environmental insurance is an effective tool for managing the financial risks associated with property transfer and acquisition. Basically there are three types of coverage available: stop loss insurance, real estate transfer insurance, and owner-controlled insurance. *Stop loss insurance* is purchased to provide protection from unexpected costs of a remediation project. The insurance will cover costs over some projected ceiling so that, if cleanup costs exceed the established figure, the additional cost is paid by the insurance company. The types of insurable risks include preexisting but previously unknown contamination, excessive remediation costs due to changes in regulations, excessive costs due to greater than anticipated contamination, and third-party or postremediation liability (migration off site, bodily harm, and loss of market value, etc.). As the environmental insurance market has become more experienced it has also grown more sophisticated. More companies entering into the field have resulted in more competitive pricing and a willingness to craft the insurance to the specific needs of the parties involved.

Generally stop loss insurance covers an exposure of up to 100 percent of the remediation cost estimate; however, variations are frequently written. The costs of stop loss insurance vary with the type of contamination, the amount of information known about the site, and the degree of regulatory or legal protection or liability associated with the project. In general, stop loss insurance is usually priced from 8 to 20 percent of the policy limit and remains in effect until the work plan is completed. Protection is provided until such time as the coverage ends. There is no meaningful standardization of this type of insurance, and special products are fashioned to meet specific project requirements.

Environmental real estate transfer insurance protects current and future landowners from the costs of remediating previously unknown contamination, third-party claims, and cleanup costs that occur after a letter of no further action is received. Like stop loss insurance, the cost of environmental real estate insurance is affected by the character of the site and the amount and quality of the information known about the site. This type of insurance usually has a renewable term of several years and must be in effect at the time a claim is made. There is no meaningful standardization of this type of insurance, and special products are fashioned to meet specific project requirements.

The scope of *owner-controlled insurance* is determined by an owner or contractor to manage the risk associated with the acts or performance of others involved in a cleanup project. The insurance vehicle can provide coverage for a variety of risks. The use of environmental insurance may be an important part of a site-specific risk management strategy. As a risk management tool, environmental insurance may relate indirectly to the specific state program by demonstrating that the developer has the capital resources necessary to complete a work plan. Although the VCP has no formal requirement for environmental insurance, the protection provided may provide the level of comfort required by a prospective purchaser. Sources of additional information about environmental insurance include the EPA publication *Potential Insurance Products for Brownfields Cleanup and Redevelopment Survey Results of Insurance Product Available for Transference of Risk at Potentially Contaminated Property,* Office of Emergency and Remediation Response, EPA 500-R-96-001, June 1996.

Environmental Justice

Studies have shown that many hazardous waste sites are located in low-income and minority neighborhoods. While it is not empirically clear as to whether the location of these facilities was based on the character of the neighborhood or the neighborhood evolved around the site, it is clear that few people would choose to live and raise their children in neighborhoods so profoundly influenced by industrial activities.

Many families moved into areas without any knowledge of the contamination or potential health risks that might exist. In the case of brownfields, neighborhoods are often faced with the impacts of contaminated sites without the economic benefits that might have once offset their proximity.

Brownfield projects must often deal with the social and economic legacy as well as the environmental concerns. Impacted communities are concerned and interested stakeholders in the redevelopment process. It is often difficult to make or substantiate scientific claims about the impact of hazardous waste sites on neighborhoods; however, current concepts of planning and environmental justice do require that future impacts be understood and discussed with stakeholders. Developers and site design professionals must recognize that brownfield sites rarely exist in isolation from the community at large. In addition to the conditions that may have existed while the facility functioned, there may be issues of continuing contamination from runoff-borne sediments or wind-borne fugitive dusts. Even in the event that there are no contamination issues, brownfield sites are often a nuisance, attracting illegal dumping, temporary shelter for the homeless, and a playground for adolescents. Local residents may desire to have the nuisance removed, but they are often suspicious about the quality and character of the proposed "improvement." In practice, it is often difficult to recognize fairness and unfairness without the participation of the community.

In many VCP programs the developer's risk management approach is subject to public scrutiny and review. In this way the interests of the community are considered in the design of the project. Adjacent neighbors in particular have valid concerns regarding the management of the construction site as well as the finished site. The nature of the contamination, if any, and the risks associated with the interim construction conditions may present a greater risk than the finished stabilized site. Fugitive dusts, uncontrolled runoff bearing sediments, and concerns with site access and construction equipment moving through neighborhoods are all construction period concerns.

Sustainability and Brownfield Redevelopment

As we begin to recognize the need to live sustainably and to find the ways of re-creating the built environment to function more sustainably, the redevelopment of brownfield sites exists as both a problem and an opportunity. Brownfield sites by definition stand in stark contrast to the principles of sustainability. The nature of such sites is that they are contaminated, underutilized properties that are visual and environmental blights. Such sites are also witness to the willingness to degrade properties, communities, and the environment with regard only for the short-term gains and without responsibility for the long-term effects. Some brownfield sites will remain so contaminated that the use of the site will be restricted well into the future. In such cases, we find we must often restrict the flow of water through the site, design the site to limit contact and exposures, and in general isolate the contaminated portions of the site from the environment at large.

On the other hand, even as we begin to define the principles of sustainable site design, we find that some brownfield sites may, in time, heal and that, with planning and nurturing, the contamination will be biologically diminished. Research into the function of landscapes as systems is raising new design possibilities. The advancement of bioremediation and phytoremediation into practical design tools will provide landscape architects with the ability to design important remediation functions into landscapes as well as beauty. If we are to make the built environment work sustainably, we must find ways to make cities function environmentally. In some ways environmentally impacted sites are among the most important design challenges.

Site Assessment Procedures and Practices

Phase I Environmental Site Assessment

Investigations into the environmental conditions found on a brownfield site are concerned largely with general site conditions and the definition of specific contaminants if any are encountered. The process of site assessment occurs over several phases, moving from a fairly prescribed *Phase I* process to a more site specific undertaking as more information is collected, typically referred to as a *Phase II environmental site assessment* (ESA). In this way the assessment process moves incrementally, using what is already known about a property in public records or memory to focused investigation of specific suspected conditions. This approach provides a rational, efficient use of financial and professional resources. In general, the most common methodology used in the professional practice of environmental site assessment is the American Society for Testing and Materials (ASTM) Practice for Environmental Site Assessments: Phase I Environmental Site Assessment Process, E-1527-97. The ASTM is a volunteer organization made up of representatives from government, industry, and academia. Its purpose is to establish standards and protocols.

The ASTM E.50 Committee is responsible for environmental assessment. Although there are many standards, the key standards for brownfield projects include the following:

- E-1527, Practice for Environmental Site Assessments: Phase I Environmental Site Assessment Process

- E-1528, Practice for Environmental Site Assessments Transaction Screen Process

- E-1903, Standard Guide for Phase II Environmental Site Assessments

- D-5746, Classification of Environmental Condition of Property Area Types

- D-1739, Standard for Risk-Based Corrective Action at Petroleum Release Sites

- PS 104-98, Guide for Risk-Based Corrective Action

It is important to realize that the ASTM standards do not prescribe an exhaustive investigation of a site. The Phase I ESA is limited to firsthand visual observation of existing conditions, reviews of existing records and historic documentation, and interviews with knowledgeable persons. The standard recognizes that a Phase I ESA is insufficient to eliminate uncertainty. Instead, the standard has been developed in accordance with the ASTM methods, as a consensus among practitioners and users of ESA information, to achieve a balance between the quality of the reports and the cost of providing them. A Phase I ESA consists of four major components:

- A review of records

- Interviews with knowledgeable people

- A firsthand site reconnaissance

- The preparation of a report

It should be noted that an ASTM Phase I ESA does not include any sampling, although in some cases sampling may be included in order to meet specific project requirements or needs. The findings of a Phase I report are the reflection of the information reviewed in the course of the ESA. The standard practice does not require the professional to verify independently any information found in the records or learned in interviews. Instead, the professional may rely on information on its face unless there is actual knowledge that information is incorrect or unless it is obvious that it is incorrect. The ASTM standards are very carefully crafted so that the specific language is very important. The standards define and use terms that have specific meaning within the ESA process. The purpose of the assessment is to identify *recognized environmental conditions* (RECs). The term refers to the presence of a condition that could indicate either actual contamination or the threat of contamination. Both hazardous substances and petroleum products are considered. Even if these materials are used, stored, and disposed of in compliance with the law, the conditions may be adequate to warrant further investigation. The standard does allow for de minimis conditions (i.e., small quantities that do not represent a material risk of harm to people or the environment).

Review of Records

Since Phase I reports are limited to available sources of information, the standard practice describes the limits to which an environmental professional can be reasonably expected to seek such information, requiring that the assessment be based on records that are practically reviewable. The standard defines *practically reviewable* as information that is "provided in a manner and in a form that upon examination yields information relevant to the property without the need for extraordinary analysis of irrelevant data. Records that cannot be retrieved by reference to the property location or geographic area are not generally considered practically reviewable" (ASTM 1998). The standard also identifies the responsibilities of the user of a Phase I ESA report to evaluate and use the report within the limits of its scope and to apply any specialized knowledge of the site conditions or the property value that might be appropriate. The objective of the records review is to obtain and review records that will help identify recognized environmental conditions in connection with the property.

To meet the test of practically reviewable records, the environmental professional need not identify or review every possible record that might exist but only sources and data that are reasonably ascertainable from standard sources. *Reasonably ascertainable* means that (1) information is publicly available, (2) it is obtainable within reasonable time and cost constraints, and (3) it is practically reviewable. *Reasonable time and cost* is considered to be a nominal cost within 20 days of a request. *Practically reviewable* means that the information pertaining to the site is accessible without excessive analysis. Information should be accessible for a limited geographic area and accessible by address, zip code, county, and so on. There are a number of companies that specialize in providing this information.

To quantify the limits of the ESA, the standard practice provides a set of suggested minimum search distances for the purposes of reviewing public records of nearby properties and activities that may affect the site (see Table 2.1). The minimum site distances are approximate and may be adjusted at the discretion of the environmental professional in consideration of the local density and the distance hazardous substances might be expected to migrate based on geology, hydrogeology, or other conditions. For example, search distance in a heavily industrialized urban area might be reduced whereas in an area where groundwater is used as the primary drinking water source, distance might be extended. As might be expected, accuracy varies from record to record and site to site. Except in cases where there are obvious mistakes or errors, the environmental professional is not obligated to make more than a reasonable effort to compensate for mistakes or insufficiencies that are obvious or in conflict with other information. If information is not reasonably ascertainable or available, the environmental professional will attempt to find information from other sources such as interviews with owners, neighbors, local officials, etc. Sources such as these are to be documented by name, address, date, and the substance of the information attributed to the source in the final report.

How far back historical research is expected to go is based on what is reasonably ascertainable and appropriate. For example, land records may go back to 1700 for a property, but if the property was undeveloped until 1960, there is little point in going back that far. Likewise, a site that has been used for industrial purposes since 1860 might bear additional research. Generally speaking, when historical records are reviewed, periods of time under the same use do not need a further investigation. For example, a site

Table 2.1 Database Minimum Search Distances

The ASTM standard recommends the following search distances from the project site; however, the environmental professional may elect to change the search distances for reasons specific to the project area.

For Sites Found on the:	Minimum Recommended Search Distance
National Priority List	1 mile
CERCLIS list	0.5 mile
RCRA TSD list	1 mile
RCRA generators list	Property and adjoining property
ERNS list	Property only
State NPL/CERCLIS	1 mile
State landfill	0.5 mile
Leaking underground storage tank (LUST)	0.5 mile
Registered underground storage tank (UST)	Property and adjoining properties

with an apartment building in 1940 that is found to have the same apartment building in 1960 does not require an interim check of the intervening years. Generally the preceding 50 years is considered an acceptable period for a historical search of title information and aerial photography. The use of previous ESA and work by others may be included in the assessment, but the source should be referenced in the report (Table 2.2).

The use of readily available information allows the site assessor to view the site over time (Table 2.3). The USGS 7.5 Quadrangle Topographic Maps may be viewed over several iterations to note changes in the character of the surrounding area and even changes in land form and drainage. These maps used in conjunction with the Department of the Interior Wetland Inventory maps and USDA Soil Surveys are often able to reveal a great deal about the past of a site or a local area (Figure 2.1).

Site Walkover

The actual site reconnaissance is the only portion of the Phase I ESA in which the professional collects information on a firsthand basis; it may also be the most important part. The purpose is to observe the property and any structures firsthand. The site assessor conducts a thorough walkover of the site including the structures. The assessor views the site from off site and points of access as well as by walking over the site in a pattern that is adequate to see all portions

Table 2.2 Sources of Site Information

Department of health and public safety
Fire department
Planning department
Zoning and building permits department
Water department
Local utilities
Local historical societies
Lists of local landfills, hazardous waste sites, spills, fires, public and private wells

Table 2.3 Physical Information Sources

USGS Geological Survey maps, groundwater, bedrock geology
USGS Geological Survey topographic maps
Soil Conservation Services soil maps
U.S. Department of Interior wetlands maps
Historical USGS topographical maps
Aerial photography
Recorded land title records
Standard historical sources
Insurance maps
City directories
Property tax files
Street directories
Building department records
Zoning and land use records
Previous site assessment reports
Environmental audit reports
Environmental permits or records
Registration of tanks
Material safety data sheets
Right-to-know or emergency plans
Site-specific reports or drawings
Correspondence

of the site. Typically site investigators will use a grid pattern that has been determined to be adequate to visually inspect the entire site. Exterior portions of a property are observed for evidence of on-site disposal or material storage. The site is assessed for the presence of stained soils, oil sheens on surface water, areas of unexplained fill, and general housekeeping. Physical characteristics of the site are carefully observed and noted (e.g., topography, aspect, drainage, existing water bodies, roads, construction type and condition of structures, roads, paved areas, water supply, sewage disposal, existing material storage area, presence of drums or tanks, odors, pools of liquid, heating and/or cooling methods, stains or corrosion, wells, floor drains, sumps, pits, ponds, lagoons, solid waste disposal). The activities of adjacent properties are also observed and reported, particularly upgradient sites. Site assessors are

Figure 2.1 Aerial photograph of port facilities. Note the visible presence of abandoned and disturbed areas.

not required to enter adjacent properties but to simply observe them from the property being investigated (Figs. 2.2 through 2.4).

Structures are inspected for floor drains, material storage areas, equipment, boiler rooms, maintenance or repair areas, utility areas, suspect building materials, and other visible signs of recognized environmental conditions. Assessors will also report the presence of odors or fumes if any are noted. Obstacles to completing a site assessment may include locked or blocked portions of a building or areas blocked by debris or conditions identified as unsafe by the assessor, and these are noted in the assessor's report.

The organization of the ESA report is described in the ASTM Standard Practice and generally will include an executive summary, documentation supporting the findings and information collected, credentials of the environmental pro-

Figure 2.2 Severely stained soils and other material residue are evident along this factory wall.

Figure 2.3 Photograph of poor storage and housekeeping. Note the apparent stained soils. Such site conditions are indications of possible environmentally hazardous conditions.

fessional performing the assessment, and the actual findings and conclusions of the assessment. Although the executive summary is intended to summarize the assessment process and focus on the findings and conclusions, site designers should read the entire report, particularly looking at the

Figure 2.4   Photograph of a well-managed material storage area.

assessment documentation, which should include copies or photocopies of historic mapping and aerial photography, summaries of interviews, and a thorough description of the site. This historic data may provide important insight to the character and limitations of site development that are not always evident to the environmental professional.

Phase II Environmental Site Assessment

In most cases Phase II investigations are limited to the study of questions raised in the Phase I ESA, although some state voluntary cleanup programs may require a more generalized characterization than is indicated by the ASTM Phase II Standard Practice. The Phase II environmental site assessment involves the collection and analysis of samples. Phase II assessments are performed when Phase I indicates the potential for or actual environmental contamination. Based on the Phase I work, the Phase II work is usually directed to a specific finding, such as an area of stained soil, a known or suspected underground storage tank, a chemical storage area, or an area of suspected contamination. The purpose of the Phase II work is usually to confirm the findings of Phase I. Sampling begins as a method of characterization to determine first the presence and degree of contamination and then to define its horizontal and vertical limits. It is, by this definition, a reiterative process.

Usually a series of sample collections is required. Each subsequent round of sampling becomes more focused and provides a greater level of information with which to determine the best remedial action approach.

Sample Planning

The collection of samples should be undertaken only after an understanding of the objectives of the sample collection has been established and the limitations of the plan have been agreed upon. Samples have limited value. The data collected from a single sample are after all really representative of only the sample itself. Moving a sample location a few feet might provide very different results. Sample plans are designed according to the questions being asked. A Phase II sampling plan is usually based on the recommendations made in Phase I for further study of specific areas of concern. In that environmental site assessments are most often conducted as part of a prospective buyer's due diligence, the sampling effort is usually interested in determining a worst-case condition rather than a general or average condition. For the buyer it is the worst-case condition, and the risks and costs associated with it, that is of the greatest concern.

Sample collection plans must also address the possibilities of multiple contaminants in different media. Many industrial sites have multiple contaminants either mixed or in discrete areas. Sampling planning must account for all these possibilities. Sampling begins as a method of characterization to determine first the presence and degree of contamination and then to define the limits and extent of contamination. Depending on the nature of the site and the objective, the sampling plan can vary widely from a very few samples to a complex three-dimensional sampling plan.

The first step in designing or evaluating a sampling plan is to understand the stated objectives of the sampling plan. What questions does the plan expect to answer? Are the objectives clearly stated? Understanding the objectives of the sampling plan is absolutely fundamental to evaluating whether the plan may meet those objectives. Having the objectives in written form also serves to communicate to consumers of the final report what questions were asked and whether the data collected support the conclusions. In the absence of clearly stated objectives, sampling data are simply information without a context. The sampling plan must also include a clear indication of the analytical methods to be used. The selection of the analytical method is a function of the objectives as well. If sampling results are to be used in conjunction with a state VCP, the state may dictate the precise methods to be used. In any case, the analytic method is an important piece of information for anyone comparing the data to later or earlier sample results.

The number of samples and the location from which they will be collected are important to demonstrate the plan's consistency with the objectives. Does the distribution and frequency of the samples meet the requirements established by the objectives? Will the samples be composite or grab samples? Generally, sampling plans are explicit about the methods of collection and the reasons for selecting one method over another. This information assists the reader of the final report in understanding the rationale of the sampling procedure. Reports will be read by people with an interest in the project but unfamiliar with the field conditions and effort necessary to collect samples. Description of terrain, cover, vegetation, topography, accessibility by equipment, and other factors influencing the degree of difficulty in obtaining samples assists the reader in understanding the report.

The sampling plan should address the stabilization of the site if necessary, the quality control procedures to be used, and the disposal of extra material, such as purge water from the development of monitoring wells. Finally, all sampling plans should contain or reference the health and safety plan, which includes the workers involved in the implementation of the plan.

TYPES OF SAMPLES

There are three types of samples: grab, composite, and integrated. *Grab samples* are individual samples taken from a specific location at a specific time. This is an appropriate choice when the size, shape, location, and nature of a suspected release are defined. Although the sample provides a measure of only one discrete point, combinations of grab samples are used to interpolate the conditions that lie between two samples. The interpolation of data is used to identify attenuation over distance or the limits of contamination. The closer the sample points, the more valid is the interpolation.

Composite samples are made up of a combination of samples. They are used to make up a "representative" sample or to produce enough material quantity for analysis. Compositing samples involves thoroughly mixing individual samples of equal weight and performing only one analysis. The results are typically multiplied by the number of individual samples for comparison sake. Analysis represents an average condition (i.e., sample locations could have higher results individually than is found in the composite). For example, a composite of five grab samples, analyzed for total lead, might be found to have 200 *parts per million* (ppm). This could mean that four samples had very low lead content and one sample had 1,000 ppm or that all five had 200 ppm. The only certainty is that in the area represented by the composite sample lead is present. Composite samples are used for initial assessment purposes where the worst-case values can be extrapolated from the results and where the sampling is performed to determine the presence of contamination. The advantage is that the cost of sampling may be reduced. The disadvantage is that in a case with a positive result, there is a fair amount of uncertainty as to where the problem may be. The value of composite sampling is relative to the conclusions to be drawn from the analysis. Composites are helpful in performing a general characterization of a site or a portion of a site; however, such samples are of little value for defining the limits of contamination.

Integrated sampling means that a composite of material is taken from the same location over a period of time, such as effluent discharges or waste streams. Integrated sampling plans are used to monitor conditions over a period of time and support judgments regarding changes in conditions. These types of programs are often used to monitor groundwater and storm water conditions; however, it might be expected that, as bioremediation approaches become more common and as we learn more about natural attenuation of contaminants, integrated sampling will be an appropriate part of projects employing these concepts.

Sampling design may be divided into one of four general groups: judgmental, random, systematic, or a combination of the first three. *Judgmental sample programs* are based on specific information about a release or contamination such as observed areas of stained soils or an area known to have been affected by a spill. In these cases the field personnel make a judgment on where to take a sample based on observation or other information. The advantage of this approach is that it tends to be cost effective and efficient; however, it is definitely biased toward the worst-case situation, and marginal areas may be missed.

Random sample programs are developed to evaluate all areas of a site, usually by dividing the site into a grid and using a random selection of grid intersections as sample locations. Since each location has an equal chance of being selected for evaluation, results are said to be indicative of an average condition. This design is selected where statistical analysis is to be used and is appropriate, or where information is to be used for legal purposes. An advantage of this approach is that it is a low-bias, sitewide approach. Its disadvantages are that grid design is often restricted by inaccessible areas or areas where sampling is not feasible (e.g., utility areas or street surfaces) and that random selection of location can result in clustering of samples.

Systematic sample programs are similar to random programs to the extent that the site is divided into a grid, but in this case samples are collected at every grid intersection. Grid patterns do not have to be square; they could be rectangular or circular (around a tank), depending on site shape and geometry. Difficult or inaccessible locations can be eliminated. The advantages of the systematic system are its low-bias sitewide coverage and its ability to eliminate inaccessible areas. Disadvantages lie in the judgment used to select the grid frequency and the limited application for statistical analysis. It is easily challenged and can be expensive.

Combination sample programs make use of both random and systematic approaches. Judgment is used to eliminate or at least minimize bias. This sampling program can be used to eliminate the biggest disadvantages of systematic or random programs, but it is not completely random, and the results can be challenged easily if the basis for selections are not carefully documented. Most Phase II sampling plans tend to use a combination approach.

SAMPLE COLLECTION

Soil samples are collected for analysis of a wide range of contaminants. Environmental soil sampling will not provide the geotechnical information that might be required for site development purposes, although with some forethought geotechnical samples can be collected in addition to the environmental samples. Typically samples are taken at several depths and over a suspected area. The depth and distribution of samples are determined by the suspected extent of contamination. Often samples are taken to bracket a suspected area with the anticipation of a second or even a third round of sampling to define the actual limits and to quantify the volume of contaminated material. It is recommended to collect as many samples as practical in the field. The actual analysis may be delayed or conducted in stages to keep mobilization costs to a practical minimum. This approach, however, may not be possible for analytes that have a limited holding time before analysis.

The physical collection of the soil samples is a function of the following factors:

- Homogeneity of the soil (presence of rock, clay, or debris)

- The ease of collection (soil density, debris or rock content, groundwater)

- The ease of decontamination

- Site restriction for equipment (topography, soils, etc.)

Shallow soil samples are typically collected with a hand auger that is manually rotated into the ground. Hand augers can be used up to 6 feet or so in depth in soft soils without interference. There are power-driven hand augers that can go a bit deeper. Sample material is collected into a tube (usually brass or plastic) that fits inside the auger. Other shallow soil sampling equipment could include a shovel, a *trier* (a hollow rod that is used to collect a core sample), a *thief* (a hollow tube within a hollow tube that is closed until a particular depth or material is reached at which time it is opened and inserted into the material to collect a sample), and a trowel.

Deeper soil samples are collected using truck-mounted equipment such as a well drilling rig or direct-push technology. Depths of from 10 to several hundred feet are possible. Hollow stem augers and split-spoon augers are commonly used to produce undisturbed samples. Soil sampling devices can be inserted into the core at particular depths to gather samples. The core is evaluated for color, smell, moisture, and composition at the time the sample was taken.

Liquid samples can be collected from drums, tanks, and surface water using dippers, glass tubes, and *composite liquid waste samplers* (COLIWASAs). Pumps can be used to assist in the collection, but pumps should be of a type and quality that do not introduce air into the sample. Groundwater samples are collected by drilling a well and installing a monitoring well. *Temporary groundwater sampling stations* are those in which a well is not installed in the boring and the bore hole is filled after a sample is collected. These are often discouraged because the results are not repeatable. Monitoring wells are always purged before a sample is taken. A well is *purged* by removing from 3 to 5 well casing volumes (determined by multiplying the total depth of the well from the ground surface to the bottom of the water column by the cross-sectional area). The purpose of the purge is to obtain a representative sample of the groundwater rather than a sample of the water that has been sitting in the well. Temperature, pH, and conductivity measures are taken. Purge water is collected into drums or another receptacle and handled according to the analysis results. Containers are labeled.

QUALITY CONTROL

Samples are collected in the field in properly prepared containers that are the correct volume for the analysis to be performed. Field personnel record the location of each sample and label the sample with a specific identification number. A transmittal form is completed that lists each sample, the time and location of collection, the specific analysis that is requested, and the name of the person that took the sample. The transmittal form remains with the samples. Whenever the samples are relinquished to another person, the person signs the form and notes the time the samples were accepted. This process is referred to as the *chain of custody,* and it provides a record of who handled the samples from the time they were collected until they were accepted at the laboratory.

A variety of laboratory methods is used for purposes of quality control in field sampling. The purpose of the quality control procedure is to identify anomalies either in the field sampling itself or in the laboratory during analysis. The most common quality control measures are the matrix spike, laboratory blank, and field duplicate. The *matrix spike* is a comparison between two duplicate field samples. In the case of a matrix spike, one sample is "spiked" with a measured amount of the contaminant, and both samples are analyzed. After an analysis is completed, the volume of the added material is then subtracted from the analysis to arrive at an accurate concentration, and the results from both samples are compared.

Laboratory blanks, on the other hand, are laboratory grade samples that are analyzed in the same way, using the same equipment used in preparing the field samples. Laboratory blanks are used in the lab to determine the accuracy of the analytical process.

Field duplicates are extra samples of the same material collected in the field and submitted to the laboratory under different numbers so that the laboratory is "blind." Duplicates are usually collected from areas suspected of having the highest degree of contamination.

GEOPHYSICAL METHODS

Geophysical methods are technologies used to identify the presence of buried metal objects or to map the subsurface features either by sounding or by profiling. *Profiling* is used to define the lateral extent of a feature such as an area of buried wastes. The result is a contour map of the area and/or object. *Sounding* is a radar technique used to determine the depth of an object at a specific location. Soundings are taken on a grid pattern to allow interpolation of the depth and area of objects.

Ground penetrating radar (GPR) provides a shallow cross section of subsurface objects. GPR can penetrate up to 40 feet in sandy soils, but it is limited to the first 4 feet in clay soils or soils containing conductive wastes. Data from GPR must be used in conjunction with supporting data from bore hole logs and resistivity or conductivity tests. The GPR coverage is affected by terrain and site vegetation. The GPR antenna is dragged behind a vehicle along a cleared 3- to 4-foot-wide path. The distance between paths varies by the type of equipment used. A typical day's survey costs from $5,000 to $20,000, which includes the interpretation of data and preparation of a report.

Electromagnetic exploration (EM) includes several techniques, each of which requires the contrasting of the conductivity of materials being screened. *Seismic refraction* is a geologic investigation tool with only limited applications in ESA work. It is used for mapping bedrock surface area, and it may be useful in groundwater or environmental pathway studies in which influences over contamination plumes are being sought. *Magnetometer surveys* are like EM surveys, and they are used to determine magnetic anomalies.

OTHER TECHNIQUES

Soil gas studies are used to identify the presence of *volatile organic compounds* (VOCs), which could include solvents, oils, gas, and cleaning fluids. The *soil air samples* are collected at known depths and locations and analyzed. Study areas are usually selected because of known or suspected dumping or disposal. The presence of VOCs in the soil would indicate contamination near the monitor point and possibly in the groundwater. Soil gas surveys are used to determine the placement of borings and monitoring points and/or wells to more precisely define the area of contamination from the decomposition of organic materials. Samples are mapped to illustrate the area of contamination and mobility of the contaminant. Samples are taken either as grab samples, where a probe is inserted into the unsaturated zone of the soil (the *vadose zone*) and air is drawn into a sample container with a vacuum pump, or as static samples, taken using a tube containing activated charcoal, which absorbs the gases. A third method does not involve collecting samples but rather takes a reading on a *photoionization detector* (PID) or *flame ionization detector* (FID) or uses an LEL meter to detect the presence of methane.

Hydrostatic testing involves subjecting an *underground storage tank* (UST) or a system of underground pipes to pressure to confirm its integrity. The system is put under pressure by introducing compressed air and then monitoring for a pressure drop.

Risk Assessment

Concern with environmental contamination is twofold: the impacts on the environment as an operating system or process and the impacts on human health. As experience with these sites has developed, it has become clear that restoration of many impacted sites to a precontaminated condition is either impossible or impractical. Cleanup strategies have started to move away from rigid cleanup criteria toward cleanup and management of impacted sites based on the quantified risk associated with the contamination, condition, proximity, and proposed use of the site.

Risk is determined by understanding who is at risk and what are the potential effects of exposure, the sources of exposure, the routes of exposure, and the time frames. As with sampling planning, the risk assessor must understand why the assessment is being performed, the history of the site, and what is known about the existing and proposed conditions. Risk assessment should include the proposed redeveloped condition as well as the interim construction condition. Risk assessments are usually concerned with risk to the human population and to the environment. Human risk is usually compared to a general population model unless a more applicable population is identified. Populations are characterized according to the exposure to contamination that occurs along specific pathways. The pathways are the identified routes by which exposure to a contaminant may occur. Common pathways might include breathing of fumes or dusts, ingestion of dusts or contaminated food or water, or dermal contact. Sensitive groups within a population such as infants, expectant mothers, and the elderly are also considered as are construction workers and persons with incidental contact on the site during construction. Finally, the anticipated end users and stakeholders are evaluated. Environmental concerns include nonhuman species and associated habitat or ecosystems.

For the landscape architect or site designer, risk assessments provide valuable information about the expected impacts of contamination on aquifers, soils, contributing watersheds, and air quality. In turn, the site designer may seek ways of mitigating these impacts in the functional design of the site. How will the runoff quality affect plantings? Will the soil be acceptable for recreational use of the site? What plant materials are resistant to low pH conditions? How is storm water to be addressed on a site where infiltration must be discouraged? Are there plants that will assist in the treatment of collected runoff?

RISK-BASED CORRECTIVE ACTIONS

Risk-based corrective actions are focused on the management of a site to control or limit risks. In such cases the remediation plan is performance based rather than focused on a specific cleanup target. These projects incorporate risk assessment practices into traditional site investigation and the selection of remedies. The purpose of this approach is to find cost-effective measures for the protection of human health and environmental resources. Remediation is based on steps necessary to prevent human or environmental exposure. The corrective action can be applied at any of the three areas of consideration: sources of contamination, transport mechanisms, or receptors. Acceptable methods interrupt the cycle of exposure either by removing or treating the source, interrupting or stopping the method of transport, controlling exposure, or some combination of those methods. Based on site information, the magnitude and immediacy of risk is determined for a specific site. Generally the process is geared primarily toward chronic problems rather than acute problems or exposures. Although there are a variety of risk assessment procedures, the consensus standards developed by the ASTM are the most commonly used in brownfield redevelopment.

The EPA has developed *risk-based concentrations* (RBCs) for use as screening levels (see Appendix 1). These provide screening levels for soils, tap water, and residential applications. The RBCs are useful tools for evaluating the degree of contamination and the acceptability of risk. Such standard numbers should be used with caution, taking into consideration all of the site-specific factors of a project. The RBCs are not accepted by all states, but they do provide a basis for comparison.

Major Contaminants

There are more than 70,000 artificial chemicals used in commerce and defense and found in the environment. A good deal is known about the health and environmental effects of about 1500 of these, but most of our concerns on brownfield sites are limited to a few individual chemicals or groups of chemicals. The Agency for Toxic Substances and Disease Registry (ATSDR), an agency of the Centers for Disease Control, has identified the Top 20 Hazardous Substances as shown in Table 2.4. For each of these chemicals, the ATSDR has prepared a public health statement. For the site designer, these contaminants may generally be discussed by the group in which they are found: metals, volatile organic compounds (VOCs), semivolatile organic compounds (SVOCs), polychlorinated biphenyls (PCBs), polycyclic aromatic hydrocarbons (PAHs), and pesticides (ATSDR, 1997).

The ATSDR/EPA Priority List of the Top 20 Hazardous Substances includes five metals: arsenic, lead, mercury, cadmium, and chromium. All metals are naturally occurring,

Table 2.4   Top 20 Hazardous Substances

Substances	Type
1. Arsenic	Metal
2. Lead	Metal
3. Mercury, metallic	Metal
4. Vinyl chloride	Semivolatile organic compound (SVOC)
5. Benzene	Volatile organic compound (VOC)
6. Polychlorinated biphenyl	PCB
7. Cadmium	Metal
8. Benzo(a)pyrene	SVOC
9. Benzo(b)flouranthene	SVOC
10. Polycyclic aromatic hydrocarbon	PAH
11. Chloroform	VOC
12. Aroclor 1254	PCB
13. DDT	Pesticide
14. Aroclor 1260	PCB
15. Trichloroethylene	VOC
16. Chromium (+6)	Metal
17. Dibenz[a,h]anthracene	SVOC
18. Dieldrin	Pesticide
19. Hexachlorobutadiene	SVOC
20. Chlordane	Pesticide

SOURCE: Adapted from the ATSDR/EPA Priority Pollutant List.

although rarely in the refined forms and concentrations associated with industry. Exposures to metals may occur by breathing or ingesting dusts or contaminated foods. In some forms metals may be absorbed by the skin, but this is a less common pathway. Metals have a variety of health effects; perhaps the most familiar are associated with lead. Lead is known to cause premature birth and low birth weight in children as well as decreased learning capabilities. Young children and pregnant women are at the greatest risk; however, long-term lead exposure can cause brain and kidney damage in adults.

Volatile organic compounds (VOCs), for example, benzene, may be artificial or naturally occurring. *Benzene* occurs naturally as a byproduct of burning. Elevated concentrations of benzene are associated with petroleum products. Benzene is made commercially and is used to make other chemicals and in the manufacture of plastics and pesticides. Most people are exposed to benzene in tobacco smoke and vehicle exhaust. Benzene contamination is associated with gasoline stations, underground storage tanks, landfill leachate, and industries that produce or use benzene. Such facilities could include plastics factories, petroleum refineries, and chemical plants. Benzene evaporates quickly, and the most common exposure pathway is through breathing. Benzene can also enter the body through contact. The most common source of dermal contact is with benzene-containing products such as gasoline or solvents. Benzene is a dangerous and harmful chemical. The impact of benzene is correlated with the concentration and length of time of exposure. Long-term exposure is known to be associated with cancer and leukemia. Immune deficiencies are also associated with benzene exposure. Even brief exposures at high concentrations can cause dizziness and headaches and even death.

Trichloroethylene (TCE) is an artificial VOC used in solvents, adhesives, paint strippers, spot removers, and correction fluid. It is also a constituent of many other chemicals. Although TCE is not known to be a carcinogen, it has been known to cause kidney and liver damage and tumors of the kidney, liver, lungs, and testicles. Short-term exposures may result in headaches, dizziness, slowed reactions, and irritation of the eyes, throat, and nose. In high concentrations loss of consciousness and even death are possible.

The Top 20 also includes benzo(a)pyrene, benzo(b)flouranthene, dibenz[a,h]anthracene, and hexachlorobutadiene, which are all SVOCs. SVOCs are a broad category of chemicals, and they have a range of toxicity factors and may be breathed or ingested, particularly in contaminated water. A variety of illnesses are associated with SVOCs. *Vinyl chloride disease* is a condition known to be associated with long-term exposure to low concentrations of vinyl chloride. The condition is manifested by damage to the liver and lung function, changes in circulation and bones at the ends of fingers, and a thickening of the skin. Exposures to high concentrations can cause dizziness, loss of coordination, headache, and even death.

Polychlorinated biphenyls, or PCBs, are artificial chemicals that were commercially produced and used as coolants and lubricants in transformers, capacitors, and other electrical equipment. PCBs have not been manufactured in the United States since 1977 because of their persistence in the environment and potential for human health effects. Exposure to PCBs is primarily through residual materials, spills, or leaking equipment. Workers have an additional exposure risk when handling PCB-containing equipment or contaminated material. PCBs readily evaporate and are distributed and returned to earth in rain or dust. Exposure occurs by eating contaminated food, breathing dust and vapors, or through dermal contact with PCB-containing materials. It is said that virtually everyone's body contains PCBs. PCBs are complex chemicals, and the direct health impacts are uncertain, although it is believed that PCBs are carcinogens.

Dioxin, among the most toxic of materials, is a byproduct of burning PCBs.

The list includes *polycyclic aromatic hydrocarbons* (PAHs), which are a group of more than 100 chemicals that are the byproducts of incomplete combustion or degradation of organic substances. PAHs are naturally occurring and artificial. As a group, PAHs have little commercial value, although some are used in plastics and pesticides. For treatment and assessment purposes, PAHs are usually considered as a group. PAHs are common substances in the environment and occur naturally at low levels. Elevated levels of PAHs are associated with oil and gas use, asphalt plants, coal-tar production, aluminum production, trash incinerators (from burning garbage), sites of fires, and anywhere coal or petroleum products are used or where wood or other organic materials are burned.

Exposure to PAHs may occur through ingestion of dust particles in food or water, breathing dust, or through dermal contact if a surface or material has a concentration high enough (e.g., roofing tar). PAHs enter the body easily and tend to be stored in fat, kidneys, and the liver, but they tend to reside in the body for only a few days. PAHs may be carcinogenic.

Pesticides are a family of chemicals with a wide distribution and persistence in the environment. In addition to serious ecological effects, some pesticides are known to have a variety of health effects on farm workers and consumers. Pesticides are breathed and ingested as well as absorbed through the skin. Some are suspected carcinogens and are known to cause tumors. Exposure to high concentrations may cause nerve damage and death.

Planning for the Redevelopment of an Impacted Site

Planning for brownfield projects is more complicated than other types of planning because of the constraints contamination may have upon the project. Fundamentally the objectives of a brownfield project are the same as they would be for any real estate development project: to construct a project that reflects the vision of the client functionally, aesthetically, and economically. Some brownfield sites may not require any change in traditional site design elements while others will require the landscape architect or design engineer to rethink even basic site design considerations. While planning law is different from state to state, few planning ordinances or laws account for the issues that might be present on environmentally impacted properties. The site designer cannot always rely on the standard design or construction methods on brownfield sites.

Conditions on brownfields may suggest that storm water infiltration should be discouraged or detained for treatment before release. Site grading may be restricted to avoid disturbances in specific areas, and work schedules may be driven by the need to stabilize sections of a site at the end of every day. Site planning may be required to incorporate passive mitigation of conditions, even the progressive treatment of the site through the selection of plant materials. Every brownfield project is different. Each has different levels of contamination, and combinations of contaminants, as well as variations in topography, drainage, and other site constraints that will directly affect the synthesis of the design solutions. Site planning activities must reach out to other professionals and stakeholders to find the design solution for a given site. The time frame of issues to be resolved on these sites may extend well into the future, beyond the design life of most development projects undertaken today. For these and other reasons, site designers find that brownfield projects are an emerging area of practice that represents a design challenge like few others.

The practicing landscape architect or site engineer is used to the role of interpreting the vision of a client and acting as a go-between with public planners and interested community members. Brownfields will provide a new dimension to this part of the professional's practice and challenge him or her to become conversant with language and concepts of this type of site design.

Involving Stakeholders

Brownfield redevelopment and state voluntary cleanup programs have evolved under the umbrella of existing public planning organizations and in the interests of environmental justice. There is some element of public involvement in nearly every voluntary cleanup program. Stakeholders may be a diverse group representing a wide range of interests and concerns. Generally speaking, it is during the site planning phase of a project that many of these concerns need to be addressed. While the site planner may not take the lead in addressing all of the stakeholders, it is a certainty that the outcome of such contacts will affect the site planning. It is important that the designer understand the concerns of each stakeholder and consider how the concern relates to the proposed project.

Stakeholders occur at many levels and in many capacities. It should be anticipated that communication with stakeholders will take place in private conversations as well as public presentations. Communication with lenders or sellers and buyers requires one level of documentation while presentations to concerned residents requires another. In either case the communication must be direct and free flowing and address the concerns of the stakeholder group. The ASTM has developed the Guide to the Process of Sustainable Brownfield Development, E 1984, which may provide the practitioner with an outline for working with the concerns of various stakeholders.

Landowners

Owners of impacted properties are faced with a number of concerns. Among the first is the issue of liability for the conditions on the property. In some cases the owner may be reluctant to allow site assessment to proceed on the property in fear of the discovery of new environmental contamination or concern over actual quantification of the contamination. The owner's concerns are twofold: first, the risk of liability for the actual out-of-pocket cost of a cleanup and second, the risk that the property value will be reduced by the anticipated cost of cleanup or simply by the perception of contamination in the local real estate market.

Owners may seek assurances from the prospective purchaser for protection against future claims and may ask to be included as an additional insured on the project. The owner can also expect the property value to be affected by the findings of the environmental site assessment.

Developers

Redevelopment of impacted properties is undertaken for a variety of reasons. Public redevelopment programs may be driven by an economic development or public policy purpose, in which case the formula for determining the viability of a project will probably not be strictly profit. Private investment into a redevelopment project, on the other hand, is driven primarily by a profit motive. Like all land development projects, the brownfield project must work "by the numbers." One purpose of the state voluntary cleanup programs has been to engage private resources in the cleanup and stabilization of impacted properties; however, the motivation of developers is to put together a successful real estate venture, one that has an environmental cleanup or management element to it.

Often developers will not be the owner of the property at the time the assessment and early planning are undertaken. In these early discussions with agencies and other stakeholders the developer must work to resolve the interests of the project, including those of the investors with the interests of the public and stakeholders. All costs of compromises and commitments required by the various stakeholders must be weighed against the projected return in the project. It is the aggregate cost of cleanup and other concessions that must be offset by other reduced costs if the private redevelopment project is to go forward and succeed.

Agencies

The interests of the local agencies and political bodies may not always reflect only the neighborhood concerns. Local officials may see the project in the context of a larger effort or plan. Agencies charged with economic development, creating jobs, and returning idle properties to the tax roles may have a perspective that differs from the local residents. Agencies that offer letters of no further action must also demonstrate a reasonable standard of care in evaluating the site and program before offering such protection. The commitment of no further action usually means the state will step in if previously unknown contamination is found. This would mean putting the state in the position of funding cleanups in such cases without a means of recovering its costs. Agency administrators must be reasonably certain that such risks are acceptably small.

Agencies also have a responsibility to provide assistance to the affected community. Outreach to the community is often facilitated through local agencies. Agency staff can assist communities by relating the experience of other communities, allowing neighborhood leaders to learn from their counterparts, and bringing technical and other resources to the community. Staff can also provide technical information to communities about infrastructure, traffic impacts, and specifics of the redevelopment proposal.

Lenders

Lenders are primarily concerned with protecting the investment in the project and avoiding any environmental liability entanglements. Also of importance to the lender is the value of the property as it is and as it will be after the redevelopment and mitigation or remediation of the environmental concerns. Appraisals of the value of a property are often given in two forms, the value of the property as if there were no environmental issues and the value with the environmental issues. The cost of the perception of contamination on the real estate market may sometimes be greater than the actual cost of cleanup.

Neighbors

Neighbors are immediately impacted by the redevelopment process. While redevelopment may stabilize or remediate existing contamination, neighbors have legitimate concerns over the impact of storm water runoff, increases in traffic, and the general change in character that will occur with redevelopment. In addition, they have concerns over the management of the site and the conditions during construction. In most cases neighborhoods do not have professional assistance in evaluating the redevelopment proposal and the technical jargon that describes contamination and redevelopment strategies.

While the concerns of neighbors are primarily focused on health, safety, and environmental issues, they also have an economic stake in the project to the extent that it will impact local property values, offer prospects for local employment, and provide opportunities for existing and new local businesses. Their concerns are often based in a sense of fairness or a perception of equity associated with the proposed improvements (Fig. 3.1).

Risk Communication for the Design Professional

Risk Assessment

Risk assessment is the scientific process of identifying and characterizing the health risks of a population. The process typically involves determining the limits of exposure and the

Figure 3.1   Residences in brownfield area.

degree of harm a substance or condition can cause in humans and then determining the actual risk to a given population. Risks are characterized as probabilities because risk assessments cannot eliminate uncertainty in their predictions. Uncertainty is built into the risk assessment because of the generalities used in describing the affected population and in the limited toxicological data regarding environmental contaminants. Risk assessments are usually based on information collected at a specific moment in time. This information is then extrapolated and used to characterize a site condition to which a population will be exposed. The assessment process does not consider changes in the pollutant over time or varying rates of exposure. Further, risk assessments necessarily make assumptions about the impacted population. Generalities are necessary; however, the actual impacts of exposure may vary significantly as a function of lifestyle choices or other exposures not included in the model. This uncertainty is even greater when several contaminants are involved. Even so, risk assessments are believed to be the best available guide for determining the effective use of resources and the protection of human health. The probabilities used to express risk usually represent the most likely probability of an event or risk. In some cases risk is expressed as a range from low to high. The lack of a precise number is the result of the uncertainty.

To qualify as a risk assessment, a study must include both toxicity data and exposure data. Studies performed on lab animals and extrapolated to human risk are not risk assessments. While risk assessments are quantitative tools, not all risk assessments are without bias. All risk assessments include certain assumptions that are internal to the calculations. There are also various models available that tend to emphasize one or another aspect of the assessment. The selection of the method and the choice of assumptions will influence the outcome of the risk assessment.

Risk Communication

Based on these investigations, the site conditions are identified, and data are analyzed to determine the risks associated with the redevelopment of the site. These risks are evaluated to identify the most effective and appropriate development response. In general, a redeveloper must choose from several standards for the cleanup of a site, and, while they differ from state to state, in general the choices include a pollutant-specific uniform risk-based standard, local background levels, federal or state standards (e.g., water quality standards), or site-specific risk-based standards.

Background levels are usually interpreted as the levels of the contaminant found in the surrounding area. To determine the background level, a statistically valid representation of the background must be analyzed. It should be noted that some states define the background level as the level of the contaminant found in a predeveloped condition. For many contaminants this is in effect a cleanup standard of zero. The use of background levels may be appropriate when the area of contamination is small and localized and removal of the material is a practical alternative.

The water quality standards refer to the *maximum contaminant levels* (MCLs) found in the Safe Drinking Water Act regulations. These are levels of contaminants determined to be safe for ingestion in drinking water, so they are very low quantities and often not an achievable or practical choice for a cleanup standard.

Risk-based standards are calculated using either standardized data or site-specific data. Uniform risk-based standards or numeric risk standards tend to be more conservative because they are based on standard data and relatively conservative assumptions. The standards are conservative because they are meant to be applied to any site without regard for specific information. Site-specific risk-based standards are derived from information regarding the character of the site, the contaminant dose, and the actual anticipated population to be exposed. The site-specific standard allows the developer to manage the risk of a site by calculating the intended use as part of the risk assessment. Clearly the site-specific standard is more likely to characterize the risk more accurately; however, the cost of developing site-specific health-based risk standards may be beyond the practical limits of the project. Uniform risk-based standards for various uses are becoming more common. The EPA *risk-based concentrations* (RBCs) (see Appendix 1) are an example of such standards. It is important to note that the standard includes concentrations for both industrial and residential conditions.

The communication of risk cannot be a one-way street. Effective risk communication is a dialogue. It is critical to appreciate, however, that the burden for the success of this communication is on the development team and on the ability of the site planner to interpret and incorporate the concerns of the stakeholders into the design. It is likely to be the site planner that makes the public presentation of the project, and he or she will be the first contact for many questions. The planner must be prepared to effectively communicate the elements of risk assessment and the specific risks of a site to stakeholders who are not technical people. The communication must describe the risk accurately but not necessarily in the dry technical language of science; in fact, whenever possible, jargon should be avoided. Further, the planner must be able to demonstrate how the proposed redevelopment will address the stakeholders' concerns. It is important to remember that the perception of risk is reality, and, once a perception is formed, it is difficult to change it. The inertia of perception is such that it takes about three times the amount of information to change a perception as it does to affirm one. Presenters should avoid framing a presentation in negative terms; words such as *never, nothing, none, not,* and *no* are to be avoided. Other words that reinforce negative perceptions are *contamination, pollution, toxic, concern,* and *dangerous.* Words such as *maybe, possibly, depending,* and other qualifiers undercut credibility. Presenters should also remember that from 50 to 75 percent of the message received by an audience is nonverbal and that the nonverbal communication has a greater impact on perceptions than does the verbal content.

The actual risk assessment data are quantitative, involving tables of data and conclusions qualified by lists of assumptions. The undigested use of such reports and data may only serve to generate suspicion or raise fears. The actual risk assessment findings must be crafted into a language and form that can be used by the stakeholders being addressed. For public presentations the use of graphics and charts to describe risk are recommended, but graphics should be simple and with no more than three colors. Highly technical presentations involving sophisticated equipment and requiring the lights to be turned on and off should be avoided. In general, women are perceived to be more credible in presenting risk. It may be better to have several small meetings with community groups than one large meeting; therefore, the description of the risk should be well thought out in advance, and it is suggested that the communication occur in the same fashion in every presentation. Community groups often discuss projects among themselves, outside of the risk communication meeting, and different examples or explanations of risk sometimes serve to raise suspicion and concern.

It is suggested that on projects with multiple contaminants that each contaminant or group of like contaminants be discussed individually, with its own explanation and graphics. The use of different colors to identify the groups of contaminants is useful for communications to stakeholders. It is common for nearby residents to have a preconceived idea regarding both the type and degree of contamination on a site. In some cases this preconception is not supported by the findings of the site assessment. In such cases it may be helpful to describe the site assessment and risk assessment process so that residents know how the work was performed.

The presentation should anticipate anger and frustration from the public at the outset of the risk communication. Even in cases where the exposures are nominal to nonexistent, there is often a sense of outrage on the part of the impacted residents. Such anger or outrage is an emotional response on which the science of risk assessment may have little effect. It is important to anticipate the emotional response and accept it as part of the process. In other cases there may be no reaction whatsoever. Presenters should be prepared to express empathy and concern.

The risk communication process must impart the facts with compassion and understanding. The communication must be thorough, honest, and understandable. Preparation for the public hearing should include the development of exhibits that graphically represent the site and the conditions found on the site. Site designers should become familiar with the type and location of contaminants on the site and prepare in advance to explain how these will be addressed. A site-specific, contaminant-specific response should be available for discussion at the public hearing. Presenters should be prepared to talk about the interim, as well as the final, site conditions, what residents can do to limit exposure, and what will be done on the site to limit exposure. The presentation should anticipate the concerns and questions that residents who might attend the hearing will ask. Table 3.1 provides a list of questions that should be anticipated in a typical public meeting. The communication should discuss the pros and cons of the project from a risk standpoint, addressing whether residents will be at a lower risk after redevelopment.

Table 3.1   Preparing for the Public Hearing

The presentation should prepare for questions such as those listed in this table. Presenters should also be prepared to listen during the presentation because risk communication is a two-way street. To be effective, the meeting must address the concerns and perceptions of neighbors as well as the findings of the site assessment.

Should we take any steps to reduce our exposures or risk?
What aren't you telling us?
What are the effects of the contamination?
Is there a danger breathing dusts from the site?
Who is responsible for the cleanup?
Who is responsible for the contamination?
How will the cleanup be done?
What levels will the cleanup be done to? Is that clean?
Why not clean it to zero?
Who is liable?
Should we be concerned if children play on the site?
Is there an increased risk during construction?
Are children at greater risk?
Are pregnant women at greater risk?
What has been our exposure in the past?
What has been done about the people who contaminated the site?
Why should we believe you?

It is helpful to provide the public with a means to characterize and evaluate the risk. The purpose of the public meetings is to provide information and to collect feedback. It may be useful to provide an analogy for the level of risk or for the measurements that are used in the presentation to provide the nontechnical participants with a means of evaluating the scale of the data. Table 3.2 provides a list of concentration analogies. These can be effective ways of communicating risk by comparing the risk to common activities or to familiar scales of measurement. Analogies should be limited to illustrating the concentration; risk analogies should be used only after careful consideration. Comparing risks with one behavior or exposure to another is a two-edged sword. On one hand, relating the risk associated with familiar activities such as driving a car or playing golf to illustrate a comparable risk from an environmental contaminant may be useful; however,

Table 3.2   Concentration Analogies

1 ppm is 0.0001%, or approximately equal to:
    1 minute in 2 years
    1 cent in $10,000
    1 ounce in 32 tons
    1 inch in 16 miles
    1 drop of water in 265 gallons

1 ppb is approximately equal to:
    1 second in 32 years
    1 cent in $10 million
    1 inch in 16,072 miles
    1 drop of water in 265,000 gallons

care should be taken to never trivialize or minimize the risk by such comparisons. If stakeholders perceive that the facts are being skewed or trivialized, the value of the presentation may be undercut by the distrust generated.

There are common pitfalls to avoid in the risk communication process such as the use of negatives or attempts at humor. The use of risk comparisons and technical jargon should be used only after careful consideration. Presenters should avoid expressing personal beliefs or opinions and should never offer guarantees or unfounded assurances. Likewise, care should be taken when refuting misinformation that the attack is not viewed as defensive, which could raise the perception that the misinformation has value. Finally, remember the attention span of most people for this type of technical presentation is 15 to 20 minutes. It is important to change speakers and keep the attention of the audience, but it is equally important to take only as long as is necessary to make the presentation.

Understanding Exposure and Risk

It is important to understand risk in the context of a brownfield project. Risk is present in any undertaking. For example, driving to work, taking a trip on a plane, eating food purchased in a grocery store, and smoking cigarettes all have elements of risk. In many cases these risks are significantly greater than the health risks posed by environmental contamination. There is a tendency to compare the environmental risks that may be inherent in a brownfield project to more common risks with the thought that, if people are able to draw this comparison, the environmental risk will be brought into a more reasonable perspective. In fact, such comparisons are rarely successful. The important difference between lifestyle risks and environmental risks is found in the fundamental nature of the source of the risk. Lifestyle risks for the most part are acceptable risks to the affected person. The individual may accept the increased risk of driving an automobile because of the increased mobility and choices the vehicle enables. In general, lifestyle risks are acceptable because the person believes there is some benefit received in exchange for the risk. Environmental contamination and the risks imposed by it offer no such quid pro quo. In the case of risks from a contaminated site, there is no positive tradeoff to offset the risk (Table 3.3).

The level of acceptable risk is entirely subjective. The pathways of exposure are any route or means of transport a contaminant may take that leads to exposure. We most often think of the most direct pathways such as breathing dusts or aerosols or exposures to contaminated surface waters or drinking contaminated groundwater. Less obvious methods of transport are the contaminants brought into homes on the clothing of workers or residents, contaminated food supplies either purchased or harvested, and exposures that occur in our daily activities in the workplace or in public. Other exposures may be due to lifestyle choices such as smoking or use of chemicals in a hobby. In any case the means of transport and the pathways to exposure are varied and can only be generalized for most populations. Risk assessment is most effective when it is applied to an individual. The greater the population addressed in a risk

Table 3.3 Risk Comparisons of Familiar Activities

Lifetime Cancer Risk 1 in 10,000	Occupational Risk	Lifestyle Risk	Accidents	Environmental Risk; Misc. Lifetime Risks
2	Insurance agent	Light drinking	Skiing or fishing	Natural radiation; watching television for 40 hours
9	Engineer, broker	Using birth control pills	Driving a car	Substances in drinking water; driving 50,000 miles
9–45	Policeman	Heavy drinking, canoeing		Living in a stone building for 4 years
	Miner		Rock climbing	2 mo of being a 60-year-old man
45–200	Race car driver		Skydiving	Working in a coal mine for 22 years
	Fireman			
>220	Stuntman			Smoking 2 packs of cigarettes per day for 15 years

SOURCE: Adapted from Russ 1987.

assessment, the greater the uncertainty in the assessment.

Exposure is a combination of the concentration of the toxin and the length of time or frequency of contact. A single low-level exposure to one type of toxin may have a very low probability of having an ill effect, but continued exposure to that same toxin, at the same level over time, may have a much greater probability of causing an ill effect. Risk is correlated to concentration and length of exposure. On the other hand, there are risks of an acute exposure to an increased level of a toxin where a single exposure for even a short period of time increases the probability of an effect. When considering exposure, one must understand if the exposure is *acute* (one-time exposure at a high level of concentration) or *chronic* (frequent exposures over time to a given concentration). The approach to the management of a risk may be a function of the exposure. OSHA has the responsibility for regulating occupational exposures, but it is not unheard of to have ambient exposures in homes and in public places that are higher than the occupational standards (Ott and Roberts 1998).

Understanding the exposure pathway is an important step toward determining an effective management strategy. If the pathway can be eliminated, there is no exposure and the risk is effectively eliminated. Managing such risk factors is an important approach to brownfield redevelopment that has direct implications on site design. By eliminating exposure pathways through the development plan, the site designer can often reduce and sometimes eliminate remediation expense. Site design approaches will be more thoroughly discussed in Chap. 4.

There is the question as to the bioavailability of the contamination. *Bioavailability* refers to the degree to which a chemical is available to or accessible by an organism. It is widely used in discussions of drugs or food supplements as to how much of the substance is actually available in an organism. Research in the bioavailability of substances in the environment is an expanding area of inquiry. It is understood that organic chemicals can be sequestered in the soil. The presence of *soil organic matter* (SOM) is critical in this process. SOM acts as a polymer combining with the chemicals and binding them to the soil particles. Under normal soil conditions these chemicals stay bound to the soil. In such cases the mere presence of a contaminant may not present a significant risk of exposure since the contaminant is not available to the organism; thus, in this case while there is exposure, there is no dose. In general, contamination is not currently reported in terms of its bioavailability; however, the research indicates the question of bioavailability is an important element of risk assessment and remediation strategies.

Risk and the Intended Use

Risk from contamination is a combination of the concentration of a contaminant and the exposure. Ultimately it is also a factor of the population being impacted. There are clear differences between the level of acceptable risk for a person employed in industry and an infant, for example. On one hand, it is recognized that certain trades and activities are inherently more risky than others. The degree of risk associated with certain activities is another consideration in the determination of an acceptable level of risk. A site-specific risk assessment that is to be used to determine cleanup or management strategies must select an appropriate receptor model for the intended use. If a site is to be used as a day-care center, for example, the appropriate receptors should be young children and the child care workers. If, on the other hand, the site is to be a warehouse, then industrial workers would be a more logical choice. The selection of the target receptor is as important as the concentration and exposure issues. Using the principle of acceptable risk may be an important factor in determining the use of the redeveloped site. Limiting site uses to industrial activities or restricting the use to prohibit food processing on a site may be one method of managing risk. While there are negative aspects to limiting site uses, it is one approach to managing the risk and the cost of redevelopment.

Nature of Impacts

Brownfield sites are most closely associated with some form of environmental contamination on the site that imposes an inherent ecological risk or a risk to human health. Risks are most often characterized as risks to human health. While contamination is a critical concern, the site development implication of the impacts of the industrial activities that created the brownfields often extend beyond the health and environmental considerations. Furthermore, the redevelopment of the site may require the regrading of a site, demolition of buildings, exposure to unburied contaminated materials, and ultimately the development of new features, buildings, traffic, green space, and storm water management facilities. Sites often have several different contaminants, each with its own characteristics. The horizontal and vertical distribution of contaminants and the concentrations will have an important influence on the remediation and design strategies selected for the site. The design professional must understand and address the implications of site conditions from the construction and development perspective.

Use of Contaminated Soils

The cost of removing and disposing of contaminated soils off site may be prohibitive. The costs of excavation, transportation, and eventual disposal are increased by the cost of purchasing and handling replacement fill material. Soils may be contaminated and yet still not meet the tests as hazardous waste. It may be possible to use nonhazardous contaminated soil in the redevelopment of a site. In cases where there is only a small area of low-level contamination, removal may be the best option because the cost of removing and disposing of the material is an acceptable tradeoff for avoiding ongoing maintenance costs, continued risk, and limitations on the use of the property. In cases where the amount of material is greater, costs may be significant and indicate that managing the contamination in place is the only practical alternative. It is important to draw a distinction between contaminated soils and hazardous soils. If soils that are deemed hazardous are to be used, the placement and handling should be considered carefully, closely supervised, and fully documented. This practice should be undertaken only with the agreement of the regulatory agency.

Construction Hazards

Although a significant amount of investigation will have been conducted before construction begins, it's always possible that some new condition will be found during the course of construction. In fact, it should be anticipated that unfavorable conditions will be encountered. For example, a previously unknown underground storage tank or an area of suspect fill material may be uncovered. Part of the construction planning should be the development of a contingency plan for this occurrence. The contingency plan should include the necessary phone contacts and interim instructions for the construction crew. It is unlikely that the construction crew will have specific hazardous waste site training or expertise to assess and deal with the situation, so instructions should be limited to stabilizing and protecting the site. Part of a contingency plan may include having an environmental contractor on call for such circumstances. A clear chain of command and responsibilities should be established in the plan to avoid confusion and miscommunication if an event should occur. The preparation of a well-conceived contingency plan will go a long way toward keeping the project on time and on budget.

Construction crews should be briefed regarding any on-site conditions that could be hazardous, and they should be instructed in what to do in the event of a spill or the discovery of suspect material or conditions. Likewise, construction personnel should also receive instruction in any health and safety issues prior to start of work. In some cases work on brownfield sites may require some practices that are not typical for construction personnel. It is important that contaminated soils or dusts stay on the site. A health and safety plan should be in use and enforced. Workers should be made aware of the conditions on the site and the practices necessary for them to protect themselves and their families. Construction site management issues will be discussed more fully in Chap. 5.

Nonhazardous Constraints

Brownfields also bring with them a wide range of development constraints not related to a toxic hazard. The uneven character of artificial land and fill material often presents a challenge on the redevelopment site. Brownfield soils are typically very poor and may require significant attention if they are to serve as a plant growth medium. Chapter 4 discusses soil recovery in greater detail. From an engineering standpoint, the quality of these soils may not be adequate for use as support for buildings or utilities.

ENGINEERING PROPERTIES OF SOIL

Former industrial sites have often experienced significant development impacts and degradation. The conditions of soils on a brownfield site may vary a great deal in only a few feet. It has been common on such sites to use significant cuts and fills to configure the site for the former industrial activities. In such cases it is important to have a good understanding of the soil conditions beyond the levels of contamination when planning the redevelopment. Some contaminants such as chromium tailings, for example, are very expansive; in the past, they were used liberally as fill material in some places. It is important for the landscape architect or site designer to understand the geotechnical conditions on the brownfield site (Fig. 3.2). Important soil characteristics are discussed below.

Bulk density is a common term used to describe the total weight of a soil for a specific volume: Bulk density equals the weight of a soil sample divided by the volume. The bulk density includes the moisture retained in the soil sample. The bulk density is an indicator of the ability of a soil to support foundations or the weight of structures. The higher the bulk density of a soil, the greater the support it can provide for a foundation. Materials with low bulk densities do not provide solid foundations. A crystalline rock has a bulk density of about 168 lb/ft^2. Soils have less than this because of pore space and low-density organic matter content.

The *Atterberg Limits and Soil Classification methods* attempt to quantify the variations in soils caused by grain-

Figure 3.2   Close-up of soil on brownfield site.

size distribution, clay mineralogy, and organic content. The Atterberg limits measure the water in a soil at a point where the soil acts as a liquid or begins plastic flow. Water is measured as a percentage of the weight of the soil when dry.

The *liquid limit* (LL) is the moisture content at which a soil tends to flow and will not retain its shape. It is determined in a liquid limit cup into which a molded cake of wet soil is placed. A V groove is cut through the patty with a tool designed for the purpose. Using a hand crank, the cut is repeatedly lifted and dropped until the soil flows to close the groove. When the moisture content is sufficient to close the groove at 25 drops such that the soil "flows," it is said the liquid limit has been reached.

The *plastic limit* (PL) is the moisture content at which a soil will deform. The soil is rolled into long threads until the threads just begin to crumble at a diameter of about 3 mm.

If a soil can be rolled into finer threads without cracking, it contains more moisture than its plastic limits; if it cracks before 3 mm is reached, it has less.

The numerical difference between the LL and the PL is called the *plasticity index* (PI). This is the range of moisture in which a soil behaves as a plastic material. Some clays can absorb water several times their own weight and would be said to have a large range of moisture content in which they behave plastically and before they start to flow. A PI over 15 is a good indicator of an expansive soil. ASTM D-4318 describes the current recommended methods for conducting the liquid limit and plastic limit tests.

The *Unified Soil Classification System* was developed by engineers. The classification is based on the amount of organic matter in the soil and grain size: *coarse grained,* meaning that over half of the soil is sand sized or larger, or *fine grained,* meaning that half of the soil is silt or clay. Within these categories are subcategories, set up according to distribution. The system is important because it is often referenced in geotechnical and environmental reports (see Table 3.4).

Porosity is the amount of pore space, and it is related to grain-size distribution and consolidation. *Permeability* refers to drainage or the rate or ability of water to drain through a soil. Clay soils usually have high porosity but low permeability and may settle considerably when loaded with a foundation, but they have lower compressibility and higher strength. Sandy soils, on the other hand, tend to have a low porosity and high permeability.

Soil strength refers to a soil's resistance to deformation or failure. Grain-to-grain contact produces friction, which is greatest in coarse-grained soils such as sand and gravel. Well-graded soils tend to have greater frictional resistance than those that are poorly graded. *Cohesion* is the measure of the capacity for soil particles to stick together (e.g., clays have a high cohesion). *Shear strength* is the measure

Table 3.4   Uniform Soil Classification System

GW*	Well-graded gravels	Less than 5% fines	Gravels
GP†	Poorly graded gravels		
GM	Silty gravels	More than 5% fines	
GC	Clayey gravels		
SW	Well-graded sand	Less than 5% fines	Sands
SP	Poorly graded sands		
SM	Silty sands	Sands with fines	
SC	Clayey sands		
ML‡	Inorganic silts; very fine sand		Silts and clays, liquid limit > 50%
CL	Inorganic clay	Low to medium plasticity	
OL	Organic silt and organic silty clay	Low plasticity	
MH§	Inorganic silts; sandy or silty soil	Micaceous	Silts and clays with liquid limit < 50%
CH	Inorganic clays	High plasticity	
OH	Organic clays	Medium to high plasticity	
PT	Highly organic soils	Peat and other organic soils	

*W refers to a well-graded soil—that is, soil that contains soil particles across a broad range.
†P refers to a poorly graded soil (grain distribution is important because it affects consolidation and settlement).
‡L refers to a low liquid limit; water content is less than 50%, and plasticity is low.
§H refers to a high liquid limit; water content is greater than 50%, and plasticity is high (very cohesive or sticky clay).

of the frictional resistance and cohesion of a soil. Field tests are preferred because soil is in its natural condition. A four-bladed vane is driven into the soil and then turned using a torque wrench. The shear strength of the soil is equal to the pounds of force applied at the time of failure.

DIFFICULT SOIL CONDITIONS

Brownfields may be particularly subject to difficult soil conditions because of the nature of artificial land, which is characteristic of such sites. Industrial sites are typically developed over a period of time during which material may be imported to the site from a wide range of sources, sometimes using waste products from an operation on site. In either case, difficult conditions may exist that were not identified as part of the environmental site assessment. The scope of the site assessment would be limited to recognized environmental conditions and would not include the engineering quality of the soil found on the site. Even if soil samples are taken, they are rarely analyzed for geotechnical characteristics as part of an environmental site assessment. Although contaminated soils may be removed because of contamination, the remaining soils may present other difficult construction problems.

Expansive soils—that is, soils that shrink or swell excessively—occur in every state. Signs of expansive soils may be extensive cracking of sidewalks, foundations, or retaining walls. These soils are typically clayey; however, expansive fills may be present on brownfield sites. Artificial land with certain waste products such as some mineral tailings may be particularly expansive, and it may not have the cohesion necessary to serve on new slopes.

Soil creep, or the slow downhill movement of soil, may be a concern in such cases. Soils with a low shear strength may be unsuitable for use in a new grading plan. In projects with significant slope or changes in grade, the use of poor artificial land soils could result in a slump or earth flow of a constructed slope under wet conditions. It is common to find unconsolidated fills containing slag or fly ash of a grade that has little or no construction value. Field tests should be conducted by a qualified geotechnical or soils engineer to determine if existing artificial land soils are suitable for proposed uses.

Redevelopment Strategies

Once the preceding considerations of environmental conditions, risk assessment, and site conditions are completed, a redevelopment strategy may be selected. The redevelopment strategy is the response method for implementing the proposed redevelopment while addressing the cleanup or mitigation requirements and addressing the site constraints. To succeed, the redevelopment program may need to have a range of concerns wider than strictly the cleanup aspects of a site or building. The site must work for the proposed program. The redevelopment plan and the environmental action plan should be inclusive. In designing a response plan that accomplishes the site program, designers must consider the anticipated costs of the redevelopment strategy. The scope of costs and impacts of the remedies are shown in Table 3.5.

The costs of remediation should be viewed as both initial costs and life cycle costs. For example, the cost of excavating and removing contaminated soils may be high; however, once the soil is removed, the on-site liability may end and

Table 3.5 Comparison of Remedy Types for 8,000 Tons of Gasoline-Contaminated Soil

Factor	Cost	Time to Complete	Liability	Maintenance	Use Restrictions
Permanent onsite by ex situ bioremediation and vacuum extraction	$1.4 million	2 years	None	None	None
Excavation with transport, offsite recycling, backfill with clean fill	$640,000	120 days	Risk of disposal site becoming a hazardous waste facility	None	None
Remove hot-spots, cap site, building restriction	$120,000	60 days	Cap failure, future use limited	Maintenance required forever	Site use limited

SOURCE: Adapted from Whitman 1997.

the use of the site could proceed without restriction. An alternative approach might be to leave the soils in place and cap the site to restrict exposure. In that case the initial expense would be reduced but the project would be committed to maintaining the cap, and the liability for the on-site condition may remain. The choice to manage a condition on site may mean restricting what the site may be used for. The restriction of site use means, of course, limiting the marketplace for the redeveloped project. If the site may be used for only industrial activities, the pool of possible users and the market value of the project are both reduced. The potential for impact from future regulation or the potential of exacerbation from anticipated activities should be considered as well as the impacts of use restrictions and costs. Lenders may be particularly sensitive to these issues if they are perceived as limiting the market value and return of a project.

The range of possible mitigation strategies includes the following:

- No action required, or do nothing

- Avoidance

- Administrative controls

- Design controls

- On-site remediation

- Off-site remediation

In some cases the degree of contamination is so low that specific action steps are not necessary. After investigation it is sometimes found that the perception was that the site contamination was far worse than the actual conditions and that the level of contaminants is below the levels that require any action or cleanup at all. In these instances, just as much communication to stakeholders can be necessary, particularly if the result is very different from the popular expectation. In other cases, small areas of contamination can be left in place and undisturbed in the redevelopment process so that no specific mitigation is required. By locating site features such as storm water management facilities away from areas of marginal contamination or by locating buildings or other impermeable surfaces such as parking over these same areas, more expensive controls or mitigation can be avoided.

Administrative controls are used to manage risks associated with contamination by limiting access through the use of deed restrictions or other limitations on future use. These controls generally limit the use of the site to a specific application or specific maintenance performance. Design controls, on the other hand, are site redevelopment features designed to reduce exposures to contamination or to provide passive treatment of contamination. Such features may include the capping of the impacted area to isolate contamination or the use of contaminant-resistant vegetation and the installation of fences or landscape barriers to isolate areas. The advantages of administrative and design controls are the relatively low cost and the fact that they may be used as temporary strategies and remediated in the future if that becomes desirable or technologies improve. Deed restrictions or other approaches that encumber the future use of the property should be carefully understood. The design professional should consider what steps are necessary to have the restriction lifted or removed should conditions improve or remediation is successfully completed at some future point. The effect the restriction will have on the perception of the property in the real estate market should also be considered. Use restrictions are more manageable if the redevelopment is undertaken for a single user and that user participates in the creation of the strategy. If the redevelopment project is to have multiple users or is going to be sold to others when completed, there must be consideration as to how the restrictions or maintenance of controls will be assured.

While groundwater and surface water contamination will be conducted on site, remediation of a soil or of other contaminated material may take place either on site or off site. Remediation technologies are wide ranging. As a general rule of thumb, the more short term and expensive the remediation, the greater the liability reduction it offers.

Actual treatment of contaminated soils may be conducted either on site or off site. Ex situ or off-site treatment is expensive because it requires the excavation and transportation of the material in addition to the cost of the treatment or disposal. Such costs begin at about $55 per ton of soil (for simply burning soil to remove hydrocarbons) and rise from there. In most cases, where ex situ treatment is selected, the material will not be returned and used on the site, and so costs may be increased if fill must be purchased to replace the lost volume of soil. The development of vitrification technology for some contaminated soils has offset this cost and handling somewhat. In these technologies contaminated soils are mixed with additives including portland cement to create a mix with a very low permeability and a relatively high strength. If volumes are adequate, these operations can be conducted on the site requiring no additional transportation. Vitrified soils have been successfully used as bedding material for roads and parking areas.

On-site treatment has become a more attractive alternative for many projects because of the cost avoidance of handling and transportation and the reduced liability of relocating a problem over public streets and disposal in another location. There is a wide variety of technologies for on-site or in situ treatment of contaminated soils. The choice of technology is usually based on the type and concentration of the contaminant, the time frame available for completion of remediation, and the budget.

The redevelopment of the environmentally compromised or contaminated site will require the landscape architect to include a variety of atypical design considerations. Typical designs may expect to involve the isolation of contaminated soils beneath paved surfaces or locate storm water facilities to avoid infiltration through contaminated soils. It may be necessary for the designer to select plant materials that are tolerant of extreme conditions associated with contaminated or artificial land sites. It is necessary to select appropriate plant materials while sometimes considering the ramifications of using an exotic species that best fills the need for the site. Phytoremediation methods rely on plant species genetically predisposed to absorb or fix a specific contaminant. The landscape architect must be familiar with the science and prepared to adapt the plant material pallet to such considerations. These issues will be more fully discussed in Chap. 4.

Some redevelopment sites are under the direct influence of upgradient sites so that run-on stormwater may contain contaminants that have direct impacts in the environmental quality of the subject site. While arguments of liability and control consume years, the landscape architect may provide short-term mitigation through collection and passive biological treatment technologies currently available. The landscape architect involved in the redevelopment of contaminated sites should be prepared to work closely with bioremediation specialists and to adapt designs to provide the environment and surfaces required for cost-effective bioremediation. In any case the selection of a remediation strategy and the site design must take into account all of the contaminants, the concerns of stakeholders, the construction constraints, the liability concerns, regulatory restrictions, and the redevelopment vision or program—all within the budget of the client.

Multiple Contaminants

In projects involving multiple contaminants, a combination of strategies may be necessary to address all the concerns. When the contaminants are coincidental—that is, located in the same area or mixed—the strategies may involve a hierarchy of responses, determining which of the contaminants presents the greatest risk and designing a response to that contaminant. It should be noted that if the treatment is pollutant specific, such as a bioremediation strategy, additional steps may be required to address the pollutants not affected by the action. Another concern is the effects of combinations of contaminants. Very little is known about the hazards and risks associated with combinations of contaminants, particularly at low concentrations. A note of caution may be appropriate when electing to manage combinations of contaminants in place. It is possible that some pollutants in combination and at very low concentrations may have some additive effect.

Remediation Technology

Remediation technologies are media specific and range from very technology intensive approaches to natural attenuation. The choice of technology may be as much a function of time frame and budget as it is the contaminant and media. Site designers should be familiar with the general types of remediation technology and how they may affect the development of a site. It should be noted that the field of remediation technology is one of ongoing innovation. Also, many technologies may be available under proprietary names. Claims of effectiveness should be weighed carefully with the documentation to confirm the appropriateness of the technology to a given application. Table 3.6 summarizes the general types of remediation technologies.

BIOREMEDIATION

Bioremediation is a process in which microorganisms such as bacteria and fungi transform contaminants to a less toxic

Table 3.6 Description of Remediation Technologies

The following list of remediation technologies includes the most common approaches; however, it is not an exhaustive list. Remediation technology continues to be an area of innovation and experimentation.

Solidification	Also called *vitrification* or *stabilization.* Removes water and changes the soil or solid medium chemically to reduce permeability and transport of contaminant by percolation.
Soil vapor extraction	Used to remove VOCs from soil through the use of vapor extraction wells. Sometimes used in conjunction with air injection systems. Contaminants are volatilized and flushed into the air for treatment.
Incineration	Controlled burning of soil or solids to convert, degrade, or oxidize contaminants. May be done on site or off site.
Bioremediation	Microorganisms used to degrade organic compounds in soils or groundwater. May be done in situ or ex situ. Many variations on technique and methods.
Soil washing	Water is used to flush through soils or medium to flush contaminants out. May involve removing soils and using mechanical agitation. Additives may be used to increase efficiency of the process.
Solvent extraction	Solvents are used to remove contaminant from soils or solid medium.
Dechlorination	Chemical treatment to remove chlorine atoms bonded to hazardous chemicals. Hydrogen or hydroxide ions used to detoxify materials.
Phytoremediation	Use of plants to remove or biostabilize contaminants in soil, sediments, or water.
Air sparging	Injection of air into groundwater to flush volatile contaminants, which are collected and treated by the soil vapor extraction processes.
Passive treatment wells	Barriers are constructed of reactive materials and installed in the aquifer to promote a chemical reaction between the barrier and the contaminant in the groundwater. Example would be a limestone barrier used to increase the pH of the groundwater.

or nontoxic state. Bioremediation is the augmenting or enhancement of natural processes to reduce or eliminate a contaminant in soil or water. In principle, the technical and economic advantage of bioremediation is the expected minimal impact of bioremediation as opposed to more invasive methods that would involve the excavation of contaminated soils and treatment or disposal. A common approach is to simply introduce nutrients into an environment with the intention of encouraging the growth of bacteria already present in a contaminated environment. As might be expected, the success of this kind of approach varies widely. The results of bioremediation have been difficult to predict, leading to wide variations in results and limited success as part of an overall remediation plan. The lack of predictability is the most significant criticism of this approach. Biotechnical research is increasing the predictability of the remediation technology and expanding the scope of bioremediation applications. Research in bioremediation includes a wide range of technologies such as biofiltering, bioreacting, biostimulation, and composting. Researchers have expanded from the use of bacteria to include fungi and enzymes. The identification of bacteria that will function in extreme environments has expanded the range of applications to more toxic environments or conditions with temperature extremes. In addition, new biologically based tools are being developed to assist in the process of site characterization and assessment.

This promising technology has experienced mixed success in field applications, and that has led to limited use of the technology on contaminated sites. Site operators are reluctant to risk remediation funds on unpredictable or unreliable approaches. The limits of bioremediation can be technical on one hand, but they are often rooted in the expectations of the users and how the technology is applied. Bioremediation is not proven technology. In some applications it has worked; in many applications it has failed. Up to now the state of the art in the field has been indeterminate. Site owners and managers have been unable to reliably predict the effectiveness of many of the available bioremediation techniques and have selected other, often more expensive, remediation options. The early approach to biotechnology had limited success, relying to a large degree on a pot-luck mixture of what might be existing in the soil already. Without accounting for the specific requirements of the site, the contaminants and the soil, such generic approaches will continue to produce uneven results.

What is needed is a complete characterization of what is on the site and what is needed in biological terms. Preliminary bioremediation assessments must collect data on the soil conditions, the contaminants, and the nutritional, air, and moisture requirements for the particular site characteristics. A biological agent may be found to be present and specifically acting on the contaminant in the existing site conditions. By collecting samples of the site soils and contaminants, a site-specific plan for use on the site can be designed. The lab can determine not only which biological agent or combination of agents would work best but also what nutrients, air, and water are necessary to optimize the process. The laboratory can also determine the most effective form of application. (For example, is it necessary to till the soil, or should it be removed and loaded into a container in slurry form? What is the necessary contact time? How much mixing is necessary?) With the conditions and parameters outlined, the predictability of the process increases and bioremediation becomes a cost-effective alternative for site remediation. The site characterization allows the development of a targeted biological solution, which increases the effectiveness and predictability of the application. The custom design of the bioremediation may provide the lowest-cost alternative on many sites.

Work is currently under way on increasing the predictability and scope of bioremediation methods. The determination methods and the application of the microorganisms may be the most important element of the bioremediation process. Successful bioremediation projects will include a thorough site characterization to determine the best biologic application and method.

Research is also under way using bacteria known as *extremophiles*. These are bacteria that live, and often thrive, at temperature extremes or in very toxic environments. For example, bacteria have been found that live in temperatures of 120°C or that grow in very toxic solvents. By using the natural ability of these bacteria to survive and function in these extremes, scientists hope to produce enzymes that will break down specific contaminants. These bacteria in the proper application may be able to provide effective remediation in extreme environments.

PHYTOREMEDIATION

Phytoremediation is an emerging technology and an exciting opportunity for expanding the use of plant materials on an impacted site. Phytoremediation uses plants to either absorb contaminants into the plant tissues, to metabolize or biochemically convert the contaminant, or to influence the level of contamination in some other way. Plant materials are selected for their inherent capability. Although genetically altered plants have been used in promising experiments, they are not available yet for general applications. Studies of phytoremediation tend to consider the capability of unaltered plant species or the genetic manipulation or engineering of a species for effectiveness with a specific contaminant. Of the two, the former has immediate interest for the landscape architect or site engineer. Phytoremediation is discussed in Chap. 5.

Life Cycle and Maintenance Planning

An important aspect of sustainable development must be understanding the *life cycle costs* (LCC) and the benefits of a development action. Costs are usually categorized as initial costs and operation and maintenance costs. *Initial costs* include the costs of environmental site assessment, site design, site acquisition, construction, and start-up. *Operation and maintenance (O&M) costs* include the general maintenance of the facilities and operation costs including energy, replacement of capital items, and expenses such as insurance. Initial costs are usually reduced by the salvage value or market value of the property. All costs are calculated in current dollars; no discounting for reduced future values are included. The purpose of calculating the LCC is to enable an owner or an operator to efficiently allocate resources and capital over the life of an asset. There are a variety of software packages on the market to support an LCC; however, the limits of the software should be carefully evaluated to be certain it has the flexibility that might be necessary for brownfield applications.

The nature of the brownfield site may require the landscape architect or site engineer to think in a different way about the lifespan of the design and the materials used in construction. Design life on brownfields may have a greater significance than on more routine sites. The presence of site contamination and its fate over time could be important considerations for the long-term feasibility of the project. In the past, risk has been routinely transferred or shared without regard or compensation. The presence of contamination on the brownfield site is an example of the transfer of risks and costs from one person to another. Environmental degradation may have benefited some at the expense of others. The businesses and activities that polluted benefited by avoiding the costs of not polluting; these costs and risks were paid for in terms of the loss of environmental quality and public health impacts. Still another transfer is under way in that the people responsible and that benefited from the contamination in many cases are not the people subsequently cleaning it up.

Design Life

The LCC process begins in the feasibility stage by defining the requirements the project must meet or fulfill. Once the requirements are identified, the design process is as much a function of the analysis as it is anything else. To understand and respond to the full range of project requirements, the outreach to stakeholders must be completed in the early steps of the design process.

Most contemporary development projects have a design life of between 25 and 75 years, although actual lifespans are difficult to project because of retrofitting and changes in use. The subject of this book is the reuse of properties that have outlived their original purpose and are being recycled into a new use or application. On some sites the implications of the decision to reuse a site may be more significant than designers and developers appreciate. Most real estate developments are undertaken on the basis that the projected return will be greater than the initial costs and anticipated O&M. Life cycle costing may be used, but it is focused primarily on the initial life of the project and the debt service. Although life cycle costing has become more common, one study found that it is practiced by less than half of the municipalities surveyed (Arditi and Messha, 1996). The LCC has been demonstrated to be an effective project management and decision tool; however, the environmental impact costs are often not considered in existing models and software. Brownfields add a new dimension to life cycle costing since the mitigation of contamination may be required beyond the design life of a given project.

The types and conditions of contamination on brownfields vary significantly; however, the LCC should consider the design life of a project as well as the lifespan and fate of the contamination. Where some toxic materials may be expected to remain relatively unchanged in the groundwater or soils, others may be actively degrading. Of those that are degrading, some may actually become more toxic. On some sites the rate of natural attenuation may be projected, and even manipulated, to identify when the contamination will fall below toxic levels. This prediction has important ramifications for the site. A site previously operated with site use restrictions may be able to have those restrictions lifted once the contamination has been attenuated or degraded. The site uses would be limited then only by the market forces and not constrained by the residual contamination. On the other hand, however, it is also possible that on a particular site, the contamination and attendant risks can be expected to survive the normal lifespan of the redevelopment project or the normal construction practices and materials.

The EPA defines *natural attenuation* as "a passive remedial approach that depends on natural processes to degrade and dissipate petroleum constituents in soil and groundwater" (EPA 1997). Other EPA documents discuss the application of natural attenuation on inorganics (EPA 1997). The apparent cost-avoidance aspects makes natural attenuation an attractive alternative. There are several elements of the approach that should be considered in the life cycle evaluation of the project. First are the degradation products of petroleum products. Although the petroleum products degrade through natural processes, the products of degradation, such as *polycyclic aromatic hydrocarbons* (PAHs) or aliphatic compounds such as octane, may be more toxic. These second-generation contaminants may be more stable in the environment, more resistant to natural degradation. In one study the contaminants normally used to characterize gasoline contamination were not found at a site after 40 years; however, there were significant levels of the degradation products (McDowell 1998).

Next are the conditions necessary for natural attenuation. Petroleum products are best degraded in an aerobic environment—that is, in soils or aquifers with a suitable permeability. Soils with low K, or hydraulic conductivity, values may not be suited for natural attenuation strategies. The North Carolina Department of Environment, Health and Natural Resources has prepared a document that provides guidelines for natural attenuation of petroleum products and suggests that only sites with a saturated K of 10^{-4} cm/s be considered for natural attenuation.

The third concern lies in the actual concentration of contamination. It has been shown that high levels of petroleum products inhibit the natural micro flora and fauna that are the processes of natural attenuation so that even in very favorable conditions the contamination may persist unchanged for extended periods of time (McDowell 1998). Other studies have shown that natural attenuation becomes slower as the temperature becomes lower (Myers and Tang 1998).

Last are the concerns over permit conditions and changing environmental regulations. Is it possible to accurately predict a rate of natural attenuation on a given site to the degree necessary to satisfy the regulatory agencies? What are the risks associated with finding several years into a project that the actual rate of natural attenuation is lower than projected? Will the agency require a more active response and what would the cost of that response be? ASTM has developed the Guide for Remediation by Natural Attenuation, E-1943, that could assist in the evaluation of this option.

In practice, many sites are abandoned because of obsolescence rather than environmental issues. These sites may have relatively small environmental impacts to contend with. Other sites may require substantial resources for cleanup prior to the actual redevelopment of the site or will require ongoing remediation processes over the life of the project. The LCC process is usually driven by one of two scales or criteria; the lowest initial cost or the lowest operating cost. LCC is intended to be a total systems approach to analyzing a project, but many models do not consider the costs of managing the environmental costs after the functional life of the project.

Performance Requirements

Projects that are driven by the initial costs may opt to address the existing contamination by managing the contamination in place. This strategy may have distinct advantages to the developer because it avoids the cost and time of a cleanup, but it may have significant back-end costs. The strategy may require engineering controls that will involve a maintenance program to assure the integrity of the mitigation or controls. These engineering controls must be managed for the life of the contamination, however, not only for the life of the project. Some types of contamination may be expected to have lifespans well beyond the typical real estate development. The engineering controls must be maintained; if they are not, the developer could risk violating a condition of the project and lose the protection of the original agreement with the authorities.

Some programs request a performance requirement to be certain future maintenance commitments are met. The failure to meet these requirements would empower the state agency to take steps to assure the maintenance was completed. The costs of the state intervention would be paid for by forfeit of the guarantee or calling for the bond. The developer would suffer the financial losses and the loss of liability protection. The latter could open the developer up to third-party lawsuits and actions by regulators.

Evaluating the Site Plan for Life Cycle Costs

Design strategies always have cost implications; however, assumptions for normal maintenance and operations may not apply on a given brownfield site.

In many projects, impermeable caps are designed to be used for parking or storage areas, and the design of these pavements is coincidental to the design of the cap. In many cases, these caps are active production areas such as container or inventory storage areas. On some sites the capped area is used for parking. The wear and tear on such pavements is significant. Deteriorating pavements are a familiar problem for most site managers. Pavements on active redeveloped brownfield sites should not be anticipated to have an effective life greater than the average parking lot.

Further, many brownfield sites involve construction of caps and parking-storage areas over fills of artificial land and unconsolidated materials, further increasing the risk of failure of the pavement and again shortening the anticipated lifespan. The LCC of these sites should include a consideration not only of shortened pavement lifespan but also the experience and loss of income that might be associated with the need to remove the impacted area for functional service for periodic maintenance or inspection. The ASTM has approved a Standard Guide for Environmental Life Cycle Assessment of Building Materials/Products, E-1991. The International Standards Organization (ISO) has also produced a document: ISO 14040 Life Cycle Assessment—Principles and Framework, which outlines the processes acceptable to ISO. Companies and organizations involved in international work, particularly with the European Union, adhere to the ISO standards.

Anticipating Obsolescence

The design life of a site is geared to the single original function of the site. The LCC process, in theory, should suggest that at a predictable point, it will become unprofitable to continue to use the site as originally intended. Many factors may influence the decision such as increasing maintenance costs, a change in the operation, falling revenues, or a change in the real estate market dynamics. When the facility no longer serves its original purpose, it is functionally obsolete. Under typical real estate practices in the United States, the facility is either sold or converted into a second rein-carnation. This second life is usually a lower-value use and brings lower revenues. In this scenario, the brownfield site may be a difficult asset to sell or reassign if the new revenues are not adequate to address the maintenance costs required. Unlike other commercial real estate, the seller may remain liable for the maintenance of the cap or other engineering controls if the new owner does not perform as required. Part of the project planning should be to antici-pate the eventual and inevitable obsolescence of the project in terms of resale and adequate income to maintain the requisite environmental controls.

The effect of including the costs of obsolescence in the LCC would be to increase the O&M costs, particularly toward the end of the project's functional life. Although the project may be required to provide a guarantee in the form of a bond of some sort in the initial stages, it is unlikely that cost would be substantial enough to act as a deterrent on a project driven by initial costs. On projects driven by the O&M costs, the costs of obsolescence may be another matter.

Deed Restrictions

Another tool favorably viewed by projects driven by initial cost concerns is the election to restrict the use of the property. Using health-based risk standards, a facility may be restricted to only industrial uses and avoid the cost of a cleanup. In these cases the property is encumbered by a covenant or deed restriction that limits its use, restricting or prohibiting other uses for the site. Developers have found that there is a reluctance on the part of many prospective tenants to become involved with such a site. In the final analysis the client must decide what level of cleanup his project needs to be successful. It is entirely possible that prospective clients may require a more stringent cleanup standard than the regulatory agencies. If a prospective tenant or buyer is sensitive to environmental issues, they may require the developer to provide assurances that all environmental liability issues are resolved. In most cases this interest lies in the tenant's desire to meet their perceived fiduciary responsibilities more so than a first interest in the actual environmental risk, but the effect is the same.

An advantage of the deed restriction approach is that with it, the initial expense of a cleanup can be avoided, but having elected to use the deed restriction does not preclude future remedial actions that might be sufficient to remove the limits on the use of the site. Should a developer choose to mitigate the site over time using bioremediation or phytoremediation, the deed restriction may provide an option for a limited use of the property until the site remediation is complete. Having completed and demonstrated the remediation results to the satisfaction of the regulatory community, the developer may be able to remove the deed restriction and limits on the use of the site. This may be an effective strategy to assist the developer in carrying the cost of the land and the remedial action.

CHAPTER 4

Storm Water Management

The development of land results in increased runoff from impermeable surfaces because of the change in the equilibrium between precipitation and the infiltration capacity of the site. For many years the customary practice was to simply to do nothing about the runoff from developed sites or, in the more recent past, to simply detain the increase for a period of time. These practices tended to concentrate the runoff into channels and pipes and increase the velocity within those conveyances, often resulting in erosion and increased sedimentation downstream. In any case, the amount of precipitation that was absorbed into the soil to recharge local groundwater was drastically reduced, even eliminated from some sites. The result was, and in some cases continues to be, an observed general degradation of the ecosystem and environmental quality exhibited by lower local water tables, reduced base flow to stream, and loss of riparian zone quality. These characteristics are especially true in densely developed urban industrial areas.

Site planners have begun to respond to these conditions and to reduce impacts through better planning and design. Practices such as taking a watershed approach when looking at an individual site or reducing the effects of concentration of storm water by providing for increased infiltration and reducing runoff have become more common. Landscape architects and site engineers must factor the brownfield conditions into their own site evaluation process and adjust the design solution to the particulars of the situation for which they have been engaged. No element of site design of a brownfield project may be more challenging than storm water management. The conditions and constraints of specific brownfield projects require rethinking some of the standards commonly employed in site design. For example, although infiltration is usually considered the most desirable approach to storm water management, on a given brownfield, site infiltration may not be an option. Many of these are urban sites that were originally constructed without on-site storm water facilities and have little space for on-site collection and treatment. While the impacted site is confounded by the constraints of the site, the final constructed design must still function in its programmed role, be esthetically pleasing, work economically, and, one would hope, advance the state of the practice where possible.

Standards of practice and design are usually the result of learning what works best through the application of professionally applied trial and error, as well as a consensus and balance between safety, utility, and cost. Standard design details are confidently employed because the work of earlier professionals has been judged as sound and effective by their peers and have stood the test of time by users. Design of impacted sites is an emerging area of practice still young enough that there are few, if any, standards that can claim the proof of time. As in most emerging fields, designs stand on the success of those practitioners and successes that preceded them.

The Redevelopment Site

Candidates for rehabilitation or remedial action may have been originally constructed without regard for on-site storm water management. Changes in use and reconstruction may provide opportunities to introduce features that promote water quality or at least mitigate poor quality runoff. *Best management practices* (BMPs) will have to be adapted for use on existing sites. The NPDES Phase II Final Rule may require permitting of facilities that were previously not required to address storm water quality.

The impact of developed land on surface waters is well documented. The construction process may contribute to the degradation of surface waters by increasing the sediment loading of streams, resulting in significant impacts on the habitat of native benthic and aquatic life. Completed development projects will have increased the impermeable surface of an area, resulting in the increase and velocity of storm water runoff. Large roof and paved surfaces also tend to increase the temperature of runoff and include pollutants associated with the operation of automobiles. Projects that include large unpaved lawn areas may contribute to the pollution of surface water through the imprudent or prophylactic use of pesticides and fertilizers.

Water quality issues are addressed in the storm water management requirements of some states, but they are not considered at all in other states. The need for a coordinated approach to nonpoint sources of pollution has resulted in several iterations of regulation. The original regulatory approach to water pollution addressed point sources such as industrial process waste and domestic sewage flows. The method was, in general, a direct end-of-the-pipe approach—essentially the installation of treatment waste to a minimum water quality standard prior to release. The National Pollution Discharge Elimination System (NPDES) point source program has had remarkable results. Pollution from nonpoint sources (NPSs) has been more difficult to regulate. NPSs are by definition not discrete concentrated or channelized flows and cannot necessarily be addressed with end-of-the-pipe approaches. Except in some industrial situations, the NPDES did not address NPSs until 1988, when the Natural Resources Defense Council (NRDC) sued the EPA for failure to develop and issue a nonpoint source program as required in the Clean Water Act. The NRDC and the EPA reached an agreement out of court, and the NPDES NPS Phase I program was developed and in place by October 1992.

The regulations addressed urban runoff from more industrial facilities, municipal storm sewers from cities serving more than 100,000 people, and construction sites of more than 5 acres. The EPA issued a final rule on August 7, 1995, for Phase II NPDES nonpoint source regulations that will extend the regulations to include commercial, retail, light industrial, and institutional facilities, construction activities under 5 acres, and municipal storm sewers for municipalities serving less than 100,000 people. Facilities affected by these regulations will be expected to apply for permits by August 7, 2001.

If NPSs of water pollution represent the largest category of water pollution sources and contribute the greatest amount of pollutants, then regulating NPSs is a rational public policy approach. Simply regulating new construction, however, would do nothing to affect the existing sources of water pollution, so it is necessary to consider remedial actions of existing facilities and perhaps most especially brownfield sites. The methods of remedial actions, however, are not as obvious. The regulations raise significant issues for existing facilities that did not account for storm water quality issues in most cases or even quantity control in many cases. Issues such as how and where to locate water quality facilities on densely developed urban sites may require creative technical and regulatory solutions developed on a case-by-case basis.

The August 7, 1995, Federal Register identified Phase II discharges as "point source discharges of storm water from commercial, retail, light industrial, and institutional facilities, construction activities under 5 acres and from municipal separate storm sewer systems serving populations of less than 100,000." This description could include malls, shopping centers, schools, churches, warehouses, and office parks, in addition to smaller construction sites, towns, and villages. In addition to brownfields, urban, suburban, and rural sites discharges will all be affected. Designers must identify ways to deal with these anticipated requirements.

Sites constructed with storm water management facilities have a distinct compliance advantage over other sites. Many on-site storm water facilities are overdesigned with regard to capacity due to conservative design assumptions and criteria. The conservative design approach may provide some, albeit limited, capacity for the introduction of best management practices in existing facilities without complete reconstruction. The comparison of as-built to design conditions would identify differences in volume, and experience with the function of a pond could identify even more. It is not uncommon to find a detention facility that does not function as designed. Variances in design versus performance include that the actual runoff collected into the pond is less than the design anticipated, the facility is overdesigned and the capacity is excessive, and the built outlet structure does not function as anticipated. In each of these cases some additional capacity may be found in the system.

The actual quantity of runoff collected and controlled by facilities is often different in practice than modeled in design (Short and Hwang 1989). Upstream development, the construction of other facilities upstream in a watershed, changes in grading and site layout, the condition of paving and the storm water facilities—all affect the performance and capacity of a facility. The combined effects of development and storm water management facilities within a watershed or subshed may provide opportunities for remedial action. A study of a developed watershed area, carefully evaluating the impacts and influence of development on succeeding storm water facilities, may reveal hidden capacity in total detention or the opportunity to provide a wide area approach to water quality. By considering the area as a whole rather than as discrete points and permits, it may be possible to achieve greater and more cost effective improvement in runoff water quality. Unlike modeling conducted in the planning stages, the evaluation of the constructed storm water facilities can look at actual performance. In the event that additional capacity is discovered, the installation of best management practices in existing facilities may be possible.

Another opportunity for the construction of BMPs on existing facilities may require relief from zoning and development requirements in some areas. For example, many commercial facilities are designed with extensive parking facilities that are rarely used to capacity. In many cases these facilities are dictated by local development standards or zoning. Remedial action may require converting some parking area to water quality facilities, and relief from zoning regulations could be necessary. Facilities with significant overcapacity might be encouraged through incentives to provide capacity for wide area facilities. Local zoning administrators may have to decide whether to have water quality protection or meet parking requirements.

Retrofitting Existing Facilities

In cases where overcapacity can be identified, existing basins could be converted completely to serve as wide area or regional water quality facilities. It may be possible to decommission a storm water basin where its function could be replaced by combining it with other facilities. In the event that capacity is found in existing systems, dry detention basins offer several opportunities for adaptation for water quality. In some cases these adaptations will have only nominal impact on the capacity and function of existing basins. The construction of infiltration beds in the bottom of existing dry detention basins or the construction of reed beds in existing detention basins are possible methods of converting a functioning dry basin from a strictly quantity control function to a quantity-quality function. In both of these cases, installation of the water quality feature would have no appreciable impact on the design function of the basin.

Design criteria for many BMPs are well established and could be applied with no modification in most cases. On sites that utilize grass-lined swales to convey storm water, infiltration channels could be installed in the channel to collect low flows of runoff and encourage infiltration. In these cases swales are modified by backfilling a trench installed in the low-flow channel of the swale, with stone almost to the existing surface. When storms occur frequently, the runoff is collected into the channel and then into the infiltration trench (see Fig. 4.20). In swales with steeper grades, the infiltration trench may be installed in reverse steps to encourage collection and infiltration.

For sites without existing storm water management facilities, it will be necessary to carefully evaluate the site and circumstances to determine the best approach for remedial action. For example, a site located higher up in a watershed may present the opportunity to acquire access or capacity in a downstream facility with excess capacity or develop on-site capability through the creative use of existing site features. For example, parking areas may be modified to include the installation of landscaped islands, which would be designed to serve as infiltration systems, or the installation of shallow detention areas in outlying parking areas on existing pavement, which would outlet to properly vegetated swales for treatment prior to release to downstream facilities.

To reduce the pollution originating on existing commercial, industrial, and institutional facilities, it will be necessary to develop methods of adapting BMPs to new applications. Existing facilities with and without storm water management facilities may be faced with treating the storm water runoff from their sites. Some of these sites may be severely constrained from installing the required facilities due to the density of development, existing site conditions, and economic factors.

Identifying the adaptations and applications will require technical and regulatory problem solving. The redesign of existing storm water management facilities may be undertaken based on evaluating as-built and current conditions and functions. Some BMPs may be applied with only nominal impact on existing function; however, other facilities may be situated in such a manner that they may be adapted to serve a wider network of sources. The adaptation of BMPs will be restricted by the space available to install the modifications and the current function of storm water management facilities. Designers will have to seek creative ways to generate the desired effect of treating site runoff with limited flexibility on the site.

The design criteria for BMPs are established to achieve the highest and most effective performance out of each application. In remedial applications, combinations of BMPs may be necessary to meet the same objectives. Remedial actions may rely on creative approaches to reduce the size necessary for BMPs by reducing or delaying the runoff directed to the facilities. In some areas a rougher paving surface or redirected off-site runoff may serve to reduce the size of facilities just enough to allow the use of existing facilities. The conservative assumptions and design criteria of original site designers may also serve as resources for mining the unused capacity of existing facilities.

Regulatory bodies must be willing to participate in finding the opportunities on Phase II sites by working with landowners to provide zoning and development ordinance relief when it is necessary. Public agencies must also provide guidance on BMP modification and facilitate practical approaches to the modification of existing sites and facilities.

Storm Water Management on a Capped Site

Perhaps the most extreme constraint faced by the designer of a contaminated site is the presence of an impervious cap. Impervious caps are constructed to seal the surface of a site, to prevent the infiltration of water through the cap and the contaminated soils, and to contain or isolate the contamination from accessibility and contact with humans or the environment. Caps differ from more common impervious covers such as paved parking areas in this need to isolate the subsurface from human and environmental exposure. Caps limit infiltration to prevent leaching or transport of the contained contaminants. The function of the cap itself is critical. Failing pavement may present the site manager with a rough-looking site and accelerate the general deterioration of a parking lot, but it presents no health or environmental risks; this is not true of the pavement used as a cap on a contaminated site. The impervious cap may also restrict the depth of soil and possible root growth area. Impervious caps and layers may also collect water in root zones and act as pots, drowning the plants. Further, the presence of a cap may preclude the construction of buildings or other heavy structures.

Impervious Caps

Impervious caps may be constructed in several ways. Until recently caps were constructed primarily of clay. Clays are

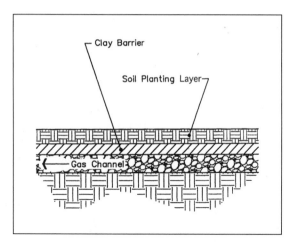

Clay Barrier

Soil Planting Layer

Gas Channel

Figure 4.1   Clay cap system. The clay barrier is kept moist, causing the clay particles to swell, which causes the clay to act as an impermeable barrier. Clay layer thicknesses vary from 1 to 3 feet.

used because of their low permeability and porosity. Bentonite is a naturally occurring clay that has been used in many applications because it is a very fine grained clay with excellent absorbency and high swelling characteristics, which have made it ideal for capping sites. In some areas local clays may be used in the construction of clay caps to keep the costs down. In such cases additives such as portland cement or soluble salts may be used to increase the density of the local clay and to decrease its permeability. Clay caps must be kept moist to maintain their effectiveness so it is common to have shallow-rooted plantings over the cap in a layered system of soil (Fig. 4.1).

In some cases macadam or bituminous concrete may be used as a rigid cap (Fig. 4.2). This is a common strategy used in redevelopment projects because of its relative low cost and its ability to also function for a parking area. The maintenance of the macadam cap requires commonly available equipment and methods. Maintenance considerations will be discussed in Chap. 6.

The use of geotextile or impervious liners has become more common as liner technology has improved. The most common type of cap used today is impervious geotextile. The success of these liners is due to the degree of proven effectiveness and the relatively low cost. Installation is fairly simple, and in most cases there is little, if any, maintenance. Geotextiles are often used in conjunction with a stone or macadam cap (Figs. 4.3 through 4.5).

Strategies for impervious caps are limited. The nature of the cap eliminates infiltration at the site of the cap and dictates that runoff will have to be collected and dispersed

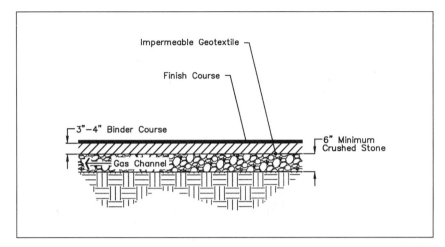

Figure 4.2 Bituminous cap detail. This treatment is used on many brownfield sites because it is a relatively inexpensive approach. It is used to double as a parking lot or storage area.

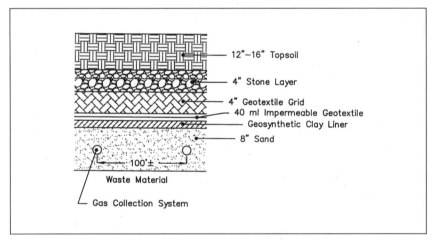

Figure 4.3 Geotextile cap system for waste areas requiring gas collection.

away from the cap. In the case of clay caps, some moisture contact is necessary to maintain the integrity of the cap so that a layer of soil and vegetation may be used above the cap. The clay cap is typically crowned to provide drainage off the cap surface and to discourage ponding (Fig. 4.6).

It is anticipated that most redevelopment projects will employ a concrete or geotextile cap rather than clay because

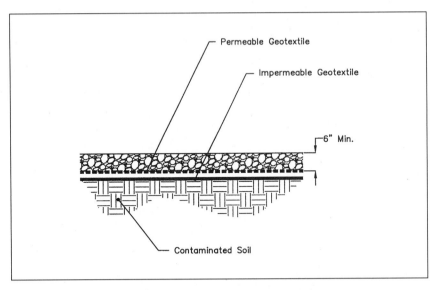

Figure 4.4   Geotextile cap system for areas requiring only isolation.

Figure 4.5   Photograph of geotextile-capped site. The presence of the shallow cap presents significant problems for planting design.

Figure 4.6 Photograph of paved parking area over a geotextile cap.

the redevelopment sites will tend to use the capped area for parking and other purposes. The use of concrete and geotextiles provides a smaller cap cross section and is usually less expensive than clay when all costs are taken into account. These materials require no moisture to maintain their effectiveness, and contact with storm water is discouraged. Unlike parking lots, the installation of subsurface collection may not be an option on the capped site since the inlets and pipes require a penetration of the cap. Exfiltration from storm water and sanitary sewage conveyances would introduce water into the contained soils. If groundwater is present, infiltration to these pipes could convey contamination off site.

A utility chase or trench, as shown in Fig. 4.7, similar in concept to those used in buildings, may be an option on some sites. The trench is designed to not penetrate the cap and provides a utility corridor that ensures isolation from the contamination for both the utilities and utility workers. The cap must have positive drainage.

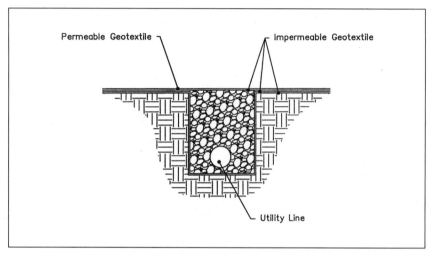

Figure 4.7 Utility trench. The location of the utility trench on some capped sites may require extraordinary measures. This trench is completely lined with impermeable geotextile. It is necessary to design these trenches with positive drainage.

Pervious Caps

Although less common, pervious caps are sometimes used as a means of containing or isolating contaminants but not restricting infiltration. Such caps might be used for materials such as *polycyclic aromatic hydrocarbons* (PAHs) where the levels indicate that protection is warranted but removal or treatment is not considered an option. In such cases layers of soil may be used in conjunction with pervious geotextile layers simply to separate the contamination from contact at the surface. Storm water may still infiltrate since the PAHs tend to remain bound to soil particles and are not water soluble. Pervious caps present far fewer problems for designers since there is no real restriction on root growth areas or grading (Figs. 4.8 and 4.9).

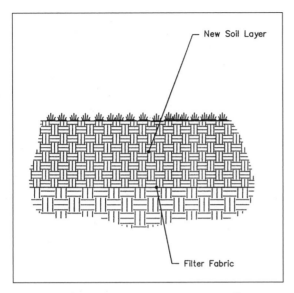

Figure 4.8 Shallow planting layer over geotextile.

Figure 4.9 Photograph of shallow soil layer and turf over a capped site.

Storm Water on the Brownfield Site

There are any number of watershed modeling approaches for determining runoff from a site, and many jurisdictions dictate which approach will be used, even which factors may be used in the analysis. Each of these systems is valuable within the limits of its assumptions and construction; however, the *rational method* is often sited as the best choice for small watersheds (Dodson 1996). The use and application of various methods are fully described in other works and in many local government documents. This book will concentrate on specific methods for storm water design on brownfield sites.

Redevelopment and water quality solutions are a matter of effective design. The redeveloped site may require some innovation in storm water management. Brownfield sites may require that infiltration be discouraged, that storm water be treated somehow on site, or that drainage onto the site be diverted from impacted areas, or they require no special considerations at all. What is more, all of these may be present on the same project. If it is presumed for a moment that the first priority is the protection of human and environmental health through design, then the second priority should be improvement of the environment through design. Before the original development, the site functioned environmentally. It offered habitat, provided a buffer for storm flows, retained water, and detained runoff so that flooding was delayed and reduced and infiltration would occur. Other functions included filtering of fine particles and a natural cleansing, as well as increased infiltration and diversion created by the vegetated and irregular natural surfaces. These functions were probably lost when the site was developed. Depending on the nature and degree of contamination on a site, it may be unrealistic, even harmful, to try to restore all of these functions. A comprehensive design should be able to identify and imitate some of the characteristics of the natural storm water management, particularly regarding the quality of the storm water when it leaves the site to the degree it is possible and appropriate.

Existing channels may require some attention to stabilization and alignment, but these should be undertaken with care to imitate the natural appearance and function of drainage ways. Consideration should be given to creating pools and ponding areas that would collect and trap water in high flows. The creation of flat area to intercept runoff and encourage infiltration might be developed to function as wetlands. Wetland pockets could prove to be an important storm water quality feature, and they might, as well, add visual interest and habitat areas (Fig. 4.10).

The creation of rougher surfaces and channels to encourage infiltration and to slow runoff should be considered. The storm water management design has a limited number

Figure 4.10 Photograph of concrete-lined channel. The lined channel provides excellent resistance to the erosive power of the moving water; however, it may contribute to increased velocities and a general degradation of the quality of water it conveys. This lined channel offers no opportunity for environmental functions such as infiltration or biological action. The lined channel, however, will not allow base flow from adjacent contaminated groundwater.

of factors within which it may work. These factors have primarily to do with the degree of roughness or capture the site may have and the speed and length of travel. *Roughness,* usually referred to as the *n* value of materials, is the degree of resistance to flow a surface offers to runoff. It is determined by the size of the materials in a channel, the amount and type of vegetation, and degree of curvature. The choice of rougher channel linings may play an important role in runoff water quality.

The design of channels is accomplished using Manning's equation (Table 4.1). The choice of the *coefficient of roughness,* called Manning's *n,* is the critical step in the use of the equation (Table 4.2). Generally a free board of at least 20 percent of the design depth or 6 inches (15 cm) is used to protect against underestimates of the *n* value and roughening of the channel by vegetative growth and incidental obstruction or debris. Design of unlined channels is usually limited by either the limiting velocity or the tractive force. The *limiting velocity* refers to the average velocity a channel will allow without suffering damage (Table 4.3).

Shape and sinuosity are critical factors in the hydraulic and environmental functions of a channel. *Shape* refers to the cross-sectional configuration of the channel, and *sinuosity* refers to the length of a channel over a given distance. Increasing the length of a channel within a given distance requires increasing the number and amplitude of curves within the distance. This increase in length allows a flatter slope over the same distance, which in turn results in slower velocities, less erosive capacity, and more infiltration. The area can be designed to contain more water in high-flow conditions and incorporate high-flow channels that operate in flood conditions. The incorporation of vegetation and pools in the channels will increase the natural capacity for retention and treatment of water-borne contaminants. Careful selection of channel bottom media and plants will fur-

Table 4.1   Manning's Formula

$$V = \left(\frac{1.49}{n}\right)\left(\frac{a}{p}\right)^{2/3}(s)^{1/2}$$

where n = coefficient of roughness
a = area cross section, square feet
p = wetted perimeter
s = slope, percent
V = velocity

Table 4.2   Coefficients of Roughness

Very smooth like glass or plastic	.010
Smooth pipe (PVC, concrete, vit. clay, etc.)	.013–.015
Straight unlined earth channels in good condition	.020
Open channels lined with asphalt	.013–.017
Open channels lined with brick	.012–.018
Open channels lined with concrete	.011–.02
Open channels lined with rip rap	.02–.035
Channels lined with vegetation 11–12 inches	.09–.15
Channels lined with vegetation 6–10 inches	.055–.08
Channels lined with vegetation 2–3 inches	.045–.06
Natural channels,* regular section	.03–.5
Natural channels with dense vegetation	.05–.7
Natural channels with irregular pools	.04–.10
Rivers, some growth	.025
Winding natural streams in poor† condition	.035
Mountain streams with rocky beds, some vegetation along banks	.040–.050

*Refers to minor streams with a top width of less than 100 feet at flood stage.
†Refers to very rough condition, erosion, etc.
SOURCE: Data from Brewer and Alter 1988, and Ferguson and Debo 1990.

ther enhance the environmental functions of storm water channels (Fig. 4.11).

Infiltration

A preferred method of storm water quality management is to reintroduce the runoff into the soil as quickly as possible to provide the opportunity for groundwater recharge. Even when it is necessary to cap a portion of a site, there

Table 4.3 Limiting Velocities for Channel Design

Material	n	Velocity (fps) for Clear Water	Velocity (fps) for Water with Sediment
Fine sand	0.02	1.5	2.5
Sandy loam	0.02	1.75	2.5
Silt loam	0.02	2.0	3.0
Firm loam	0.02	2.5	3.5
Stiff clay	0.025	3.75	5.0
Shales, hardpan	0.025	3.75	5.0
Fine gravel	0.02	2.5	5
Coarse gravel	0.025	4.0	6.0

SOURCE: Adapted from Barfield, Warner, and Hann 1987.

Figure 4.11 Photograph of artificial sinuous channel. The channel lengthens the flow path, allowing for a flatter slope and lower velocities. The natural gravelly bottom allows for plants to root and infiltration. Note the width of the channel available for high-flow conditions.

may still be opportunities to encourage infiltration in other areas. Infiltration does provide some treatment and filtering as the storm water passes through the soil particles and comes into contact with various biological agents present in the soil. These cleansing aspects of infiltration are determined by the length of the pathway through the soil and the properties of the particular soil. In any case, infiltration affects or removes only particulate matter and pollutants that might attach to soil particles. Water-soluble pollutants such as nutrients, pesticides, or salts will travel through the soil medium because they are dissolved in the water. To effectively deal with these pollutants, the design must provide for a biological treatment through contact with algae in wet ponds or microorganisms in wetlands or in rich soils or provide for extended retention within the soil matrix.

Another reason to consider infiltration is the loss of groundwater recharge that accompanies a typical detention basin development. The Chester County Planning Commission in Pennsylvania has developed some conceptual models of development for its planning purposes. They found through a study they commissioned that the typical developed square mile in the study area lost about 10 inches of recharge water (storm water runoff) each year. This 10 inches would represent 40,785,879 gallons of water each year. By using infiltration systems where it is possible, this kind of loss can be significantly reduced. About 70 percent of the homes in the United States use well water, so protecting and managing our groundwater resources is an important and necessary undertaking.

There is significant experience with and knowledge about using soil as a filter medium (e.g., in ground sewage disposal systems). In storm water management, just as in the design of on-site sewage disposal, there must be guidelines. The Environmental Protection Agency requires a 2- to 4-foot vertical separation from the bottom of the infiltration facility to the seasonal top of the water table or bedrock. The feasibility of infiltration is determined in a 4-point test (see also Table 4.4):

1. The soil texture is in a class with an infiltration rate that permits adequate percolation of collected water through the soil.

2. There is an available ponding or dewatering time of 3 to 7 days.

Table 4.4   Properties of Soils by Texture

Texture Class	Effective Water Capacity	Minimum Infiltration Rate	Hydrologic Soil Group
Sand	0.35	8.27 in/h	A
Loamy sand	0.31	2.41 in/h	A
Sandy loam	0.25	1.02 in/h	B
Loam	0.19	0.52 in/h	B
Silt loam	0.17	0.27 in/h	C
Sandy clay loam	0.14	0.17 in/h	C
Clay loam	0.14	0.09 in/h	D
Silty clay loam	0.11	0.06 in/h	D
Sandy clay	0.09	0.05 in/h	D
Silty clay	0.09	0.04 in/h	D
Clay	0.08	0.02 in/h	D

3. There is adequate space to provide a vertical depth of a minimum of 2 to 4 feet, minimum between the infiltration bed and bedrock or the seasonal high water table.

4. The site topography (slope), nature of the soil (fill, stability), and the location of foundations, utilities, wells, and similar site features are conducive to the collection and conveyance of runoff.

Infiltration systems should be used only on soils with adequate drainage. Soils with high clay or fine silt may have percolation rates that are too low and sandy, or gravelly sand soils may have a percolation rate that is too high. The former will not drain and will tend to clog sooner with runoff-borne fines, and the latter will drain too quickly for treatment. Infiltration systems may have removal efficiencies as high as 70 percent for metals (this number does not include soluble metals) and 80 percent for nitrogen and phosphorus (Oregon DEQ 1998). It is important to remember that infiltration beds will not affect soluble contaminants, and on brownfield sites they may be designed and used in conjunction with other treatment facilities such as filter strips or settling basins.

Local use of groundwater as a source of drinking water should be investigated when considering the use of infiltration on brownfield sites. It is recommended that infiltration should not be used within one-half mile of a public water supply system that depends on groundwater (Center for Watershed Protection 1995). In the presence of a source of drinking water, the concentration and type of contaminant present on a given site might suggest a greater distance or an alternative treatment and control method.

The designer may also elect to use a variety of different filter media depending on the anticipated contaminant or desired treatment. Although stone is the most common medium for storm water infiltration, other materials may be used instead of or in conjunction with the stone in infiltration systems for brownfield sites. It is important to distinguish between these filter systems and more common infiltration devices. Maintenance on some systems will increase as the medium used is able to trap more and finer particles. The filter medium on brownfield projects may require special handling when it is removed.

SAND FILTERS

Sand filters were among the first wastewater treatment systems devised and are still used in many systems today. The sand filter is an effective method for removing suspended solids, but it has no designed biological treatment capacity and cannot remove soluble pollutants. In general, the sand filter is at least 1.5 feet deep (0.45 m) and should be used in conjunction with other media or systems to address soluble contaminants. Sand filters have been designed using a layer of peat to increase the efficiency to 90 percent of suspended solids, 70 percent of total phosphorus, 50 percent of total nitrogen, and 80 percent of trace metals (Pitt 1996). The peat-sand filter is usually planted with a cover of grass to increase the removal of nutrients and provide filter surfaces for the deposition of films. The combination of peat and sand is a very effective filter, although effectiveness can be increased still further when the filter is used in conjunction with a presettling facility (Fig. 4.12).

Filters of peat or composted materials are a relatively new technology and have a much greater removal efficiency, up to 90 percent removal of soluble metals, 95 percent of suspended solids, and 87 percent hydrocarbon capture as well as high rates of removal for other materials. The peat compost filter has only moderate rates of nutrient removal (40 percent of total phosphorus and 56 percent of Kjeldahl nitrogen) (Pitt 1996). Peat by itself is an effective filter material, but it releases an effluent with a greater turbidity. The compost used in such filters should be of deciduous leaves. The peat compost filter requires maintenance and a change of filter material approximately once every 2 years depending on loading.

FILTER STRIPS

For the purposes of design, the infiltration basin serves the same function as the detention basin, to offset the increase

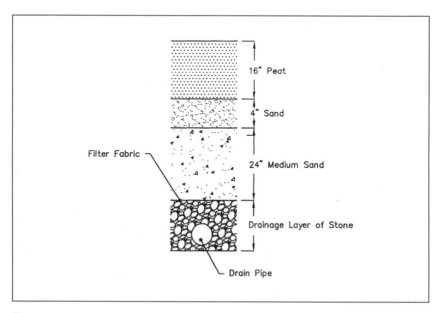

Figure 4.12 Sand/peat filter medium.

in runoff from the developed site. The infiltration basin outlets its volume of storm water through the pore space in the soil rather than through a surface outlet structure. This allows for some recharge of the aquifer and minimizes the pollutant impact on the receiving surface water. In general, infiltration basins have a large surface area to provide the maximum possible soil surface contact for the collected runoff; the greater the surface area, the faster the volume can infiltrate into the soil. It is important to remember that oil and grease, floating organic material, and fast-settling solids need to be filtered from the infiltration basin. This may be accomplished through the use of a vegetative filter strip, which acts as a filter by slowing surface runoff velocity and providing many surfaces that act as filters or surfaces for the deposition of grease and oil (see Fig. 4.5). The vegetated filter strip removes particulates such as metals and phosphorus by filtration through the surfaces of the vegetation and promotes some infiltration as runoff is slowed. The surfaces of the plants also act as surfaces for the deposition of contaminants that might exist as films in the runoff such as hydrocarbons. The presence of a healthy soil medium and plant community provides some inherent microbial action on the contaminants present in the runoff. The microbial action will continue even after the surge of storm water has passed. Properly designed and constructed filter strips may have a particulate trapping efficiency of up to 95 percent (Tourbier et al. 1989). Contact time or the time the water is in contact with the vegetation should be maximized by slowing the velocity of the runoff and by designing the strip to be as wide as possible. Velocities should be no more than 1 *foot per second* (fps) (0.3 m).

Filter strips should be designed with a minimum of 2 percent slope and should not exceed 4 percent. If the slope of the filter strip is less than 2 percent an infiltration underdrain may be required. The vegetation selected for filter strips is usually grass. The filter should be a minimum of 15 feet (4.4 m) wide. It may be necessary to use sod in order to allow the strip an opportunity to secure and establish itself. Native sod-forming grasses are recommended; tall fescue, western wheatgrass, ryegrass, and Kentucky bluegrass are all recommended for filter strips. The filter strip should be designed to receive a perpendicular sheet of runoff as a concentrated flow will limit the effectiveness of the filter strip and may damage it (Fig. 4.13).

INFILTRATION TRENCHES

An *infiltration trench* is another method of capturing water and allowing for recharge as shown in Fig. 4.14. The infiltration trench is generally 2 to 10 feet deep (0.6 to 3 m) (Figs. 4.15 and 4.16). The depth is constrained by the same criteria as the basin (i.e., depth to bedrock or the seasonal high water table). The trench is lined with filter fabric and filled with stone. The spaces between the stone provide the storage area for the runoff. Void space of backfill is assumed to be in the range of 30 to 40 percent for aggregate of 1.5 to 3 inches (4 to 8 cm). *Void space* refers to the spaces between the solid particles of the fill. Although an emerging spillway is usually not designed for an infiltration trench, the design and construction should consider and address the circumstance of an overflow. An observation well should

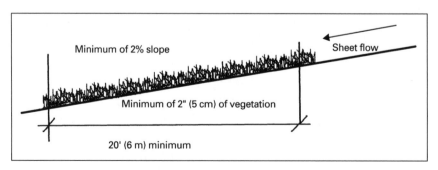

Figure 4.13   Vegetative filter strip.

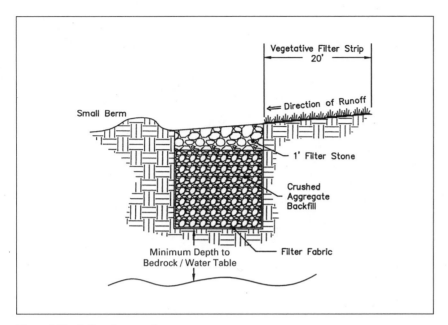

Figure 4.14 Infiltration trench.

Figure 4.15 Note the use of this planted island used to intercept flow from the parking lot. The direction of flow is from right to left. Curb stops allow for even distribution of flow into the island. A solid curb on the downslope side helps to retain some of the water.

Figure 4.16   Photograph of finished infiltration bed. Note the observation wells not yet cut off to surface level.

be installed in the infiltration trench as shown in Fig. 4.17. The observation well can be used to monitor the sediment level in the trench and to monitor the dewatering time (Maryland 1993).

The amount of void space, referred to in most standards as the percentage of voids, is variable by the type of material. The National Stone Foundation suggests that 35 percent voids is a good rule of thumb. Trenches designed using this rule have functioned well within expected performance standards. A more accurate percentage of voids can be calculated:

$$n = 1 - \left(\frac{d}{G \times 62.4} \right)$$

where n = percent of voids
    d = dry density of stone
    G = specific gravity of stone

The dry density of a particular stone is usually available from the quarry where stone is graded to specifications. If more specific data are not available, the mean specific gravity of 2.6 is used.

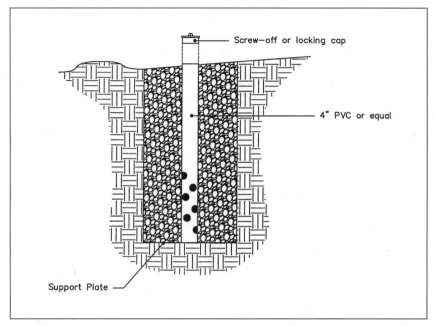

Figure 4.17   Observation well.

Methods adapted from the infiltration basin and trench include dry wells, swale traps, and catch basin traps. These facilities are designed to collect and trap the storm water in the earliest stages of the runoff process. Typically these types of facilities are small in size and located throughout a site. Through the cumulative effect of small collection facilities, the increase in runoff due to the development is offset.

DRY WELLS

Dry wells are small excavated pits that are backfilled with aggregate in the same manner as the infiltration trench. The primary difference between the dry well and infiltration trench is the means by which the water is collected into the system. Where trenches are located parallel to the contours and extend along a certain point in the site to intercept the runoff, the dry well collects runoff directly from a roof drain or outfall.

Dry wells are used primarily to collect the runoff from small areas such as a roof or section of a roof. In design, the dry well must meet the same tests as the infiltration basin or trench; however, the dry well has no treatment capability. In most applications the dry well is situated in a visible location near a structure, and the appearance of the dry well at the surface is important. A *soil filter* is used in most cases to make the dry well disappear from view. Figure 4.18 shows a dry well in which the soil filter consists of the last 1 foot of the space simply being filled with top soil.

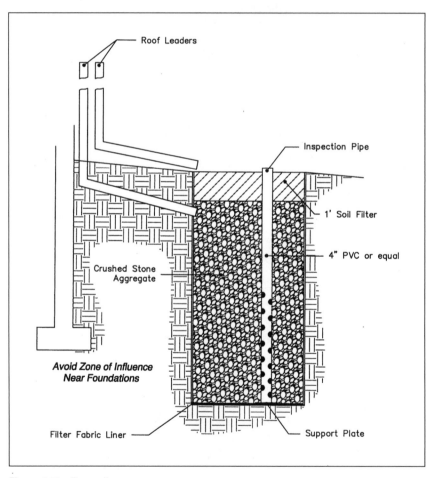

Figure 4.18 Dry well.

The infiltrator portion of the *catch basin infiltrator* is not visible, as it is located at the bottom of a catch basin, shown in Fig. 4.19. The sizing of the catch basin infiltrator can be geared toward the more frequent storms. This may allow the rest of the conveyance system to be sized differently and result in reduced construction costs. For example, if the infiltrator can accommodate a 1-year storm, downstream facilities may be able to be reduced slightly in size if the 1-year storm will always be detained. The lower volume of flows may mean smaller pipe sizes and lower costs.

The *swale infiltrator* acts similarly to allow infiltration of low-flow, frequent storm events, but it provides the capacity through which large infrequent storms can pass, runoff that could not be easily infiltrated through the soil. Swales

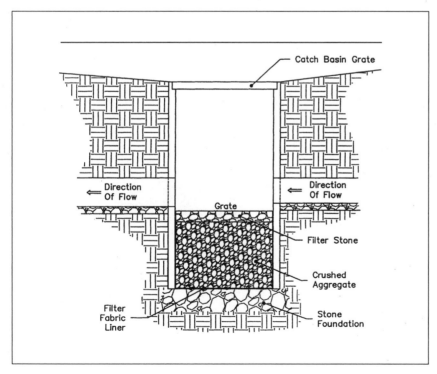

Figure 4.19   Catch basin infiltrator.

remain the choice of conveyance systems because they are superior to pipes in many ways (Fig. 4.20).

The swale infiltrator may also be used to introduce biological treatment to the storm water. The media for the swale may serve as surfaces for bacteria and other microorganisms to attach and to act as biofilters of the storm water as it passes through. The velocity of water through the media must be controlled if contact time between the biological agents and the water is to be adequate. The actual time will be a function of the toxins and the ability of the specific biological agents to consume or act on it. Determination of this will require some bench testing by a microbiologist. Once provided with the requirements, the site designer may design the swale accordingly.

Control of the water through the swale media is a function of slope and media size. The rate of travel through the media may be determined by the equation:

$$Q = 0.4 \left(\frac{h^{1.57}}{L^{0.57}} \right) W$$

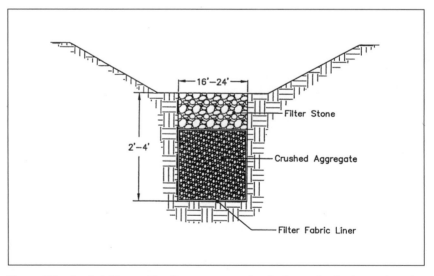

Figure 4.20 Swale infiltrator. The filter stone must be sized to resist the force of moving water in the swale. This method may be used on new construction or on existing swales.

where Q = volume of water
     h = depth of water
     L = flow path length
     W = width of channel
     0.4 = hydraulic conductivity, K

The formula is adapted from work completed at Pennsylvania State University, which looked at the use of gabions filled with 6 inches (15 cm) stone as basin outlet structures that would allow a discharge less than the predeveloped rate (Aron et al. 1992).

Bioswales

Bioswales increase the treatment capability of retention by adding the biological elements of the filter strip to the infiltration trench. Quite a lot of work has been done with bioretention strips and basins, but, in spite of a good deal of variability, all systems are a combination of filtration and biological action by soil-plant communities and infiltration. These have been effective innovations for the treatment of urban runoff and can be adapted to some brownfield sites. The bioswale uses a grass strip as a filter to reduce runoff velocity and to remove particulates. The swale employs a medium of sand or other material with a topsoil cover to further filter the runoff and as a medium for microbial growth and rooting medium for swale plantings.

The bioretention swale has received high marks for treatment of the first flush of runoff. Hydrocarbons are degraded and metals are bound to organic constituents in the topsoil layer. As a system, the bioswale has very high removal efficiencies: up to 92 percent of the total suspended solids, 67 percent of the lead, from 30 to 80 percent of the total phosphorus, and 75 percent of the total petroleum hydrocarbons as well as other materials (King County 1993).

The difficulties with any bioretention on brownfield sites will be related to the toxicity of the runoff and the space available for a properly sized facility. Although the bioretention approach may enable the treatment of contaminants in concentrations greater than might be allowed by regulation or permit, in general, bioretention basins are used to polish the runoff. Removal capacities of bioretention may vary over the course of a year with weather and climate, and some contaminants require significantly more contact or residence time than others. It may not be possible to design the bioretention facility to treat all of the contaminants present in runoff; instead, most facilities are compromises of treatment capacity, available space, and cost. Further, the design of bioretention may vary according to the contaminant to be treated or removed.

The size of bioretention facilities may also present a problem on tight urban brownfield sites. These sites often have little or no space for bioretention of a type that might be designed for new construction. Bioswales offer something of an alternative. For example, where bioretention basins typically include a permanent pool of water, the bioswale may not. The bioswale will tend to be a more linear design, perhaps better suited to the limited space or difficult topography of an urban site.

Bioswales provide additional storage above the swale and will act as ponds in more extreme storm events. There is a nearly permanent shallow pool, but the retention time in the swale is usually designed to be from 60 to 120 hours to maximize the efficiency of the biological treatment and settlement. The permanent pool acts as a nursery to maintain the biotic component of the swale. Bioretention swales are sized in much the same way as ponds; the size of the pond determines its retention time. Detention may be calculated as follows:

$$\frac{Vb}{Vr} = 2.5$$

where Vb = wet detention permanent volume
   Vr = mean runoff volume

The use of turf grass infiltration strips also increases the efficiency of the bioretention swale. These forebay strips are designed using the same parameter as described earlier. The bioretention swale acts as a swale in that it does convey storm water; however, its longitudinal grade is so shallow, usually between 1 and 2 percent, that the water is retained much longer to allow settlement and biotreatment (Fig. 4.21).

Ponds

The most common methods of managing storm water runoff are detention or retention basins. *Detention basins* are usually dry basins that fill with water only during a rain. They work by delaying the storm water so that it is released at a rate that mimics the predevelopment flow. A *retention basin* holds the water in a pool. The only outlet is through emergency spillways that allow the basin to overflow in a con-

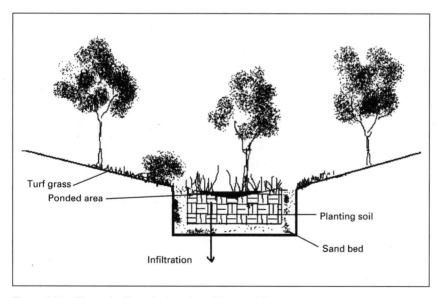

Figure 4.21 Bioswale. Note the location of the sand filter.

trolled manner if it should become too full. The retention basin loses water through infiltration and evaporation. These basins are often part of a larger plan that incorporates storm water management into water features.

Detention basin effectiveness is a function of the drainage area in which it operates and the location of the basin in the watershed. The lower the basin is in a watershed, the less effective it is in making a positive or beneficial effect on flood reduction in the watershed itself. It is possible that a properly constructed but mislocated basin could actually make a downstream flooding problem worse. The basin functions by detaining the water it collects and then releasing the water at a rate that is equal to the predeveloped rate. The development of a site results in more runoff so that, at an equal rate of discharge, it will take longer for the runoff to be discharged.

When it rains, it takes a period of time for the runoff to collect and run to the low points. In a watershed this lag time can be hours or days, depending on the size of the drainage area. Before a site is developed, areas low in the watershed may collect water, which may run off before the main portion of the flood travels down to that point in the watershed. The runoff from the lower end is discharged before the flood arrives. After development and the installation of the detention basin, this increased runoff is stored and its discharge is delayed. In some cases the delay may be long enough to coincide with the "flood." In such cases the basin actually makes the flood worse by contributing more water to it. The project, and certainly the downstream landowners, may be better off without the basin.

Locating a basin far up in a watershed can be difficult as well. If a basin is too high in the drainage area, it can be difficult to collect enough water in it to offset the increase in runoff due to development. Clearly the basin must be located with careful thought and analysis if it is to serve its purpose (Sloat et al. 1989). Site designers must study existing drainage patterns and pathways to identify opportunities that exist on the site. Much consideration should be given to using existing drainage paths. Where increase in flows and velocities will occur, it may be appropriate to enhance existing drainage ways to account for the increase rather than obliterating them in favor of a new path. The drainage patterns on a site have developed over time and can often be converted into effective drainage ways for the new development. In some cases these drainage ways, left in place throughout the site, double as a green way and walkway for pedestrians, combining the necessities for drainage with the desirability of open green space.

The design of wet ponds and wetlands is usually a matter of balancing the site constraints with the purpose and objectives of a pond (Fig. 4.22). It is generally a balancing act between cost, site issues (such as slope or drainage area), the appearance of the finished product, and the function the pond is needed to perform. On sites where infiltration is not an option, an alternative to the infiltration and recharge methods is the development of a wet pond or a retention basin. Basins may be designed with an impermeable liner to prevent infiltration into subsurface soils. The advantages of a wet pond include an effective process of the removal of certain pollutants through settling in the permanent pool. The geometry of the pool is an important aspect of the pond's capability to remove or reduce pollutants. Ponds are sized with regard to the flow of water through the pond, pond volume, depth, and the expected particle sizes to be encountered in order to allow for the necessary settling time. The activity of plants and microorganisms necessary for the reduction of pollutants occurs primarily at the bottom of the basin. The shape of the basin (geometry) must minimize currents within the basin and maximize the travel time from the point where storm water enters the pond to any point of outlet or overflow.

Figure 4.22   Photograph of constructed bioretention pond.

The surface area is usually designed also in relation to the depth of the pond to avoid *dead storage,* or areas that do not get mixed into the rest of the pond. Pond depths will vary according to the purpose. The *marsh zone,* or *littoral zone,* is usually 6 inches to 2 feet (0.15 to 0.6 m) deep and provides the most effective removal of nutrients and some other pollutants (Table 4.5). The design of the basin should also include an area equal to 33 percent of the pond surface area that is from 3 to 6 feet (1 to 2 m) deep for fish. An additional 25 percent of the pond should be at least 3 feet deep (1 m) and within 6 feet (2 m) of the shore. This combination of shallow and deep areas provides a combination of the effects and uses of the pond.

The minimum drainage area to be considered for the wet pond should be adjusted according to the rainfall characteristics of an area, the amount of anticipated runoff, the type of land use, pond geometry and depth, and the settling rate of the expected particulate. The state of Maryland has developed area and volume parameters for the design of wet

Table 4.5 Suggested Plants for Littoral Zone Planting

Common Name	Scientific Name	Planting Depth, Inches, cm
Duck potato	*Sagittaria latifolia*	12 (30)
Common three square	*Scirpus americanus*	6 (15)
Softstem bulrush	*Scirpus validus*	12 (30)
Sweet flag	*Acorus calamus*	3 (8)
Buttonbush	*Cephalanrthus occidentalis*	24 (60)
Rose mallow	*Hibiscus moscheutos*	3 (8)
Rice cutgrass	*Leersia oryzoides*	3 (8)
Spatterdock	*Nuphar luteum*	60 (150)
Arrow-arum	*Peltandra virginica*	12 (30)
Lizards tail	*Saururus cernuus*	6 (15)

SOURCE: Adapted from Jarrett and Hoover 1979.

ponds that serve as an excellent guide. The first parameter is the ratio between the drainage area and the pond surface area. The recommended range of the ratio is from 10 to 50. This range could represent a 1-acre pond in a 10-acre watershed or a 10-acre pond in a 500-acre watershed. Again, these recommendations should be evaluated for the specific rainfall characteristics of the area under consideration.

Another key parameter is the volume ratio where the wet pond volume is divided by the mean runoff volume. Studies have indicated that the larger a surface area of a pond, in general, the greater the pollutant removal efficiency. A pond can be made deeper to achieve water quality, but increased depth is not as effective as a larger surface area. The smaller the area ratio (larger pond surface), the greater the efficiency of the pond in removing pollutants. If the volume of a pond is much greater than the volume of runoff coming into the pond, a longer residence time will be required. The residence time is important because the settlement of pollutants will occur primarily when the water is not moving in the pond. Studies have shown that two-thirds of the incoming sediments will settle out in the first 24 hours. The reduction of phosphorus, however, will take up to 2 weeks in the basin in order to achieve significant reductions. Phosphorus is a pollutant with serious water quality consequences. The volume required for a 2-week storage volume is very large. Volumes this large will affect the pond's ability to function as a detention basin and meet the peak discharge control requirements. The combination of purposes—storm water detention and maintenance of water quality—must be carefully balanced.

A volume ratio of 2.5 is suggested in order to achieve 70 percent removal of sediment loads, or a residence time of about 9 days. The 9-day residence time is recognized as a middle ground, providing water quality improvements but avoiding the large volume required for the 2-week residence time (Fig. 4.23).

Bioremediation in Ponds and Wetlands

The level of biological activity, or biological productivity, in ponds, and especially in wetlands, is thought to be among the highest of any natural system. The potential for these systems for treating or stabilizing toxic materials is only

Figure 4.23   Photograph of regional retention pond and constructed wetland.

recently becoming clear. The design of wetland treatment systems for failing septic systems, feedlot runoff, and wastewater treatment facilities and the application of bioretention systems to maintain storm water quality point to the methods that might be used to improve runoff water quality. While brownfield water quality issues may be complicated by the presence of toxins, the use of bioremediation technologies in conjunction with storm water management design may represent an important element of brownfield site design.

Assuming toxicity is low enough, swales and ponds can be designed to provide the proper amount of detention time for bacteria and microfauna to act on the contaminants. The design of these facilities would be contaminant specific as well as site specific (i.e., the nature of the contaminant or combination of contaminants would dictate the nature of the biological agents). The characteristics of those agents would in turn influence the design. Site designers will have to work with biologists to identify the design parameters to accomplish the contact time and conditions that achieve the best treatment result.

The advantages of incorporating bioremediation into the site design are numerous. First, by combining the two functions, site disruption and delays are minimized, and the cost of removing material off site is eliminated. The cost of bioremediation is less than active or mechanized treatment processes. Bioremediation acts to eventually eliminate the contamination or reduce it to a level where liability is eliminated, and once remediated, the contamination is gone. The disadvantage is often the length of time necessary for the bioremediation to be completed. Site designers should work closely with biologists to determine the design parameters necessary to provide the microbiological elements of the design with the most favorable environment (Table 4.6).

Table 4.6   Comparison of Costs for Storm Water Management Facilities

Practice	Construction Cost	Annual O&M	Useful Life, Years
Infiltration trench	$0.20–$1.20/ft^3	3–13% of capital cost	25
Vegetated swale	From seed $4.5–$8.5/linear foot	$0.50–$1.0/ linear foot	50
Vegetative filter strip established with existing vegetation	$0	$50–$200/acre	50
	From seed $200–$1000/acre	$800/acre	50
	From seed with mulch $800–$3,500/acre		50
	From sod $4,500–$48,000/acre		50
Sand filter	$1–$11/ft^3	Probably 7% of construction cost	25
Wet pond	$0.05–$1.0/ft^3	0.1–1% of capital cost	50
Bioswale	Not available	Not available	Not available

SOURCE: Adapted from EPA-840-B-92-002, January 1993.

CHAPTER 5

Planting Plans

Saving Existing Vegetation

Even brownfield sites have trees and vegetation. Although in many cases these are volunteers or specimens in very poor condition, sometimes valuable specimens are found on impacted sites. In other cases masses of volunteers may be valuable because of the mass or plant community they nurse even though they have little value as individual specimens. These valuable trees are often destroyed or damaged in the course of construction. Mature trees may serve a variety of roles in the redeveloped landscape, although sometimes the effort to save a poor-quality tree or a tree in poor condition is greater than the value of the tree. A careful evaluation of the existing vegetation should be undertaken as part of the predesign site evaluation.

Trees may serve functional roles in addition to being a desirable element of the redeveloped landscape. The root systems of trees may provide stabilization to the soil, and the activity of some nurse trees will actually promote soil health. Thus, these trees may have an important restorative role on the brownfield site. Trees are damaged most often

Figure 5.1   These young trees have shown tolerance for the soil and moisture conditions and have become established on this brownfield site.

during redevelopment from cuts and fills because the balance between the roots and the soil is disturbed. The disturbance between the tree roots and the soil essentially interrupts the balance the tree had established with its supply of air and water. In some cases the disturbances may weaken the structural base of the tree as well. Tree roots grow and develop partially as a function of the air and water available in a given soil. Trees also contribute to the health of the soil and may be an important part of a long-term, low-cost site recovery strategy (Fig. 5.1).

Depth of a fill is important in determining the impact on selected trees. Soils on construction sites are generally left compacted and are nearly impermeable to the trucks and equipment driving over them. Even without removing or adding soil to the base of a tree, the compaction from construction vehicles can damage trees. When a layer of soil is added to the top of a grade, air and water are restricted from the root zone; generally the deeper the fill, the greater the restriction. Depth of fill is only one issue in determining the effect of a fill on a particular tree and the steps that must be taken to overcome the impact. Other factors include the type and the health of the tree and the type of soil. As shown in Table 5.1, some species of trees are more tolerant than other species, and a healthy tree of any variety will withstand the stress of a fill better than a damaged or weak tree (Zion 1968).

The soil is a dynamic ecosystem in which a complex relationship between microorganisms, organic matter, soil structure, and chemistry is maintained. The soil texture of the fill

Table 5.1 Common Trees and Their Tolerance to Cut and Fill

Most Affected	Less Affected	Least Affected
Sugar maple	Birch	Elm
Beech	Hickory	Poplar
Dogwood	Hemlock	Willow
Oak		Plane tree
Tulip tree		Pin oak
Evergreens		Locust

will be at best minimal simply because of the mechanical action of disturbances. *Soil structure* refers to the formation of soil aggregates, or distinct clumps of soil, that reflect the organic and mineral content and the beneficial effects of plant life and microorganisms. The soil structure is a very important factor in how a plant is able to grow. Soils with a fine texture or particle size, such as clays, will tend to have a greater impact as fills because their fine particle size will fill available pore space through which air and water would travel to the tree roots. Even shallow fills of clay can severely damage a tree. Soils with a coarse texture, such as sandy or gravelly soils, cause the least amount of damage to trees because air and water move through the soil more readily. In most cases a shallow fill of several inches of gravelly soil, or soils of the same kind as the tree is growing in, will have no long-term effect on a tree. The tree is able to compensate by extending its roots into the new layer. This upward extension of roots is more difficult in a deeper fill because of the loss of soil water and air and the absence of pore space.

Evaluating Trees

To determine whether the condition of a tree is adequate to warrant the effort and expense of being saved, an evaluation of the tree should be performed. Although a variety of methods exist with which to base an evaluation, they generally have certain elements in common. These elements include comparing the tree to the characteristics of the species as displayed by the specimen such as form, color, shape, and overall condition. The evaluation also must address the health of the tree and its general appearance and vigor. Beyond the characteristics of the tree, however, the evaluation must also consider the location of the specimen, now and in the proposed site condition.

A method developed by James Urban, ASLA, considers these elements but goes on to weigh the average growth of the tree and the available soil volume as well. Urban's method was specifically developed for trees in a city situation. Although Urban's method may not have been developed for brownfield sites specifically, it is applicable. It is straightforward and full of common sense and bears repeating:

1. *Excellent condition:* No noticeable problems, regular and even branching, normal-sized leaves, normal color

2. *Good condition:* Full grown with no tip die back, may have minor bark wounds, thinner crowns, slightly smaller leaf size, or minor infestations

3. *Fair condition:* One or more of the following—minor tip or crown die back (less than 10 percent), small yellowed or disfigured leaves, thinner crown, significant limb wounds, recent large branch removed that minimally affects shape, large insect infestation, any problem that should be repaired without long-term effect on the plant's health

4. *Poor condition:* Any of the following—crown die back from 10 to 25 percent, significantly smaller, yellowed, or disfigured leaves, branch removal that affects the crown shape in a significant way, wounding to the bark that will affect the tree's health

5. *Very poor condition:* Any problem that is so significant that it grossly affects the shape or the health of the tree; little hope for the tree's survival

6. *Replace:* Some green seen, but no hope for the tree's survival

7. *Dead*

This fundamental approach can serve as a guideline to evaluating the trees on a given site (Urban 1989). The decision to save the tree must also include the cost of doing so as well as the benefit.

Planting over Impervious Caps

Planting over impervious caps presents a series of problems to be evaluated. Capped sites are often limited to grass cover or left with stone or pavement as armor for the cap. The integrity of the cap is critical and must be considered in whatever approach is taken to developing a site plan. If the cap is of clay or a modified soil mixture, plant roots may have to be restricted from penetrating or damaging the structural and containment integrity of the cap. In such cases where a shallow layer of soil is placed, it may be possible to grow grass, groundcovers, and other low plantings that do not require a deep soil medium. Introducing trees and shrubs or masses of plant materials may require introducing planters, graded terraces, and berms to the site to provide the necessary planting bed size.

One approach to planting design on sites with impervious caps is to treat the cap as if it were a roof-top garden. The analogy holds to the extent that roof-top gardens must be careful to protect the integrity of the roof as a seal as well as the support for the garden. Caps act to support the garden as a foundation, and penetrations of the cap are generally avoided; however, they differ from roof-tops in several important respects. The site redevelopment design may involve the introduction or reconfiguration of underground utilities, and some form vehicular traffic is generally anticipated.

While the integrity of the cap is critical, it may be necessary to penetrate the cap to install utilities (see Fig. 4.8). The decision to open the cap should be based on the nature of the contamination, the risks to workers, the public, and the environment, and the costs compared to alternatives. It may be necessary to acquire permission from a regulatory agency to open the cap in some cases. Penetrations of the cap should be undertaken using a well-thought-out plan that includes minimizing the length of time and the size of the area to be exposed. The installation of utilities will involve excavation of suspect material. The excavation process will require extraordinary oversight and control of excavated material. Contingencies should be planned for inclement weather and allowance for delays in the schedule. Also, it can be anticipated that after the installation of utilities and bedding materials and expansion of excavated soils, there will be excess material to be dealt with. The cost of disposing of the anticipated excess should be considered when evaluating alternatives to penetrating the cap.

A similar approach might be used for locating planting areas over a cap. The same concerns exist as in the utility trench; however, islands of vegetation may be located in areas where contamination is lower or no cap is required (see Fig. 5.2). In any case a depression in the cap might be provided to allow for deeper soils if properly planned. Such a depression would require positive drainage in wet areas.

Improving Impacted Soils

The vigor and appearance of the restored site is a function of the choice of materials and the cultural methods applied to the site. The degraded soils typically found on former industrial sites have poor structure and require special attention when drawing up planting and stabilization plans. The use of soil amendments and tolerant plant species, as

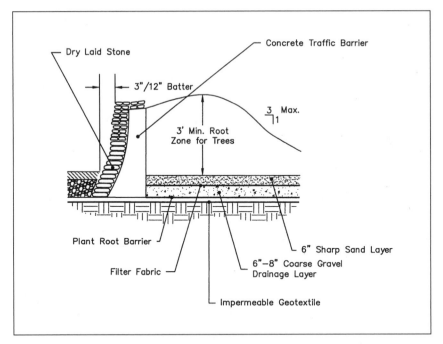

Figure 5.2   Planting island for developing planted islands and berms over capped sites.

well as preparation, installation, and maintenance, are all part of the brownfield site planner's concerns. The earth disturbance associated with a remedial action destroys the structure of the soil. Soil structure is the arrangement of soil particles into aggregates of the mineral soils particle and organic matter, and it is related to the success of efforts to vegetatively stabilize the soil. In the disturbed remedial action site, the granular structure of the soil is destroyed through the operations of grading and compaction. The loss of soil structure results in a decrease in soil permeability and an increase in erodability. Soils with a granular structure naturally allow for infiltration and resist erosion. Increased runoff and erodability result from the earthmoving activities, and timely planned attention to stabilizing the site is critical to a successful project (Brown et al. 1986). In addition, the graded and compacted surface is generally not ideal for establishing vegetation without specific steps to prepare the soil, an appropriate selection of materials, and a plan for maintenance (Fig. 5.3).

Ideally, the first step in determining the soil for planting should be the analysis of representative soil samples to determine the soil texture, organic content, available nutrients, and soil pH. A reputable laboratory should be used. On sites where significant amounts of fill have been brought on to the site, it may be necessary to a collect a number of samples in order to correctly identify the conditions that exist on the site. The finish grade of a site is often a hard, bare smooth surface. This dry, hard, compacted, and infertile condition is not conducive to establishing a vegetative cover. The soil sample provides basic information, for a relatively modest cost, that allows the revegetation plan to address the specific requirements of the site rather than using a standardized approach of so many pounds of fertilizer and so much adjustment made to the pH. Although the standard approach may work, it is just as likely it will not. The soil analysis allows the best combination of soil amendments

Figure 5.3 This photograph illustrates the variance in soil quality that might be anticipated on even a small site. The darker soil is stained black with petroleum residues.

and cultivation methods for success on the given site. The knowledge gained by the soil sample allows the designer to use the right amount of the right material the first time. Often this is less expensive than the guesswork approach.

The typical site will bear the impacts of compaction and possibly contamination and may have been subject to extensive clearing and grading, which may have resulted in large exposed, disturbed areas. Grading and compaction may result in a dry, compacted, and infertile material with little resemblance to the original soil. On many redevelopment sites fill is brought from off site, often from a myriad of sources. The results of these activities are unpredictable if not unproductive soil. In most cases the depth of soil considered for permanent revegetation should be up to 30 inches (0.75 m) deep. Establishing plant growth without characterizing the soil may produce uneven, happenstance results. Once grading is nearly completed, soil samples should be taken (see Table 5.2).

These tests will provide the fundamental data for determining the characteristics of the soil and the cultural

Table 5.2   A Soil Sampling Method

A method for collecting soil samples can be found in the U.S. Environmental Protection Agency Process Design Manual for Land Treatment, Section III (1977). Essentially the following steps are recommended:

1. Subdivide the area into homogenous units, and, if necessary, subdivide these into uniform-size areas of 5–40 acres.

2. Establish a grid to locate sampling points. Composite samples of each area should be composed of between 10 and 20 samples. Care must be taken to use uniform-size cores or slices of equal volume and/or of equal depth to develop the composite.

3. Test for:
   - Standard water pH and/or buffer pH
   - % organic matter
   - Cation exchange capacity
   - Particle size distribution
   - Salinity
   - Available nutrients

requirement and amendments necessary for a successful revegetation effort. In addition to examining the soil, a visit to the area surrounding the site to identify local vegetation can provide important information on native plants. This is important to correlate the native species climate and precipitation requirements for the proposed vegetation. It is important to notice differences that might occur at various elevations, slopes, exposures, and aspects. This information can influence the revegetation plan in a manner that will encourage a design that can be sustained through the season and through climate extremes such as drought or wet years, or heavy winds or snows (Darmer 1992). It is necessary for the designer to have accurate topography for the site as well as climactic information and data about site hydrology. The revegetation plan can be based on these collected sources of information.

Seed bed preparation generally occurs after "finish grading" is complete. Generally the surfaces left to be seeded are hard and smooth and not ready to be seeded. Graded slopes that are to be seeded should be 2:1 or flatter. Steeper slopes may require special treatment if vegetation alone is to be used to stabilize the slope. The interim condition between finish grading and a stable vegetated slope is a fragile one. On slopes steeper than 3:1, stepping the slope is sometimes used to help vegetation become established. Slopes should be left in a rough condition. A smooth slope is a more difficult surface on which to establish vegetation than a slope left with clods and imperfections. Another version is the stair-stepped slope in which the final grading is done with a serrated blade drawn across the slope, parallel with the contours (see Fig. 5.4). Using this method, the surface is left with many locations for seed to become established. Seeds blown or washed from one location are likely to be deposited in microsites created by the "steps" in the slopes. Gradually, over time, the edges of the stairs wear down and debris from above fills in the trough, leaving the smooth desirable surface.

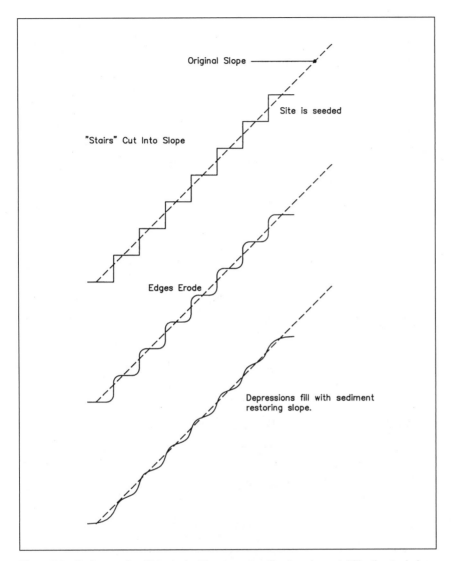

Figure 5.4 Stair-stepping. This method has been an effective slope stabilization technique on mine recovery sites using native plant seed mixtures of grasses, forbs, and trees. The soil amendments are incorporated; then, using a serrated blade, the final grade is made across the slope. The slope is seeded. The slope face will erode and, as it does so, restore a natural grade.

Compaction is a problem that extends deep into the soil. Simply "scratching up" the seed bed will not provide for infiltration of air and water beyond the thin, weak layer of loose soil at the surface. Although an initial stand of vegetation may germinate and appear vigorous, the compacted subsoil restricts root growth and infiltration of water and will eventually result in the concentration of salts in the topsoil, limiting successful plant growth. In addition, the slower-growing deeper-rooted plants will not establish on the site (Craul et al. 1991). The soils may require deeper conditioning prior to seeding by the use of equipment that is able to plow to a depth of up to 30 inches. Once these cultural operations are complete, final seed bed preparation can begin. The amounts of fertilizer, pH, and organic additives should be determined by the soil tests. In lieu of site-specific data, the general specifications for the site should be followed (Perry 1991).

The soil analysis reduces the risk of failure because the specific requirements of the site can be determined and recommendations can address the best treatment and amendments to prepare the site. Repeated seedings and the poor performance of seedlings requiring more guesswork and may cost more than doing it right the first time. In most locales the soil conservation service, agricultural extension, or agricultural college provide general information on fertilizers and soil treatment, and in lieu of a soil sample and analysis, these recommendations can be an adequate fallback. Another source of information is the National PLANTS database maintained by the Natural Resources Conservation Service of the U.S. Department of Agriculture. The database is found online at the following address:

http://plants.usda.gov/plantproj/plants/index.html

The planting plan is usually completed in the planning stages of a project; therefore recommendations on soil treatment are made without the benefit of soil analysis or knowledge of the actual site conditions at the time planting is to be done. Soil samples should not be taken until the site work is nearly complete in order to gather a representative sample. The contractor and the designer should discuss the stabilization plan at the time of installation to update and revise the plan.

In addition to fertilizer and pH treatments, organic matter is commercially available from modern composting operations. Specifications for commercially composted material should be written and reviewed carefully. Materials used for these purposes have diverse sources, and the potential for unwanted trace elements and contaminants should be evaluated. A standardized analysis, at a minimum, should be received from the supplier of composted materials.

Finally, the restoration of such difficult soils may also benefit from the introduction of additional organic matter, mycorrihzae fungus, and other natural microbiotic additives that have become commercially available. While these fungi and bacteria may be introduced as part of added organic matter or in conjunction with the root masses of plants, the more focused introduction of these materials may provide an important start-up to the soil. These living components of the soil play important roles in the plant-soil relationship and in turn participate in the stabilization of the soils and of contaminants. While it is true that organic matter itself will promote these same results, commercial soil additives may play an important role in establishing the landscape by accelerating the process. The use of *polyacrylamides* (PAMs) and *polysaccharides* can assist in developing and maintaining soil structure and permeability. These materials serve the soil by reducing the loss of fines to erosion, maintaining soil structure, and aiding the soil in holding soil water. In addition to helping to stabilize the soil and promoting vigorous plant growth, the improved soil may play an important role in reducing the bioavailiability of contaminants; however, some studies have shown that chemical soil conditioners may reduce the cation exchange capacity of soil.

Cultural Operations

The vegetation will require the soil to be a medium that provides a site for germination and growth, allows moisture and air to permeate through the soil, and provides nutrition and structural stability. After the site is "finish graded," the cultural preparation of the soil seed bed is undertaken. The seed bed will usually require more than simply spreading a few inches of topsoil if the area is to sustain more than a weak cover of thin vegetation. If the plants are rooted in only the first 6 inches of soil, they are subject to stress because of extremes in moisture, temperature, and the collection of salts, in some areas, in the soil. Deeper-rooted plants will not establish at all in this environment because of the hard, unbroken layer of compacted artificial land. The properly prepared soil will encourage germination and root growth. A soil structure will develop, and long-term stabilization will begin.

The decisions as to what cultural equipment and methods should be employed are site specific, made on the basis of site characteristics such as the amount of compaction, soil type, slope, season, climatic factors, and the available equipment. The broad range of implements includes familiar agricultural equipment such as disc and chisel plows, as well as less common equipment such as subsoilers and land imprinters. Some types of equipment are listed and compared in Table 5.3.

In addition to the attributes of the soil, the conditions on the disturbed site must also be considered when choosing plant materials. The surface provides no protection for the plants, and mulches protect only the early stages of the plants' growth. The climatic extremes of an area are often made even worse on the unprotected site. Wind will dry the unprotected surface more quickly and erode the unprotected soils. Rainfall impact on unprotected soils can have a considerable impact and result in significant and costly damage. Young seedlings are particularly susceptible to damage from wind, rain, and heat-cold stress.

On capped sites, there may be a desire to restrict infiltration but also to have a sustainable vegetative cover. This

Table 5.3 Comparison of Cultivation Implements

Implement Type	Depth	Characteristics
One way disc plows	To 30-inch-deep penetration	Improves infiltration and percolation, root penetration
Offset disc plows	To 18 inches	Good for sites where weeds have become established; excellent means to break up surface compaction
Chisel plows	To 12 inches	Limited value in badly compacted soils; good only for short-term results; good in rocky soils
Subsoilers	To 30 inches	Better suited to breaking up middepth compaction than to seed bed preparation
Land imprinters	To 6 inches	Works well on rugged sites; does not reduce compaction
Contour furrowers	To 12 inches	Cultivates, furrows, and seeds in one operation; can be used on slopes up to 20%
Gougers	To 10 inches	Seed bed preparation; does not reduce compaction
Klodbusters	Surface	Seed bed preparation only
Cultipackers	Surface	Final treatment just before or just after seeding

cap, such as over a landfill, diverts soils water away from the underlying materials but has sufficient soil above to support the vegetative cover (Rogoshewski et al. 1983). Blending soils to create a soil medium with a greater absorption capacity might also be part of the plan. Soils of different particle size can be combined to increase the permeability or moisture-retaining capabilities of a soil. Layering is another means that, when done in conjunction with a barrier or blended soil, could be part of the revegetation plan. Trees and shrubs will grow better in a soil that is about 30 inches (0.75 m) thick as opposed to thinner soils, like the grasses and legumes. Compacted soils act to resist root growth, so that even routine root ball planting

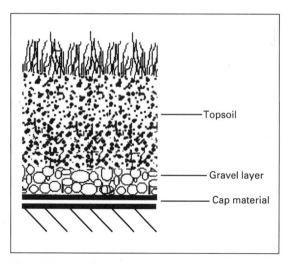

Topsoil

Gravel layer

Cap material

Figure 5.5   Layering.

methods may be inadequate in disturbed soils. The heavily compacted soils do not provide an opportunity for root penetration so that the excavation process smoothes the soil surfaces in the excavated planting pit, further reducing the already limited pore space and the transmission of air and water (Fig. 5.5).

Seeding should be performed as quickly as possible after "final grading." Generally, the most efficient seeding method for large areas is with hydroseeding. In this method, seed, fertilizer, mulch, and lime are applied in a single operation. For level areas, seed drills are often used, but several passes are required to apply all the constituents. All cultural seeding operations should be performed at right angles to the slope (parallel to the contours). If the plan includes shrubbery, trees, or seedlings, they must be planted by hand (Goldman et al. 1986).

Mulches

Mulches are generally recommended for all revegetation efforts. The choice of materials and range of characteristics are so broad that careful thought and consideration should be given to the selection of a mulch. The complexity of the choice aside, the role of mulch to the vegetation plan should not be overlooked. To different degrees each mulch material provides the following attributes: insulates soil against temperature extremes, protects runoff, reduces evaporation, encourages infiltration, and holds the seed in its place. Different materials perform these tasks with different degrees of success. In addition, the means of application and the availability may also be important considerations. Cost is also a consideration; some material can be purchased and installed for as little as $1800 per acre (wood fiber) while other material costs as much as $18,000 per acre (jute matting) (Goldman, Jackson, and Bursztynsky 1986). Table 5.4 compares some of these attributes.

Selecting Plant Materials for Impacted Sites

The redevelopment site may be a difficult environment in which to establish vegetation. In addition to concerns relating to the poor quality and character of the soils, there are also problems related to the disturbed environment of any construction site. The unstabilized surface provides no protection from the climatic extremes of different seasons. Wind will dry the unprotected surface quicker and erode unprotected soils. Rainfall impact on unprotected surface can cause significant damage. Young seedlings are susceptible to damage from wind, rain, and heat stress. In areas where summer temperatures may reach 100°F, the hard surface could result in 130°F temperatures at the soil surface.

Table 5.4   Comparison of Mulch Types

Material	Advantages	Disadvantages
Straw	Low cost, biodegradable, light color	Must be anchored in place, added cost of nets or tackifiers, contains weed seeds, short application distance
Wood fiber mulch	Holds seeds or plants in place; inexpensive, can be hydroseeded, stays on slopes	Does not resist rainfall
Netting/fiber	Resists rain and erosion	Expensive, absorbs erosive force of water, must be in contact with soils
Netting	Good slope protection	Expensive, must be in contact with soil

SOURCES: Adapted from Goldman, Jackson, and Busztynski 1986, and Brown et al. 1986.

Plant materials selected to revegetate a site must be able to establish quickly in a harsh environment. In general, native species are a good choice. The native species have a predictable performance and growth habit in the general soils of the area and in the climatic conditions. It is key to the success of the revegetation plan to allow for the extremes of the environment, not only the average conditions; the dry summer and especially harsh winter must be anticipated in the plan. Native species may be best suited to respond to these variations. Introduced species should be carefully evaluated before they are used. The EPA has prepared recommendations for reestablishing vegetation on severely disturbed remedial action sites, and the guidelines are relevant to the brownfield redevelopment site (see Table 5.5).

The growth habit and cultural requirements of selected plant materials are the key factors in selecting plant material (Table 5.6). Constraints on establishing and maintaining the plants include the various climatic conditions and cultural requirements, but selection of plants must consider the growth habit, rooting depth, and rate of establishment. The time of year for seeding is also an important consideration. The rate of maturation from germination will be affected by the temperature and precipitation. Some cool season grasses will not germinate in high temperatures, or, once germinated, they will suffer from the extreme temperatures; in contrast, warm season grasses require higher temperatures to germinate. The plants selected for the revegetation plan must be compatible with each other as well as resistant to insect damage and diseases. The long-term permanent stabilization plan should include grasses, legumes, shrubs, and trees. Generally speaking, perennials are best planted in the fall, and annuals should be seeded in the spring. When working on brownfield sites, it may also be necessary to identify species that are tolerant of conta-

Table 5.5 Criteria for Selecting Plant Materials

For selecting grasses and forbs:

Availability of seed
Resistance to erosion and traffic stresses at the site
Adaptability to critical conditions such as pH, soil texture, drainage, salinity, and wind erosion
Adaptability to climate of site such as sunlight, exposure, temperatures, wind, and rainfall
Resistance to insects, disease, etc.
Compatibility with other plants selected
Ability to propagate
Consistent with long-term maintenance plans and succession plan

For selecting shrubs and trees:

Availability in required quantity
Capability to produce root systems as required by the site characteristics
Ability to become quickly established
Tolerance of site conditions, acid, saline, wet, droughty, and compacted soils
Compatible with principals of secondary succession
Ability for vigorous growth after relief of moisture stress; regrowth after damage
Ability to reproduce
Value to wildlife
Ability to create islands of fertility by creating a point of accumulation for organic matter, detritus, and nutrients
Ability to withstand traffic stresses
Resistance to insects, diseases, and other pests
Compatibility with other plants selected for the project
Relative maintenance requirements and costs
Tolerance for site-specific stresses

minants from the site or that are shallow rooted to avoid penetration of caps or liners.

Selecting and Planting New Trees

Selecting a tree begins with selecting a site for the tree. A tree that will thrive on a residential lawn may not grow well on a city street. Although shallow-rooted trees are ideal for city conditions, they will tend to damage sidewalks and curbs. The shallow roots exposed to the surface are often damaged by the pedestrian traffic in an urban environment. Tall trees may interfere with overhead wires. Some trees are grown for their shape or beauty and require a view from a

Table 5.6   Plant Materials for Brownfield Sites

Grasses:

Bluestem, big, *Andropogon gerardi,* and little bluestem, *Schizachyrium scoparium.* Native to eastern United States and prairie but has adapted to all regions of the United States. Warm season, perennial grass. Slow to develop, but established stands require little maintenance. Will tolerate poorly drained soils. Lower pH limit 4.5.

Buffalograss, *Buchloe dactyloides.* Warm season grass. Prefers loamy and clayey soils. Good drought resistance. Rapidly establishing sod former. Used in western states, Great Plains, and Southwest. Tolerant of saline-alkaline soils.

Tall fescue, *Festuca arundinacea,* and cultivars. Adapted to acid or alkaline, droughty and wet soils, soils of sandstone or shale origins, good for intermittent channels, drought resistant, bunch-type. Cool season, perennial grass. Lower pH limit 4.5. Moderate rate of establishment. Kentucky-31 cultivar widely used to reestablish vegetation and stabilize surface mining sites. Low aluminum tolerance.

Switchgrass, *Panicum virgatum.* Adapted to infertile and saline soils but short-lived in northeastern United States. Grows best mixed with birdsfoot trefoil, variety "Blackwell" used widely. Moderate aluminum tolerance. Lower pH limit 5.0. Adapted to wet and dry soils.

Reed canarygrass, *Phalaris arundinacea.* Good for drainage swales and gullies. Tolerates saline-alkali soils. Cool season, sod-forming perennial grass. Lower pH limit 4.5. Moderate rate of establishment. Widely adapted but thrives in northern half of interior United States.

Deertongue grass, *Paricum cladestinum.* Native cool season, perennial grass. Acid tolerant, drought resistant, adapted to infertile soils, strong volunteer characteristics. Moderate to slow rate of establishment. Lower pH limit 4.0. High aluminum tolerance.

Rye, *Secule* var. Annual cool season grass with rapid rate of establishment. Used as a quick cover with companion grasses with slower establishment rates. Widely adapted to all regions of United States. Lower pH limit 4.5.

Annual ryegrass, *Lolium multiflorim.* Annual cool season grass with quick rate of establishment. Survives well on coarse sandy soils, temporary cover only. May compete with companion species. Lower pH limit is 4.5. Low aluminum tolerance.

Perennial ryegrass, *Lolium perenne.* Perennial, cool season grass with rapid rate of establishment. Rapid establishment rate, but short-lived perennial (2–3 years) that does not successfully reseed itself. Used as companion grass to others with slower rate of establishment. Lower pH limit 4.5. Low aluminum tolerance.

Redtop, *Agrostis gigantea.* Perennial, cool season grass with a moderate to rapid rate of establishment. Sod forming, spreads by rhizomes. Relatively short-lived and will give way to companion grasses with slower rates of establishment over several years. Lower pH limit 4.5–5.0. Low aluminum tolerance.

Table 5.6   Plant Materials for Brownfield Sites (*Continued*)

Switchgrass, *Panicum virgatum.* Native warm season, perennial grass with a moderate to slow rate of establishment (2–4 years). Widely adapted to United States. Cultivar blackwell widely used on minesites in eastern states. Usually a companion grass to quicker establishing annual grass. Lower pH limit 4.0–4.5.

Timothy, *Phleum pratense.* Cool season perennial with a moderate rate of establishment. Best adapted to cool humid northern half of United States. Relatively short-lived (5 years). It is recommended that it be sown with legumes. Widely used as forage crop.

Weeping lovegrass, *Eragrostis curvula.* Perennial, warm season grass used for quick cover. Rapid rate of establishment, but may be short-lived (3–4 years). Used in mixtures with longer-lived, but slower to establish grasses and legumes. Lower pH limit 4.0. Moderate aluminum tolerance.

Forbs and Legumes:

Alfalfa, *Medicago sativa.* Perennial, cool season legume with a moderate to rapid rate of growth. Best adapted to northern half of United States. Best performance on nonacid, fertile soils. Lower pH limit is 5.5 but does best near 7.0.

Crownvetch, *Coronilla varia.* Perennial cool season legume. Lower pH limit 5.0. Slow rate of establishment (3–4 years). Rate of establishment is slowed by lower pH. Will provide continuous, maintenance-free cover once established. Moderate aluminum tolerance.

Common lespedeza, *Lespedeza striata* var. *Kobe.* Warm season annual legume. Tolerant to high levels of manganese in soils. Quick rate of establishment. Limited geographical adaptation. Lower pH limit 4.5.

Serica lespedeza, *Lespedeza cuneata.* Warm season perennial legume with slow rate of establishment. Lower pH limit 4.5. Moderate aluminum tolerance.

Trees and Shrubs:

Red-osier dogwood, *Cornus stolonifera.* Native shrub best suited for moist areas along drainage swales or ponds. Dense root system good for stabilizing banks. Tolerates light shade. Lower pH limit 4.5. 6–15 feet (1.8–4.7 m) tall.

Silky dogwood, *Cornus amomum.* Native shrub. Tolerates shade better than red osier and is more tolerant of acid soils. Lower pH limit 4.0. May be started by direct seeding. To 10 feet (3.1 m).

Indigobush, *Amorpha fruticosa.* Native widely adapted shrub-legume with intermediate tolerance to shade. Lower pH limit of 4.0. Native to eastern states. Used successfully for stabilizing mine soils. Slow rate of establishment. Excellent soil-conditioning characteristics because of nitrogen-fixing capability. May be started by sowing seed. Not used on sites above 2,500 feet.

Autumn olive, *Elaeagnus umbellata* var. Native shrub with nitrogen-fixing capabilities and intermediate tolerance to shade. Adapted to eastern states. Lower pH limit 4.0.

Viburnum, *Vinburnum spp.* Native shrubs. Lower pH limit 4.0. Nanny berry *V. Lentago* and mapleleaf viburnum *V. acerfolium* more tolerant of acid soils than others. Witherod *V. cassinodes* and *V. acerfolium* tolerant of dry sites. Low salt tolerance.

(*continued*)

Table 5.6   Plant Materials for Brownfield Sites (*Continued*)

Trees:

Loblolly pine, *Pinus taeda.* Native conifer with lower pH limit 4.0. Fast-growing, adapted to a wide range of soils.

Scotch pine, *Pinus sylvestria.* Conifer. Greatest natural range of any pine. Grows in many different conditions. Wide variation in appearance and tolerances depending on sources of plants. Does well in dry to somewhat poorly drained soils.

Black locust, *Robinia pseudoacacia.* Native hardwood tree. Nitrogen fixer. Can be seeded directly, adapted to wide variations in soils, good leaf litter, but should be used in mixtures. Good salt tolerance. Not desirable near residences. Rapid rate of growth.

Red maple, *Acer rubrum.* Native hardwood tree adapted to a wide range of soils—wet to dry, fine to course, pH of 4.0–7.0. Grows best on well-drained loamy soils. Wide range. Low salt tolerance.

Silver maple, *Acer saccharinum.* Native hardwood tree adapted to a wide range of soils—wet to dry, fine to course, pH of 4.0–7.0. Grows best on well-drained loamy soils. May be multistemmed. Wide range. Resistant to effects of smoke and soot.

River birch, *Betula nigra.* Native hardwood tree. Adapted to poorly drained soils and may be used where soils are too acid for other trees. Lower pH limit 4.0.

Hackberry, *Celtis occidentalis.* Tolerates soil pH to 5.0, tolerates soils from poorly drained to excessively drained.

Gingko, *Gingko biloba.* Resistant to effects of smoke and soot. Tolerates city conditions well.

Red oak, *Quercus rubra.* Tolerates city conditions well. Good salt tolerance

London plane tree, *Platanus x acerfolia.* Resistant to effects of smoke and soot.

Honey locust, *Gleditsia triacanthus.* Resistant to effects of smoke and soot. Tolerates city conditions well.

Norway maple, *Acer platinoides.* Tolerates city conditions well.

Hawthorn, *Crataegus spp.* Good salt tolerance

Hybrid poplars, *Populus spp.* Crosses of native and introduced species. Performance of varieties varies from region to region; local knowledge may be best reference. Lower pH limits to 4.0.

Gray dogwood, *Cornus racemosa.* Rapid growth. Tolerates wide range of soil conditions including wet soils; colony former.

distance to appreciate. Each site must be recognized for its characteristics and constraints when selecting the right tree.

The brownfield site issues must be considered in combination with the purpose or desirable attributes of the tree before making a selection. Fortunately, given the many species and varieties of trees, a fit is usually available for most combinations of site and purpose. Locating trees should be done with an understanding of the cultural requirements of the tree and the intended impact or value to the site. There is no single source of plant information available or in general use, and nearly every book includes its list of recommended trees. Often these lists have a strong regional flavor, which can be valuable. Selecting trees that enhance the site and will tolerate the conditions on the site requires a local knowledge.

Contemporary standards for planting trees are quite different from the old tree pit planting method. Research has led to the modification of techniques so that the site conditions are taken into account. Three different categories of planting have been identified: *street lawn, residential,* and *pit.* These methods each represent a condition that is far different than estate planting, on which the old method was based.

The primary difference in these categories is the amount of soil space available to the tree. A great deal is known about the way in which trees grow and the requirements of growth. Most roots of trees are very small, ranging in size from a pencil thickness to a hair. These are the feeder roots that absorb and transmit nutrients and moisture to the plant. These roots grow *up* toward the surface to form mats in the first few inches of soil. These roots grow and die back in response to conditions near the surface. Periods of root growth occur in moist seasons, and die back occurs in the hot dry summer and cold winter months (Urban 1991).

The fundamental need of tree health—which should be considered for existing as well as new trees—is adequate room to grow. For new trees the location of planting should consider the tree's size in 5, 10, and 25 years. In the case of existing trees, the location of proposed improvements may restrict growth, or the growth of the tree may become a nuisance or cause damage. This aspect of living site elements should prompt some consideration of the impact of the plant over time in a given location.

Planting Trees

The actual selection of a specific specimen should be done with a critical eye and by a qualified person. The elements of selection include a straight trunk with well-balanced growth and a symmetry throughout the plant. Trees with double leaders or deep Y's should be avoided. Bark should be intact and not swollen, cut, bruised, or cracked. Trees that drip on cars, such as birches, elms, lindens, and willows, are a poor choice for planting near parking areas. The average lifespan of city trees is less than 10 years. Some lessons can be learned from the causes of these tree losses. The single most common cause of city tree mortality is drainage. Tree pits along city streets or in some compacted urban soils are simply pots that have no drainage. Water collected in these pits does not drain away and the tree is drowned. Tree pits designed for city environments or environments with poor drainage should include a means of draining excess water from the pit (Urban 1991) (Figs. 5.6 and 5.7).

The next most common cause of tree losses is mechanical damage from wire baskets, wire from staking, tree grates, or tree wrap. All these devices are intended to support or protect the tree at some point in its move from the nursery to its ultimate location, but if they are installed improperly or left in place too long, these devices will become the cause of death. All wire or wrapping around a root ball should be cut away to allow the roots to grow beyond the root ball without restriction. Even biodegradable materials such as burlap remain in the soil years after the plant is installed.

Tree staking is a practice that is debated. Staking a tree is a practice left over from the time when most planting was

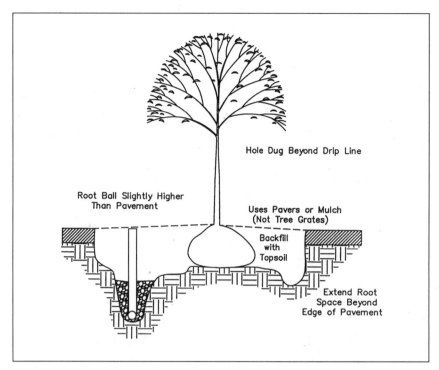

Hole Dug Beyond Drip Line

Root Ball Slightly Higher
Than Pavement

Uses Pavers or Mulch
(Not Tree Grates)

Backfill
with
Topsoil

Extend Root
Space Beyond
Edge of Pavement

Figure 5.6 Tree pit. The tree pit addresses major causes of urban tree mortality. It allows for growth and effective water and air exchange with the soil. This illustration is substantially based on the work of James Urban, ASLA.

of bare root plants. A balled specimen should not require staking in most cases; however, if stakes are used for plantings on slopes or for security reasons (to avoid plant theft), it should be necessary only for 6 months or so. Tree wrap is used to protect the tree from animals and vandals.

Tree grates are common in urban environments and are used to protect the tree from the damage of pedestrian traffic. The rings are designed so that as a tree grows the ring can be cut back allowing the trunk room to grow; however, in today's cities with shrinking maintenance budgets, this is usually not done. One alternative to the tree ring is to install pavers over the tree root zone. The pavers allow some water to penetrate to the roots and can easily be removed as the tree grows (Figs. 5.8 and 5.9).

Figure 5.7 An effective method of watering trees in the field. The buckets are wired together around the base of the tree and three holes are drilled in each bucket, which allows the water to gradually infiltrate around the newly planted tree.

The installation of trees in tree pits can be designed to increase the life expectancy of the tree and to reduce the cost of replacing dead trees. This would be to create continuous tree pits or troughs that extend the length of the street or parking areas. Each tree root zone is connected to the others. The pavement over this tree pit could be of pavers. A study by the Cornell Urban Horticultural Institute found that using pavers over these tree pits was a viable method both from a plant vitality standpoint and a long-term feasibility standpoint. Although some decrease in initial permeability was noted, the long-term effectiveness of the paver system was only nominally affected.

The study made several recommendations to be considered in the design and installation of these systems. Pavers should be dimensionally small so that the number of joints and intersections is increased. In placing the pavers, it was recommended to use a maximum joint width of 1/4 inch along with coarse sand in the joints over crushed stone if a stabilizing base material is used. The primary joint should be made to run parallel to existing contours to intercept as much runoff as possible.

Tree Wells

By planning for and constructing tree wells, existing trees can be saved. Trees used for the construction of tree wells should be chosen for their immediate and long-term value

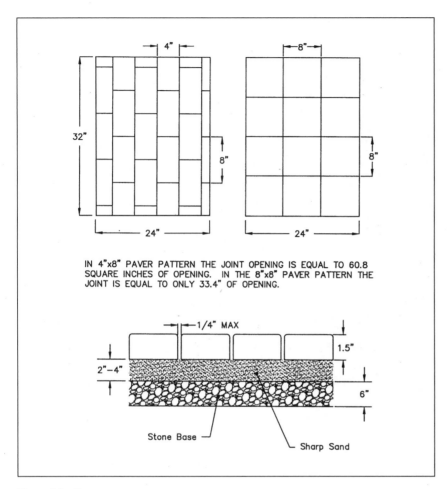

IN 4"x8" PAVER PATTERN THE JOINT OPENING IS EQUAL TO 60.8 SQUARE INCHES OF OPENING. IN THE 8"x8" PAVER PATTERN THE JOINT IS EQUAL TO ONLY 33.4" OF OPENING.

Figure 5.8 Paver.

and contribution to the landscape to justify the cost and effort of the tree well. Old or damaged trees may not offer the longevity necessary to justify the additional expense; a young tree could be planted at less expense. The number, size, and quality of trees on a given site must be considered in making the decision to construct a fill protection. On a lot with many trees, the cost of saving one or two trees may not be attractive, whereas on a lot with few trees, the cost of saving a single specimen might be very attractive.

Figure 5.9   Pavers around the base of a tree are used to replace iron grates. Note the presence of pipes to facilitate water and air exchange with root zone.

The site should be prepared before the grades are raised. All vegetation should be removed from the area affected and the soil worked. Fertilizer and soil enhancements should be added in accordance with specifications provided by manufacturers, nursery personnel, or a landscape architect. Once the soil is worked and the amendments have been introduced, care should be taken to not disturb the area with construction equipment or vehicles. The best method to protect the root zone is to isolate the area with a temporary fence.

Tree wells must be designed to provide the tree with air and water and also to provide drainage away from the trunk. There are as many designs for tree wells as there are applications and designers; however, there are some fundamental principles common to all successful designs. To provide drainage away from the tree trunk and allow air to the area of the root zone, a series of 4- to 6-inch perforated plastic pipes are laid radially from the root zone. The drain tiles should be installed with a positive slope *away* from the tree. The drain tiles should extend to or just beyond the drip line of the tree (see Fig. 5.10).

Once the drain tiles are in place, the well is constructed. The choice of material for the well can be varied. For shallow wells of 1 to 3 feet, bricks or stone can be used. These should be laid up in an open joint (i.e., without mortar). This is sometimes referred to as a *dry joint*. A batter of at least 3 inches per foot should be provided. In deeper wells it may be necessary to construct the well with a greater structural stability. In such cases timber tree wells are often used. These structures allow the use of stabilizing features, such as a deadman, to be incorporated into the design (see Fig. 5.11). In either case the well should be constructed allowing at least 2 feet from the trunk of the tree in all directions.

A means of drainage at the drip line is often provided. This may be a series of drain tiles on end and extending into

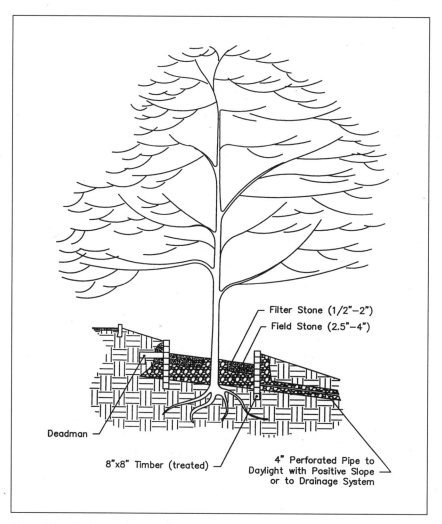

Figure 5.10 Timber retaining wall in tree well.

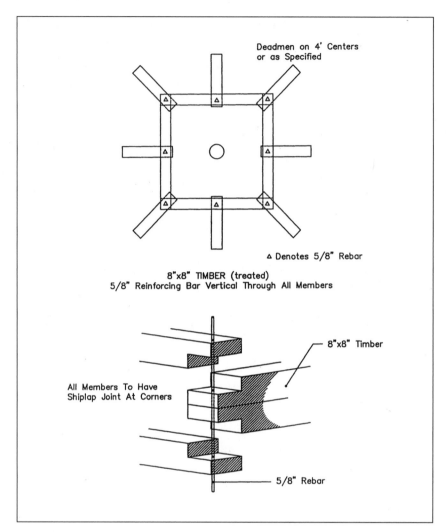

Deadmen on 4' Centers or as Specified

△ Denotes 5/8" Rebar

8"x8" TIMBER (treated)
5/8" Reinforcing Bar Vertical Through All Members

8"x8" Timber

All Members To Have
Shiplap Joint At Corners

5/8" Rebar

Figure 5.11 Timber deadman.

a gravel or stone bed or an actual gravel or stone channel provided to direct water to the root zone. Once the tiles and well are in place, a layer of stone 2 to 4 inches in diameter should be installed over the pipe and cultivated soil. This layer should not exceed 18 inches or 25 percent of the depth of the fill, whichever is least. It may be necessary to support the well or the drip line drain pipes with additional rocks (Figs. 5.12 and 5.13).

The layer of rocks or stone must be of a material that will not react with the trees or soil chemistry in such a manner as to harm or inhibit the plant. The layer of rocks is covered with a finer "filter" stone to a maximum depth of 12 inches or to within a foot of the ultimate grade. A layer of straw or filter fabric is installed on top of the filter stone. This prevents, to some degree, the soil fines from washing into the spaces between the stones and rocks, at least until the soil can begin

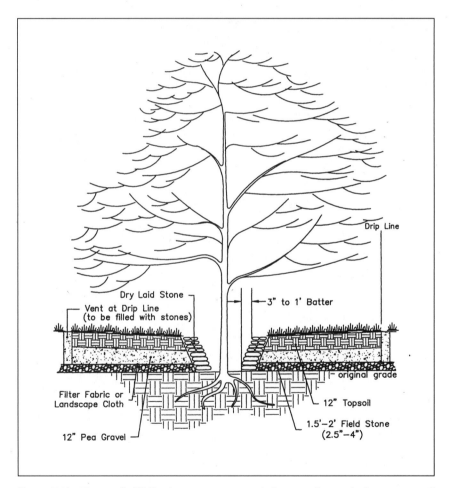

Figure 5.12 Tree well. While there are many variations on the methods, a tree well requires planning and care to be effective: The greater the sensitivity of the tree species the more care required.

Figure 5.13 Timber tree wells around mature trees. In this case approximately 5 feet of fill was successfully placed around the base of these mature trees.

to form some structure. Topsoil is then placed up to the finished grade. If vertical drain tiles were used at the drip line, these should be filled with small stone to prevent debris from filling and blocking the hole.

Trees in Cut

It is more difficult to protect a tree from a change in grade that involves removing soil from its base. If soil is to be removed, it is probable that some root damage will occur, including the removal of some roots in the process. The roots most likely to be damaged or removed are the smaller roots on which the tree relies for feeding. The rooting characteristics of a tree will have some bearing on the degree of impact the disturbance will have. Elms, for example, are deep-rooting trees and will tolerate a modest change in grade. Shallow-rooted trees, such as conifers, are difficult to save and protect in cuts. Table 5.1, which shows trees that are tolerant of fills, might be applied in reverse for cuts or reductions in grades.

It is key to the success of removing soil that the operation be done by hand to minimize damage to the roots.

Steps can be taken to reduce the damage by promoting a new root growth at a lower level, but these efforts require at least one full growing season before the removal takes place and are rarely used. Construction site management is important to assure the decision and efforts to save a tree are successful. Care taken during the construction process can minimize the risk of damage by subcontractors or careless operators. The procedures to protect selected trees would begin by clearly marking or identifying the specimen in the field. This can be accomplished by simply marking the trees to be saved with surveyor's tape and marking the trees to be removed with paint on the trunk. After marking or identifying the trees in the field, the next step is to communicate the plan to save the trees to the field crew so that everyone knows the plan.

Other steps that should be employed to protect the trees during construction include installing snow fencing around the root zone or, better yet, routing site traffic away from the specimen. Trees with low hanging branches that are likely to be damaged by construction vehicles and activities should be pruned or the protective fence extended to encompass the low branches. Debris disposal and material storage areas should be kept at least 50 feet away from the root zone. If damage does occur to the tree, it should be evaluated and repaired or mitigated immediately.

Where slope stabilization by tree planting is required, the slope should be mulched with woodchips to a depth of 4 to 6 inches (0.1 to 0.15 m) on the slope immediately upon completion of grading. Woodchips should be approximately 2 inches (5 cm) square in size, and the mulch should be applied uniformly over the planting area. Trees should be of a species that is adapted to growing on slopes. Seedlings should have had two full growing seasons in nursery beds prior to planting. Seedlings should be set vertically and roots spread carefully in a natural position in the planting hole. All trees should be thoroughly watered the day they are planted. All excess excavated material should be used as a curb for water retention. The area should be fertilized with approximately 500 pounds of 10-10-10 fertilizer per acre, worked into the slope prior to the application of the woodchips (Figs. 5.14 and 5.15).

Vegetative Screens

Among the effects of land development, and redevelopment in particular, there is the inevitable mixture of land uses. Areas of transition or mixed uses often require careful planning to offset the impact of conflicting uses. The use of trees and other plantings to screen or buffer the impacts of these areas is a common practice (Fig. 5.16). To design an effective planted buffer, it is critical to select plant types with site-appropriate characteristics. Buffer plantings can be designed for a variety of purposes or combinations of purposes: (a) a visual screen to block unwanted views, to mask glare, or to

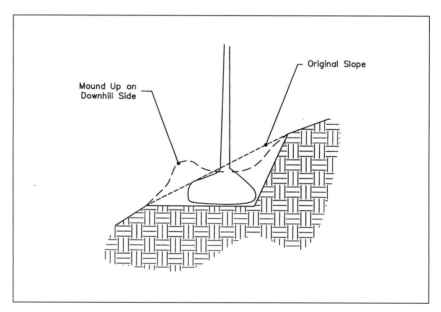

Figure 5.14 Hillside planting. The ball should rest on undisturbed soil.

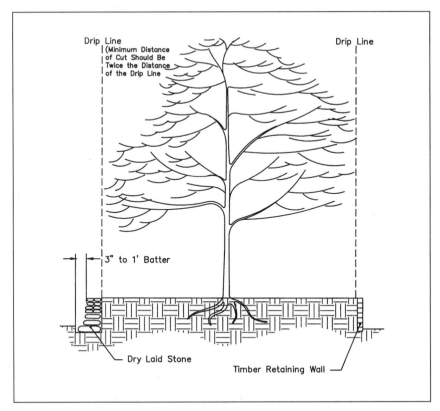

Figure 5.15 Tree in cut. Note that the location of the cut should be well beyond the drip line to allow for growth of the tree and to protect the existing feeder roots. The distance of the cut should be adjusted for the age and size of a tree.

direct the viewer to a particular feature, (b) a barrier to deflect or absorb sound, (c) a filter to collect airborne dust and particulates, (d) a source of shade and protection from the sun for purposes of comfort and/or energy efficiency, and (e) as a wind breaker.

The design of the visual screen is probably the most common purpose for buffers along residential areas (Table 5.7). The function of the visual screen is usually to block an unwanted view. This is usually accomplished by a simple row or rows of shrubs and trees. Unless carefully planned, such arrangements may not be effective at actually restricting the

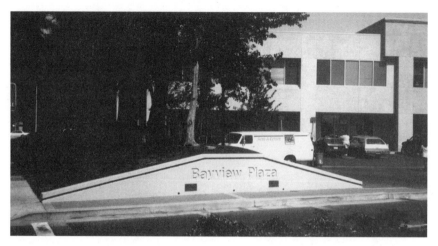

Figure 5.16   Photograph of a planted berm. Note the depth of the berm necessary to provide the deeper root zone required by trees and how the berm height contributes to the screening effect.

view. Instead, they may simply serve to frame the unwanted view. In addition to screening the unwanted view, the well-designed buffer can affect other intrusive influences such as highway noise or fugitive dusts from adjacent commercial or industrial sites. Through the use of screens and buffers, it is often possible to mitigate a negative influence and enhance the character of the site or minimize the impact of the redevelopment on a neighboring site (Fig. 5.17).

Planting for Energy Savings

Tree masses have characteristics that have several significant impacts on their immediate environment. The shade from a tree will lower temperatures by as much as 10 degrees from surrounding areas. Shade also reduces evaporation from the area affected. The combination of these effects is a localized reduction in the relative humidity. Of particular interest to the design of buffers is the size and location of plants in order to take advantage of this localized influence. Actual distances and plant heights are a function of a site's latitude, but, generally speaking, a site is shaded on the south to

Table 5.7 Trees for Buffers

Tree	Resists Smoke and Soot	Fast Growth	Thick Growth	Tolerant of City Conditions
Ash		X	X	X
Birch	X			
Catalpa	X			
Gingko	X	X	X	X
Hawthorn	X			X
Hornbeam	X			X
Locust		X		
Norway maple				X
Honey locust		X		X
Linden				X
White pine		X	X	
Scotch pine		X	X	
Junipers			X	
Elms	X	X	X	

SOURCE: Adapted from Bingham 1965.

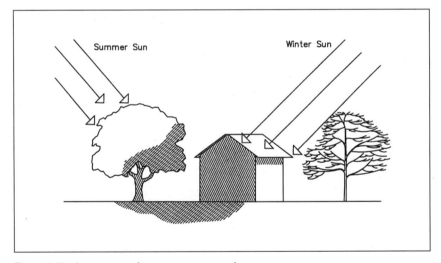

Figure 5.17 Locate trees for energy conservation.

southwestern side in the summer. In winter these would provide valuable warming from the sun. The plan might also
include the planting of successive plant types—that is, a
combination of plants that would include fast-growing
plants that would ultimately be removed and replaced by
slower-growing but more desirable species.

Plants with compact, tight growth patterns will tend to be better screening plants. These plants create a dense, soft collection of surfaces (leaves), which tends to absorb sound and provide surfaces for the deposition and filtering of dusts (Fig. 5.18). A basic element of the design of buffers is the location of the buffer with regard to the source of the nuisance and the point of observation. Locating the screen is a site-specific consideration, but, generally speaking, the buffers are more effective if they are located closer to the source of dust or noise. In the case of energy concerns, such as windbreaks or shade, the buffer should be located closer to the building.

Planting for Sound Reduction

Sound will attenuate over distance; therefore, the buffer is more effective closer to the source. This is also true of fugitive dusts or airborne particulates. The dimensions of the screen are also important. Width may be limited by property lines, but ideally screens will not be limited to single

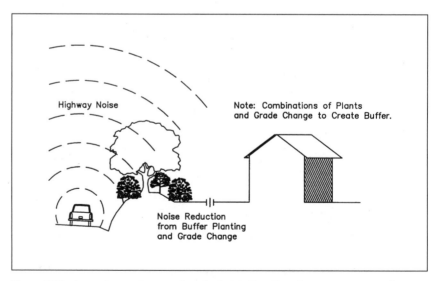

Figure 5.18 Locate trees for sound and wind buffer. Sound attenuates over distance. Buffers designed to absorb sound should be composed of multiple textures and should be several layers thick. Ideally, these buffers should be located close to the source of the sound.

properties and will extend as deeply as required to be effective. The height of the buffer is also important. Although there is no formula for precisely determining the exact width and height of a buffer, careful thought and consideration of the nature of the nuisance can be an effective guide. Sound dissipates at a predictable rate over distance. Dusts and particulates settle out of the air at a predictable rate. By understanding these characteristics, a designer can effectively use the materials and site characteristics to the advantage of the project (Fig. 5.19).

It is possible that a row of trees can actually make a problem worse, which can happen if it has been poorly located, directing a sound or diverting the prevailing wind to where

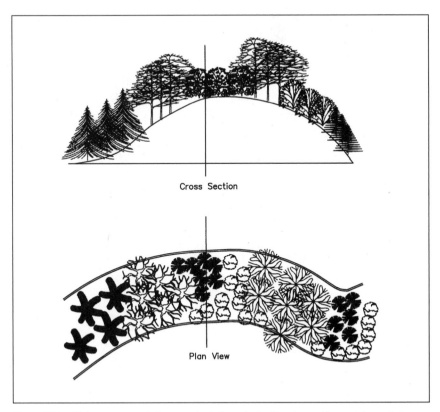

Figure 5.19   Noise, unwanted views, and wind can be buffered or redirected through the use of well-placed and well-thought-out buffers.

it is not wanted. It is known that several rows of trees are more effective than a single row and that several rows of combinations of different plants is more effective still. These increases in the density of the buffer can sometimes be accentuated even further through the use of graded berms to elevate the screen and provide a dense base for the screen.

In choosing plants, the design should specify a material that will mature relatively quickly and that will not become a maintenance problem. Of course, the plant materials chosen must be able to tolerate the nature of the nuisance. Furthermore, the buffer must be designed with the impact of seasons in mind. A solid wall of evergreens is not the only solution to screening issues. Although deciduous trees will not offer any significant screening from views, sound, or dust in January, it may be in some cases that there will be no activity to be screened at that time. People tend to remain indoors with windows and doors shut much of the time. Distance from a nuisance can be used to some advantage by the designer to determine a blend of conifers and deciduous trees.

The rules of thumb for a buffer design are that the buffer should be located closer to the source of noise or dust and that the depth of the buffer mass should be relative to the strength or magnitude of the nuisance (i.e., the louder the noise, the thicker the screen). The height of the screen is as important as the width. Combinations of plants are more effective than single types of plants. Probably because of the different textures and surfaces, a variety of plants may be used to deflect and absorb sound. Grading can enhance the effectiveness and visual interest of the buffer (Fig. 5.20).

Phytoremediation

Phytoremediation is an emerging science and area of interest for landscape architects. The general types of phytoremediation were discussed in Chap. 3. The advantages of

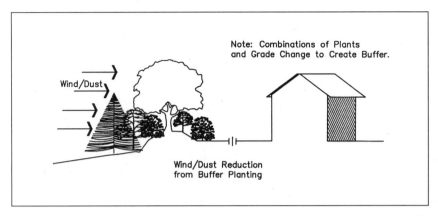

Note: Combinations of Plants and Grade Change to Create Buffer.

Wind/Dust

Wind/Dust Reduction from Buffer Planting

Figure 5.20 Building buffers for wind and dust filters requires the use of multiple textures and layers of plants. Buffers for dust reduction should be located as close to the source of the dust as is feasible.

phytoremediation are found in the relatively low costs of phytoremediation and the high volume of materials that can be treated. The disadvantages are generally found to be in the length of time necessary for the phytoremediation process and in the application limitations. Phytoremediation is limited to the *rhizosphere,* or root zone, of plants and by the specific soil conditions. As mentioned previously, the soils of impacted sites can be very poor. For vegetation to be part of an effective strategy, the soils must be conducive to vigorous plant growth. The levels of contamination must also be low enough to allow the plant materials to survive.

Types of phytoremediation include phytoextraction, rhizosphere biodegradation, phytodegradation, phytovolatilization, and hydraulic control. *Phytoextraction* is also referred to as *phytoaccumulation* because plants absorb contaminants and incorporate the material into their stems and leaves. Plants are selected for their ability to absorb a specific metal or contaminant. This method is used most commonly for the reduction of metals or hydrocarbons in soils and groundwater. Plants are harvested and composted or incinerated. Alfalfa and fescues have been used successfully for these applications as have junipers and poplars.

Rhizosphere degradation refers to the degradation of contaminants by microorganisms around the roots of a plant. The plant provides nutrition to bacteria and fungi, which in turn biodegrade substances encountered in the soil as part of the symbiotic relationship with the plants. This is a natural process of plant and soil health that has been found to be effective with soils contaminated with low levels of petroleum products. Grasses and clovers have been used successfully. Phytodegradation occurs as a metabolic process within the individual plant. Some plants produce materials that catalyze the degradation process within the plant. Research has identified some success degrading aromatic and chlorinated aliphatic compounds. This type of phytoremediation has been effectively used in field trials with *trichloroethylene* (TCE), herbicides, and petroleum. *Phytovolatilization* is similar to phytodegradation in that it occurs as an internal, metabolic process of some plants. In this approach plants absorb contaminants at their roots; the materials are degraded internally, and then the volatilized by-products of degradation are released through the leaves as part of the plants' respiratory processes. In experiments with yellow poplar trees, the trees were able to volatilize up to 90 percent of the TCE absorbed.

The last type of phytoremediation is the *hydraulic influence of plants*. Some trees may be used to act as living pumps. These plants are selected for the ability to take up large quantities of water. For example, the yellow poplar mentioned above will draw about 30 gallons of water per day, and cottonwoods may absorb and process up to 350 gallons of water every day. Such trees used in mass may affect a localized reduction in the elevation of the water table.

Phytoremediation is an exciting approach to healing impacted sites because it is a relatively low cost application and it is aesthetically pleasing. Though phytoremediation techniques have suggested many promising uses, the applications are limited in several ways. The reach of phytore-mediation is fairly shallow and limited to the root zone of plants, or the contaminants may be present at levels that are toxic to the plants. The rate of remediation is also limited by the plant's capability to process the contaminant, and not all contaminants can be sorbed by plants. The capability of the plants will be effected by weather and seasons. Finally, phytoremediation may simply effect the transfer of the contamination from one medium to another.

Much of the current knowledge has been developed only recently; however, there are applications for this new information on many redevelopment sites. The plant list in Table 5.8 is a summary of available information on specific plant materials used in reported phytoremediation projects. No genetically manipulated or engineered materials were used in compiling the list, although significant results have been achieved in field trials of such plants. Likewise, commercially available trademark plant materials were not included on the list, though the number of such materials is growing rapidly. The area of phytoremediation is an area of rich research possibilities for landscape architects and site engineers.

Table 5.8 Plants with Known Phytoremediation Applications

Plant	Application	Contaminant	Medium
Hybrid poplar	Phytovolatilization	Trichloroethylene	Groundwater
Poplar	Phytovolatilization	Carbon tetrachloride	Groundwater
Alfalfa	Phytoextraction	Petroleum hydrocarbons	Soil, groundwater
Juniper	Phytoextraction	Petroleum hydrocarbons	Soil, groundwater
Fescue	Phytoextraction	Petroleum hydrocarbons	Soil, groundwater
Clover	Phytodegradation	Petroleum	Soil

SOURCE: Information adapted from Milton Gordon, Stuart Strand, and Lee Newman, *Final Report: Degradation of Environmental Pollutants by Plants,* 1998, U.S. EPA, Washington, D.C., and U.S. EPA, *A Citizen's Guide to Phytoremediation,* 1998.

CHAPTER 6

Design and Site Management Issues

T he design professional's role during construction is no less important than it is during the planning and design process. The construction phase is the implementation of all the preceding effort, and in this phase the project plans speak most often for the design professional. As much as there is a tendency to draw a bright line between the design and construction phases of a project, in practice, this does not occur. The designer must think through the construction process as he or she designs; he or she must build the project in his or her mind to anticipate and account for difficulties. The design plans must reflect that process and level of thinking.

Project plans do not exist entirely on plan sheets. In the contemporary marketplace, most plans go through a review process and must be substantiated with design reports and permit applications. The processes for approving plans and granting permits usually entails some performance criteria or conditions under which the site is to be developed and operated. The design professional must be certain the project plans reflect these conditions and needs to effectively communicate them to the contractors.

Working with Construction Contractors

The site plans must express the methods and materials to be used to meet the aims of the environmental concerns as well as the site development concerns. Material substitutions that might be the normal practice may not be acceptable on the brownfield site. Poor workmanship or substandard materials may contribute to a recontamination or exacerbation of a condition with significant environmental and economic consequences. Poor practices increase the health and safety risks for workers and neighbors. Plans and details regarding these aspects of the site work must be complete and unambiguous. This is especially true if the site work calls for a method that is unusual or varies from a more common local practice.

The design plans may require close coordination with or even incorporate the work of other professionals. It may be necessary to indicate the locations of samples or monitoring wells on the design plans. Situations in which the design may require that a monitoring well be abandoned should be closely coordinated with the environmental consultant. Abandoning monitoring wells often requires the agreement of local or state regulatory personnel. In areas of known contamination or where special practices are required, the drawing should reflect this information graphically and include appropriate notes.

The site designer will be called upon to think through the construction sequence and staging. The temporary construction condition will have to be addressed in the project *erosion and sediment control plan* (ESPC). The preparation of erosion and sedimentation plans is usually completed well in advance of construction before a contractor is even selected. At the outset of construction, the general contractor should review the construction sequence in the ESPC and discuss changes with the site designer prior to beginning construction. The site designer will also be called upon to develop or to participate in the development of a site management plan as part of the ESPC and the NPDES general permit.

Erosion and Sediment Control

The damage and impacts of erosion and sedimentation are well documented and familiar results of land disturbances. Recognition of the importance of reducing these impacts and preserving the natural resources has been responsible for the passage of laws and regulations at all levels of government to address erosion and sediment control. At least 18 states have passed sediment control laws since Maryland enacted the first law and program in 1970. Although the laws differ in scope and enforcement, the intent and impacts were clear; the protection of surface water quality required the regulation of significant earth disturbances. The presence of the ubiquitous filter fabric fence and other control measures on construction sites are evidence of these laws.

On the federal scene, the Clean Water Act and the recent National Pollution Discharge Elimination System (NPDES) regulations for nonpoint source pollutants (NPSs) promise to have impacts as well. The NPS regulations require controls and compliance on construction sites of 2.02 hectares (5 acres) or more. The construction project may be required to give notice of intent to use the general permit under the NPDES nonpoint source program. The general permit process has also been adopted by states with their own programs. Simply put, the general permit is issued to everyone at the time the regulations take effect. Anyone wishing to use the permit must file a notice of intent with the appropriate agency. Individual states may adopt the federal program or develop one of their own. One effect of the regulations is that states that did not previously have erosion and sediment control laws are now required to meet the federal standard. For states that did have laws and regulations but where exemptions or voluntary compliance weakened compliance and enforcement, tighter standards should result from the NPDES regulations. All of these concerns normally encountered on a construction site become even more of an issue on the site with contaminated soils. The control of sediment on the brownfield site is a critical site management issue. A poorly managed site could create environmental and health and safety conditions that are worse than those of the original preconstruction site. At the very least, because of the sensitivity to the perceived conditions on such projects, good housekeeping is an important function.

The lessons from those states that have had programs for 20 or more years should tell us that erosion and sediment programs require more than a set of rules and guidelines if they will succeed in the field. Unfortunately, in many cases, erosion and sediment control plans are the last thing designed and the first thing installed. Installation is haphazard or incomplete, and maintenance is limited to responding to complaints and inspections. The development of the erosion and sediment control plan should include the management of the facilities through the entire project—not simply the instructions for how to start and end the construction phase of the project. As with any element of a project, it must be thought out and planned and responsibility and resources must be assigned, performance expectations communicated, and performance monitored and confirmed from time to time. As enforcement of the new regulations begins to occur, site work contractors will necessarily begin to develop and adopt operating procedures that reduce the risks of violations and enforcement actions.

The actual ESPC is usually completed by the site designer so that the analysis of the site, the selection and sizing of facilities, and the specification of materials are the site designer's responsibility. Of all the causes of erosion and sediment control failure, the construction contractor actually has control over only three: compensating for seasonal differences, installing facilities, and maintaining facilities. The designer is responsible for all other aspects of the erosion and sedimentation plan. During the study of a plan, while preparing for the start of construction, the contractor should review the erosion and sediment controls and sequencing to be assured that they work. Erosion and sediment controls are sometimes designed without regard for the dynamics of a construction site. Designs tend to address specific moments in the course of the site work and not the constantly changing site conditions. The contractor should review the erosion and sediment control plan to be sure that there is adequate room to store excavated or excess material. In cases where storage is required, the contractor should also consider whether there is a practical pattern for the use of heavy equipment and if it is possible to stage contaminated materials and avoid contamination of new areas or recontamination of cleaned areas.

Temporary drainage conditions may also present a problem if not planned for. The installation of sediment traps and basins may have to incorporate an interim step or two if significant changes in grade are proposed. The contributing area to a sediment trap may change dramatically several times during the period of construction. These interim steps must be provided for in the plan.

The first impact on a site is the earthwork. As the site is regraded to provide the necessary shape and surfaces on which to construct the proposed site elements, the risk of erosion and sediment pollution to streams and lakes, as well as the problem of blowing dusts, increases. The grading changes made to the site can result in redirecting site drainage away from existing drainage patterns. The temporary construction drainage pattern is often not considered in the project planning and can become a serious problem if not managed properly. The impact could result in off-site damage to surface water quality, or conveyance of contaminated sediments off site, which in turn could lead to fines and increased project costs, in addition to public relations and credibility damage.

Even on the brownfield site, the loss of wildlife habitat or tree masses can often cause an emotional reaction from a community (Fig. 6-1). The simplest construction project fosters a wide range of emotional reactions from a community. The loss of open space and green areas is often met with resistance and misunderstanding. This reaction can occur regardless of the real habitat value or quality of these areas; just the change and construction activity attracts attention. The early identification of these habitat areas and drainage patterns must be completed in the planning stages and then must be carried through to the construction phases of the project. If the early work identified a habitat that was to be saved, among the most important steps when site work begins is to identify and isolate those areas in the field. Critical habitat areas or areas that are to serve as buffers to such areas should be clearly marked in the field, and operators should be instructed as to the purpose of the marks. Tree masses that are to be saved should be identified, and individual specimens should be protected by fences or barriers to isolate them from the busy construction activities (see Chap. 5).

The most common environmental impact of most disturbed sites besides the initial loss of cover is the temporary influence of storm water runoff in the forms of erosion, sedimentation, loss of soil, and the degradation of downstream water. The clearing of the vegetation obviously disturbs the relationship between the vegetative cover and the soil. In the absence of the vegetation, the soil is more prone to ero-

Figure 6.1 Neighbors of this urban landfill protested the development of the site because of the loss of habitat for certain wildflowers and birds and other animals.

sion, water is unable to soak in as easily, and it is more difficult for vegetation to be established. The loss of cover means the loss of plant surfaces which intercept and deflect the energy of the falling rain before it contacts the soil. In turn, this plant protection allows the soil structure to remain intact, allowing for gradual infiltration of water through the soil and resistance to the erosive forces of wind and rain.

The design and management of sites usually address the long-term protection of sites from erosion and storm water damage, but often the temporary construction condition is forgotten during the design stage. Dealing with the dynamic, often complex storm water runoff conditions that exist on a construction site as an afterthought can be an expensive experience.

Minimizing Erosion

By minimizing the amount of area that is to be disturbed, there can be a reduction in the amount of runoff increase and in the facilities necessary to handle it. The reduced runoff translates immediately to a reduced risk of erosion but also a smaller requirement for storm water facilities. If vegetated areas exist on brownfield sites and they are of sufficient quality, efforts to retain them may be rewarded in several ways. The areas of preserved vegetation may act as adequate buffers between disturbed areas that reduce the amount of active erosion and sediment protection required. Likewise, the less clearing and grubbing that is done, the greater the degree of infiltration capacity is preserved. Although some inconveniences may occur during construction, there are substantial cost savings involved by the reduction of disturbed area.

THE EROSION PROCESS

Erosion is the uncontrolled transportation of soil either by wind or water. In most site construction cases the primary short-term concern is erosion due to an unstabilized soil surface and the impact of precipitation and runoff. It is generally understood how erosions works. The mitigation of these mechanisms is the focus of erosion control. In general, erosion begins with the loosening of soil particles through freeze-thaw or wet-dry cycles, or from the impact of falling rain.

Erosion is defined by the manner in which it is moved rather than by the cause. *Splash erosion* is simply the result of raindrop impact on unprotected soils. Through the repetitious hammering of raindrops, soil particles are gradually moved downhill. This is a process of concern to builders with sites that have unprotected soils exposed to the weather. The larger the raindrops and the greater the slope, the farther downhill the soil particles will move and the greater the risk of erosion. As this process develops, the soil is broken up, the soil structure is degraded and the process of erosion is accelerated. Even on flat slopes the destruction of the soil structure is detrimental, resulting in a hard soil crust when it dries. The crust limits infiltration and increases runoff and further erosion. Soils without structure are difficult mediums in which to establish vegetation, exacerbating the erosion cycle.

Sheet erosion occurs where there is a uniform slope and surface, and runoff flows in a sheet. Erosion in these instances usually is limited to the loose soil particles. Sheet erosion rarely occurs in other than a limited form in the field. Sheet flow tends to concentrate into more defined flows as it is channeled by the irregularities of a site.

The channelized flow results in the types of erosion most think of when the subject comes up: rill and gully erosion. *Rill erosion* is characterized by small channels that often abraid and intertwine, while *gully erosion* is identified by the large channels that are obviously damaging. Where a rill is at worst only a few inches deep, a gully can be 10 or more feet deep.

The impacts of erosion and sediment extend from the aesthetic impacts to the easily quantified cost of dredging reservoirs to recover lost capacity. The U.S. Army Corps of Engineers spends an estimated $350 million annually to dredge rivers and harbors in the United States. Sediment-filled rivers, reservoirs, and harbors cannot be used for shipping or recreation. The material dredged from these reservoirs is often the most productive and fertile fraction of the soil matrix. The loss of soil as an agricultural resource can have a direct impact on the productivity and feasibility of that operation. To replace topsoil with commercially available topsoil would cost at least $20 per cubic yard ($26 per cubic meter) or about $4.6 billion each year in the United States. Taking these replacement costs and the dredging costs together make a compelling economic argument for erosion and sediment control.

PRINCIPLES OF EROSION AND SEDIMENT CONTROL

The essence of the principles of erosion and sediment control lies in the fundamental difference between the prevention of erosion and the control of sediment (Table 6.1).

Table 6.1   Principles of Erosion and Sediment Control

1 Design development to fit the site and the terrain.
2. Schedule earthwork and construction to minimize soil exposure and enhance stabilization.
3. Retain existing vegetation to the extent possible.
4. Stabilize exposed areas as quickly as possible.
5. Minimize the length and steepness of slopes.
6. Keep runoff velocities low in the temporary and final conditions.
7. Prepare drainage ways for increased flows and velocities.
8. Trap the sediment on the site.
9. Inspect and maintain controls.

SOURCE: Adapted from Goldman, Jackson, and Bursetynsky 1986.

Erosion prevention is an exercise in anticipation, while sediment control is a reactive undertaking. Although it may not be possible to have site development without some earth disturbance, often the amount of disturbance extends well beyond the area required. The necessary sediment control features such as filter fences, sediment traps, stone filters, check dams, and sediment basins are installed according to the disturbed area. The less area disturbed, the fewer controls necessary and the lower the cost of site control (Figs. 6.2 through 6.4).

Sediment control is, in effect, planned damage control. These efforts are geared entirely toward collecting, directing, capturing, filtering, and releasing sediment-laden runoff after erosion has occurred. By reducing the amount of erosion through design, the cost of site development can be reduced. In this marketplace where every dollar counts, the savings can help make a project successful.

The design and layout of a site must consider and address the physical characteristics of a site. The new features such as roads or buildings must fit onto the site and minimize the needs for large cuts and fills. This requires that the plan accommodate the site and the arrangement of the features in a manner that maximizes the integrity of each of them. By minimizing the disturbance and the excavated area at the design level, the designer begins to mitigate the impact of

Figure 6.2 Filter fabric fence is installed on a relatively constant grade at the toe of a slope. The fabric is secured in the ground.

Figure 6.3 Filter fabric fence secured across the opening of a catch basin is an effective sediment control.

development. The design must retain as much of the original terrain and character of the site as is feasible. Roads should be designed to be parallel to contours as much as possible. Buildings should be located to minimize significant grading changes. The disturbance and earthwork should be limited to necessary areas only, and the disturbed areas should be

Figure 6.4   Sediment traps offer simple and effective sediment control. Note the detained water in the photograph and the sediment marks on the stone filter outlet.

as small as possible. If practical, strips of existing vegetation should be left in place between disturbed areas. If a project is phased, small areas should be graded individually to minimize time of exposure and vegetation should be left in place between these areas. The time of disturbance should be scheduled to minimize risk of erosion and to maximize growth conditions in order to restabilize the site. On many brownfield sites the entire site is paved or under impermeable cover so the retention and use of vegetation is limited.

The finished grading of the site should mimic the original terrain to the degree possible. This is especially true if the original character of the site was considered an important element of the project. If the views and terrain are features that prospective buyers would be attracted to, then it is important to maintain the sense that they are undisturbed and the site is as natural as possible. The most important aspect of this is the quality of the grading. New slopes should be graded to appear natural by being uneven, irregular, rounded, and undulating surfaces. It may be a unique opportunity to restore some of the site's original character.

Slopes should be constructed with irregular inclinations rather than a single grade across the entire face of a slope. The distance between the top of slope and the toe should vary, providing for different slope lengths. Designers must appreciate the need for the natural softer forms of artificial land and must also be designed to meet the expectations of the ultimate user.

STABILIZATION

There are two distinct types of stabilization on disturbed sites: temporary and permanent. *Temporary stabilization* generally is used on a portion of a site that has been disturbed and is to be left in a disturbed state for some time prior to final grading and stabilization. This might apply to soil stockpiles or temporary access points. The means of temporary stabilization would include vegetation, geotextile fabrics, and/or stone. Temporary stabilization methods are generally inexpensive to purchase, install, and remove. The rule of thumb used in most areas is that, if an area is to remain in a disturbed condition but with no further activity for more than 20 days, temporary stabilization is called for; however, the guideline must be tempered by local conditions, time of the year, and other relative information.

Permanent stabilization, the finished surface of the developed site, includes vegetation, paving, geotextiles, stone, or combinations of these. In most cases the permanent stabilization of a site will be composed of vegetation and paving of some type. Vegetation is the least expensive cover material to use in most applications; however, in areas of high traffic (pedestrian or vehicular), paving is the obvious choice. Where occasional traffic might occur such as in maintenance roads or emergency access ways, a combination of vegetation and paving might be desirable. A number of products are available for use in stabilizing turf and as vehicle support systems. These systems minimize paving and therefore reduce runoff and the required supporting network of pipes and detention basins (Fig. 6.5).

For areas outside of parking and cartways, vegetative cover is usually used. As already discussed, one effect of construction activities is the destruction of soil structure, which inhibits the soil as a medium for plant growth. Soil structure is the arrangement of soil particles into aggregates in combination with organic matter and microorganisms. The aggregates include pore spaces for the movement of water and air through the soils. The loss of soil structure increases erodability and reduces permeability of the soil. Before vegetation can be expected to grow and become established in this difficult environment, the soil and the site must be properly prepared. Although preparation does not immediately restore the soil structure, it does provide the elements necessary for the soil to heal itself over time (Fig. 6.6).

Erosion and Sediment Controls

The site designer must take the responsibility to be sure that the design fits the site. After a thorough evaluation of the site characteristics, the design process must synthesize a solution

Figure 6.5   Stabilized turf parking area.

Figure 6.6 Trees planted on a newly graded slope will eventually play an important part in stabilizing the slope.

that respects the character and constraints of the site and accomplishes the design program. Elegance in design could be expressed as the solution that does both well. Development, by definition, means changing the site. In the case of redevelopment, that site has already been changed once and often for the worse. The designer may have to go beyond simply respecting the site and may need to consider the necessity to heal the landscape as well. The design solution must account for the site constraints and promote the environmental function of the finished landscape.

The period during construction when the site is disturbed is when risks of erosion and sedimentation are the greatest. The ESPC must deal with the interim conditions when soils are being moved, there is a lack of cover on disturbed areas, and new grades are being established. The proper design of slopes, grades, and channels is critical. The designer should carefully evaluate the plans and specifications for erosion and sedimentation facilities to be sure the design and construction sequence is practical.

The installation of filter fabric and other filtering devices is visible on many construction sites; however, the material is only as good as its installation and its maintenance. The use of filter fabric is limited to relatively small drainage areas and sheet flow conditions. Different states and local governments have regulations pertaining to the use of filter fabric fence. Limits range from no more than 100 feet of uphill area contributing to the fence to several acres depending on cover and topography. Long stretches of filter fabric should be interrupted with stone outlet filters at low places. Although filter fabric fence is to be installed along a slope at a constant elevation, in the field inevitably there are low places or places where water will collect behind the fence. The outlet filter provides some relief to inundated filter fabric. The outlet filter should be constructed of AASHTO No. 57 stone or its equivalent and be located at low points in the fence. The stone filter acts as a sediment trap to allow the slow release of water that collects behind the fences as well as the settling of sediment (Figs. 6.7 and 6.8).

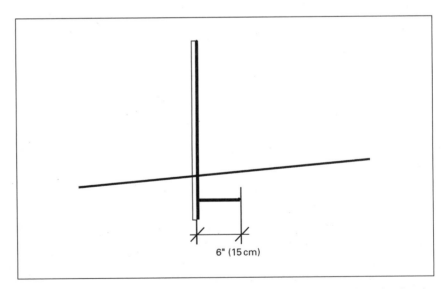

6" (15 cm)

Figure 6.7 Filter fabric fence. Note the filter fabric is secured with an L-shaped tuck at the bottom.

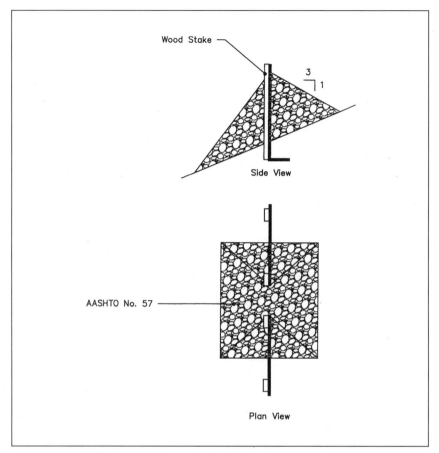

Wood Stake

3 | 1

Side View

AASHTO No. 57

Plan View

Figure 6.8 Stone filter. Stone filters are installed in the low points along a filter fabric fence or may be used in places where filter fabric is stressed. The fabric is removed and replaced by the stone, which also acts as a sediment filter.

DRAINAGE DESIGN

The slope, the erosivity of the soil, and the velocity of runoff, among other elements, must be accounted for in the design of collection and conveyance systems. The final design solution must consider the practicality and constructability of the design. The ESPC addresses the conditions leading up to the final stabilization of a site. Determining the proper interim protection and the installation of protection are important parts of the ESPC design. Designers often use standard details to describe the construction of swales and channels.

They should be sure to evaluate the detail for constructability on a given site (i.e., whether it makes sense and can be built). They should consider factors such as the effect of a vegetated swale over an impermeable cap and whether there is enough soil coverage to provide for a root zone and to resist scour at higher flow velocities (Figs. 6.9 and 6.10). See the discussion in Chap. 4 on channel design.

The reasons for channel failure include high volumes and velocity of runoff, erodible soil character, steep grade, and/or unstable channel. Since most redevelopment sites have already been graded and tend to have a fairly uniform grade, existing storm water conveyances may be used rather than constructing a new system. If channels are to be developed, however, the proper installation of geotextiles and channels are key to the stability and function of the channel, even if required only until the site is stabilized. Most geotextiles are designed for specific applications of velocity and grade. Permanent geotextiles may be appropriate for channels with velocities that exceed the limits of the soil. The proper installation method is every

Figure 6.9 This dramatic failure of a drainage system constructed in fill underscores the importance of proper construction as well as design.

bit as important as the fabric selection (Figs. 6.11 and 6.12).

Repair of badly degraded or eroded sites may present special problems for the redevelopment project. In areas where erosion damage has already occurred, it may be necessary to take extra steps to control the runoff velocity until the swale or impacted areas are stabilized. In such cases the eroded channel may require a relocation of the channel or a temporary redirection of the runoff until a stabilized channel can be constructed. It is necessary in some cases to completely excavate the eroded area and replace it with carefully compacted and graded fill. These damaged areas should be excavated back to stable soil. The replacement material should be "keyed" into the soil and compacted as shown in Fig. 6.13. The cause of the failure should

Figure 6.10 Properly constructed and lined channel. The fabric is installed so that it has continuous contact with the soil.

be assessed to avoid a reoccurrence. The site designer should determine whether the velocity was greater than anticipated by the design or if the soils are of a different

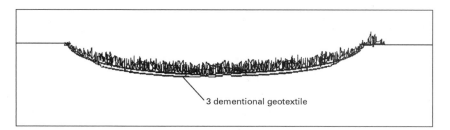

3 dementional geotextile

Figure 6.11 Fabric-lined swale.

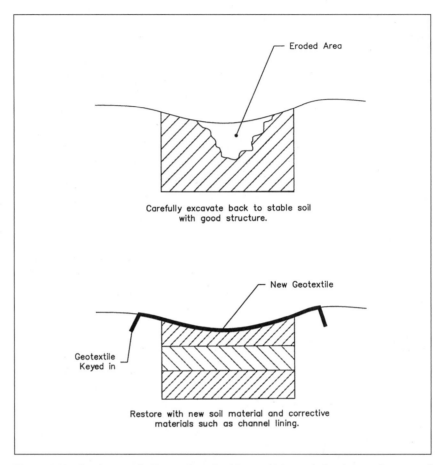

Eroded Area

Carefully excavate back to stable soil
with good structure.

New Geotextile

Geotextile
Keyed in

Restore with new soil material and corrective
materials such as channel lining.

Figure 6.12   Erosion repair. Excavation should extend beyond the damaged area and extend into stabilized soil. The new soil should be compacted in layers. The shape of the excavation should "key" the repair in place. The source of the original erosion should be resolved.

character. It would also be critical to determine if the installation is in accordance with the design. In any case, merely replacing the material without accounting for the cause of the failure may result in another failure. The designer should anticipate the need for additional temporary protection until the vegetation is clearly established, particularly if the cause of the erosive volume and velocity of water has not also been abated (Figs. 6.14 and 6.15).

SLOPE DESIGN

It is better to have a longer, flatter slope than a short steep slope (see Figs. 6.16 through 6.20). All cultural operations should be at 90 degrees to the slope (across the face of the slope, not up and down). Methods of increasing rate of vegetative stabilization on slopes include *stair stepping, tracking, hydroseeding,* and using mulch or blankets (see Fig. 5.7).

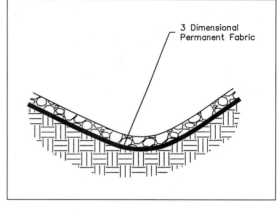

Figure 6.13   Riprap-lined swale.

Mulch and erosion control fabrics act to shield the soil from the destructive power of raindrops and runoff until the slope can be stabilized with vegetation or other means. Where infiltration systems are being used, it is necessary to protect the new system from inundation during construction and from compaction by construction equipment. Runoff and sediment

Figure 6.14   This riprap-lined swale was installed to collect and convey runoff from a new slope. The grades involved result in higher velocities than an unprotected channel could convey.

Figure 6.15 This swale has failed because it was not properly protected after construction.

Figure 6.16 The use of tracked equipment to roughen graded surfaces can play an important role in erosion resistance and establishing vegetation. The tracked surface, in comparison to the untracked surface, is rough, offering many microsites for seeds and for infiltration.

should be diverted from the infiltration system during construction to avoid the introduction of fines into the infiltration area before filter strips are established. Disturbed areas can be protected by upstream diversions and temporary vegetated buffers. As always, the less disturbance, the less opportunity for erosion and sedimentation. Native plants often are best suited to the site and are sometimes already well established. The existing roots act to bind soils, and the above-ground surfaces act to deflect rain and slow any runoff. Native plants may be better suited to the regional character and are preferred choices; however, an existing stand of nonnative vegetation should be carefully assessed before removal. The stabilization of the site and the tolerance of the exotic species to harsh site conditions may be of significant value. Perhaps the reintroduction of native plants would be better managed over time rather than on a wholesale basis. In any case, it is the tolerance for the conditions known to exist on the site that must be the deciding criteria.

The design criteria of sediment traps are usually specified by regulatory agencies; however, a general rule of thumb is that the temporary sediment trap should have 2,000 ft^3/acre

Figure 6.17 Photograph of slope with geotextile. The temporary geotextile provides protection from precipitation and allows the seeds to establish.

of drainage area and that the drainage area for any single trap should be limited to a 5-acre maximum drainage area. Different types of outlet structures are devised for different circumstances; however, they all share the same purpose, which is to release slowly the collected runoff to allow time for the sediment to settle out and be retained on the site. Solutions for damaged areas may require the use of geotextile grids, infiltration channels, or geotextile fabric, depending on the velocities and volumes being conveyed. The use of polyacrylamide and soil microbiota

Figure 6.18 Photograph of slope with geotextile after 4 weeks. Note the presence of the early vegetation.

Figure 6.19 Photograph of unstable slope. The cut slope was not properly stabilized at the time of construction and has eroded to a point where a significant overhang has developed.

additives may also promote the development of soil structure (Figs. 6.21 and 6.22).

Sediment trap outlet structures must be designed to drain the trap at a rate of between 3 and 7 days. Since the rate remains in that range regardless how full the trap becomes, a stage outlet structure is necessary. The choices range from a filter stone berm to a riser outlet structure.

Figure 6.20 Photograph of the slope in Fig. 6.19. The slope has lengthened and stabilized. Note the bench graded in to lengthen the slope.

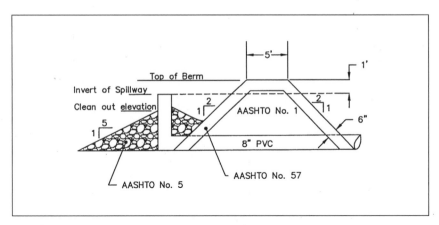

Figure 6.21 Typical sediment trap. Sediment traps are usually limited to a contributing area of 5 acres and sized to allow for 2,000 cubic feet (51 m³) of runoff storage per acre. Local authorities usually require sediment to be removed from traps when the storage capacity of the trap is reduced to about 700 ft³ (18 m³) per acre.

The rate of water through the stone may be calculated using the formula given in Chap. 4 for the rate of infiltration through a stone medium. The design of the staged riser requires calculating the discharge rate for various volumes on the trap. This requires designing a riser with a vertical

Figure 6.22   Photograph of sediment trap for large project. Note the staged outlet structure in the center of the photograph.

series of holes sized to allow the minimum drainage period but not to exceed the maximum regardless of the depth.

The formula for designing the staged riser is as follows:

$$Q = Ca\sqrt{2gh}$$

where Q = flow, ft^3/s

a = the area of the opening, ft^2

g = 32.2 (gravity)

h = depth of flow over opening (head)

Using the formula, the designer can construct a table showing the flows for various openings at various depths.

Site Management

Erosion and sediment control of disturbed construction sites is ultimately a management responsibility. Most failures of controls are failures of management and are largely due to the absence of a planned and programmed approach. Construction management can best respond to the erosion and sediment requirements of a site by developing and adopting operating procedures that include such an approach. A dialogue between the designer and the contractor to exchange ideas and solutions can be an important step in the successful erosion and sediment control plan. The designer is in the best position to initiate this meeting. If a contractor has not been chosen at that point of the project, a meeting with a qualified contractor may be just as valuable. Experience indicates that the closer this working relationship, the better the site controls work. The site manager has an interest in these early stages because eventually he or she is responsible for implementation. The entire thrust of the management plan should be aimed at controlling the causes of failure and maintaining the integrity of the site controls.

The *general management plan* for a construction site may be included in the erosion and sediment control plan. The purposes, however, are different. The erosion and sediment control report exists primarily to communicate site and design information. The management plan contains information on operations and performance and is concerned with executing the design. Although it would be expected that each plan is a reflection of the needs and concerns of the individual site, some characteristics can be presumed to occur in both.

The installation of control features requires adequate information and detailing in the plan. The plan should include construction details for the various facilities that are to be installed. This would include the routine details but also more specific information such as staple patterns on erosion control fabrics or invert elevations on sediment trap dewatering outlets. The adequate installation of controls begins with understanding the construction details.

The typical *erosion and sediment control plan* includes a construction sequence and, when appropriate, phase lines. The designer often is required to make assumptions about the project that may not be true later on. The construction sequence should be reviewed and understood. Items that cause conflicts or are no longer accurate should be addressed with the designer so that a revision can be made in the report. Too often these details are overlooked or discounted as unimportant until there is a problem later in the project and the contractor is found to be "out of sequence" with his or her approved plan and permit. This small detail is suddenly disproportionately important and can cause delays and even fines. Site designers must continue to participate in the site design by working with the contractor to revise the ESPC when necessary.

The ability to respond to problems is an important aspect of site management, particularly on brownfield sites where there is an increased risk of discovering additional contamination or unanticipated site conditions. A *project directory* is a simple tool. It is merely a directory of the phone numbers, addresses, and fax numbers of the various people involved in the project. The list normally includes the names and numbers of the owners, the project engineer, the project surveyor, the municipal engineer, the site manager (and an alternate or two), as well as any subcontractors or others that might be important. The list should also include the names and information of the regulatory and enforcement personnel.

The directory should include an identification of the responsibilities of each person listed or an explanation of why the name is listed. Such a directory will help the project team respond to emergencies and problems much faster and smoother and may be important in keeping the project on schedule. It may also be helpful in avoiding fines and enforcement actions.

PROJECT START-UP

The *project start-up meeting* is a fundamental element of the management plan. It is the site manager's responsibility to organize the start-up meeting. The meeting should be attended by the site designer, erosion and sediment control plan designer, local enforcement personnel, and supervision and staff from the project. It may be appropriate to have others attend as well such as municipal representatives or environmental regulators.

The site plan should be used to guide discussion. If phases are involved, the delineation and field recognition of phase lines should be discussed. The construction sequence should also be reviewed. The first meeting should include a review of the scope of the project and a review of the grading operations, specifically including identifications of areas of significant cuts and fills, and sensitive areas such as wetlands or floodplains. Areas of concern such as contaminated soils or underground storage tanks or pipelines should also be discussed. The erosion and sediment controls that will be used throughout the project, maintenance schedules, and repair plans should be reviewed. The meeting should include a discussion of any special material handling requirements and known site hazards. The health and safety (H&S) plan requirements should be presented, and the procedures for an emergency response introduced. A site walkover should be conducted to familiarize everyone with the start-up condition of the site. This is particularly important if there is existing erosion or sedimentation occurring. Minutes should be taken during the meeting and distributed afterward to all the attendees. A copy of these minutes should be kept in the project log.

Once the earthwork has begun and the project is up and running, the site manager's attention will be diverted from the erosion and sediment control plan. By assigning a staff person to monitor the schedule, the manager can be sure the routine inspections and maintenance items are being addressed. Routine inspections are scheduled at frequencies that reflect the site characteristics, the time of the year, and the condition of the site. A hilly site that is fully disturbed during the rainy part of the year will justify more frequent inspection than the same site partially stabilized during a dry season.

INSPECTIONS

Inspections themselves are relatively inexpensive, requiring only a visual check in most cases to ascertain the condition and any corrective action that might be required (Figs. 6.23 and 6.24). The use of a small tape recorder makes notetaking almost effortless. It is unreasonable to assume that the schedule set out in the beginning of a project will be met perfectly throughout the project. Some flexibility is appropriate in the system. In most cases, adjusting the schedule by 2 or 3 days is not a problem, but inspections should be made after every significant rain or melt event without exception.

From the start-up meeting and throughout the project until final stabilization is confirmed, a *logbook* should be maintained by the person assigned the responsibility to oversee the erosion and sediment control plan. The purpose of the logbook is to record the routine inspections and maintenance as well as the general progress and activity on the site. A well-maintained logbook is a record of performance and compliance with the plan. The log should reflect the routine inspections, as well as any corrective actions taken, and should include photographs. Copies of meeting minutes and contacts with regulatory personnel are also pertinent. It may be appropriate to keep records regarding precipitation or weather that is relevant to actions and decisions taken and records of the required inspections after storm events, including photographs. The logbook becomes a record of significant progress, including conformance and progress as outlined in the construction sequence.

It is not unusual during the course of a construction project to have changes. The changes may occur because of a change in the project or a change in site conditions encountered during the construction process. It is common to have changes in the erosion and sediment control plan as well. These changes are often a response to an unforeseen condition such as a concentrated flow of runoff where one was not anticipated. The site manager must have the flexibility to respond to the problem quickly. In fact, anything other than a quick response would be inconsistent with the objectives of the plan. Once the response is made, however, a note should be made in the logbook, and the owner, site engineer, and regulator should be notified. A copy of the notice should be kept in the logbook.

Although the objective of site management planning is to eliminate problems through anticipation and control, the nature of the construction site and conflicting agendas is such that problems will arise. It may not be practical to try to address every conceivable problem that may occur on a site in the course of construction. Instead, the plan must rely on the training and commitment of the project management. The better prepared and knowledgeable the project manager is, the more likely problems can be identified and addressed early. The adversarial tone that has characterized the relationship between site managers and regulatory personnel must give way to a sound working relationship. Experience with problem solving on disturbed sites has shown that on sites where there is open communication and an exchange of ideas between the parties, problems are addressed routinely. In these cases there are fewer enforcement actions taken and fewer problems overall. The basis for the relationship is the knowledge each player has in the role and interests of the other. Such relationships are built over time and with effort on everyone's part.

The brownfield site plan may include unusual specifications, particularly regarding capping or isolating materials to be left in place or in managing contaminated excavated

Figure 6.23   This properly installed filter fabric fence has continued to perform in spite of much needed maintenance.

materials. Contractors and construction crews not familiar with the extra effort and practices required on the brownfield project may require precise instruction. The landscape architect or site engineer should meet with the contractor to review the unusual practices or methods to ensure that the need for compliance is understood. This meeting should be confirmed in writing. It is a common practice in redevelopment of such sites to require the staging and use of excavated materials to occur in very specific ways that are not common practice on

Figure 6.24 It is not uncommon for filter fabric fences to be found performing extra duty, beyond the scope of their design.

other construction sites. Even a temporary lapse in this discipline may prove to be costly. Frequent site visits may be necessary to ensure compliance with the design intent.

It is always sound professional practice to communicate in writing. While this may not be practical in the effort to support ongoing construction, the design professional should document all instructions or concerns in writing. Phone conversations and meetings should also be documented in the project file. It is also recommended that the design professional maintain a personal diary in which discussions are recorded. These practices may provide the design professional with important support and defense in the event of an incident on the construction site.

Preparedness, Prevention, and Contingency Plans

The NPDES Nonpoint Source Program includes construction sites among the regulated industries. The regulations encourage the construction managers to have a *preparedness, prevention, and contingency plan* (PPCP) to assist them in the day-to-day management of the project and in the effective response in the event of an emergency. On some redevelopment sites the PPCP may be required, particularly if the site operates under an RCRA permit or is among the industries in the standard industry classification codes listed in the NPDES regulations. The PPCP is as much a plan to avoid problems as it is a response plan. The PPCP is project and site specific but will share some common elements from plan to plan.

A key element of the plan is a copy of the site plan itself on which the areas of key activities are designated. The plan should show the site entrances and exits, loading and unloading areas, material storage areas, staging areas, drainage appurtenances, truck wash areas, the location of phones and fire hydrants, and any other pertinent facilities. This site plan will provide an important reference in the event of an on-site emergency. The purpose of the PPCP is to anticipate the conditions or circumstances that might occur on a given site in order to prepare a response in advance of the occasion of an actual event. The plan serves to anticipate and therefore modify site activities to avoid the need for a response and to formulate a plan for response should it be necessary. The plan should identify the responsible person on-site. A call list should be prepared that includes the names and numbers, including pagers, of the responsible person, alternates for that person, and various support personnel. Support personnel could include the site engineer, landscape architect, local emergency services, and cleanup contractor. The call list should be distributed to all appropriate personnel and posted conspicuously on site.

The PPCP should identify the location of material disposal sites including truck washouts and material recycling areas (Fig. 6.25). As personnel start work on the site, they should be apprised of the location of these facilities and the site housekeeping and management practices. All personnel should be trained in the proper response to a spill or other incident. The discussion should include directions for response to minor spills and more significant events. The most important part of the PPCP is the training of on-site personnel. While all on-site personnel should be made aware of the site rules, it is not necessary to include all personnel in the response training. A select group of personnel should be trained in the location of response equipment, control and cleanup methods, and disposal practices called for in the plan. A record should be kept of all training.

Figure 6.25   Signs help to manage the construction site.

The PPCP includes a list of the materials stored on the site as well as the location of storage, the point of disposal, and the method of disposal. The location and inventory of the *emergency response equipment* (ERE) should also be included. Typically emergency response equipment is limited to absorbent material, sheets of 8-mL plastic, gloves, disposable coveralls, overboots, duct tape, brooms, shovels, a small set of nonsparking tools, a chemical fire extinguisher, a first-aid kit, and a camera. The storage area should also include a copy of the PPCP and the call list.

The range of materials possible on a construction site are too numerous to address here; however, certain materials can be expected to be on virtually every site. Procedures for these materials should be determined on a site- and project-specific basis. In general, the procedures for common materials or types of materials are fairly similar.

Materials Management

Fuels and volatile petroleum products should be stored in approved containers and stored out of doors in a secure, covered area or indoors in a properly ventilated area. Bulk storage of these materials (55 gallons or more) should be held in a containment area sized to contain 110 percent of the largest single container within it. In the event of a spill or a rupture or leaking tank, the released material will be contained. In the case of small spills, absorbent material will be used to collect the material. Contaminated absorbent material should be collected in an open container that is stored in a well-ventilated area until disposal (Figs. 6.26 and 6.27).

For spills that are too large to be collected by available materials but that are in the containment area, the integrity of the containment should be confirmed and secured. In the case of highly flammable materials, the local fire department should be called to assess the condition and determine if the use of foam is required to suppress the volatile mate-

Figure 6.26 Fuel tank inside containment.

Figure 6.27 These fuel cans are stored in a containment to collect any spills. The containment itself is placed over two pieces of plywood to further protect the soil.

rials and reduce the risk of fire or explosion. For less volatile materials, a recycling recovery firm can be called to remove the contents.

For spills that occur outside of the containment area, the absorbent materials should be used to control the flow. Care should be taken to protect surface waters, drainage pathways, and storm water conveyances from contamination. Contaminated soils should be excavated and collected and stored on plastic sheets until disposition is determined. In all cases the responsible person should assess the situation and determine whether there is a need or requirement to report the incident to the authorities.

Construction chemicals may include paint, acids, cleaning materials, solvents, adhesives, and any number of other materials. All construction materials should be stored and disposed of in accordance with the manufacturer's instructions, safety and health regulations, and waste disposal regulations. Materials brought onto the site in greater than incidental or retail quantities should have a *material safety data sheet* (MSDS) on file. Like petroleum products, large quantities of liquid materials should be stored inside a secondary containment. Cleanup of liquid materials should follow procedures similar to petroleum products. Materials that represent a special hazard such as burns from acids or fumes from solvents should be labeled, and the proper safety equipment should be available on site to deal with the spill (Fig. 6.28).

Nonhazardous solid waste should also be covered under the PPCP. Nonhazardous solid waste would include wood, concrete, scrap metal, plastic, masonry products, roofing materials, and other building products and debris. Material should be collected into separate containers for recovery and recycling. Burning and burying wastes on site should be discouraged.

Wash from concrete trucks should be directed to a designated area. Rinse water from concrete washout can be haz-

Figure 6.28 Photograph of oil spill on construction site. This spill is located in what is to become a storm water management facility.

ardous to aquatic ecosystems. The washout area should be located away from drainage paths and surface waters. The washout may be designed as a sump to collect the rinse and allow evaporation to remove the water. The remaining residue and asphalt wastes should be collected and recycled or disposed of properly as construction wastes.

Practice Management Issues

For many firms site design for brownfield redevelopment will be the first time they have dealt with environmental contamination as part of the design process. Beyond the design concerns are issues relating to the management of the firm itself. Like so many other management issues, it is necessary to tend to these administrative details for the firm to live up to its professional responsibilities and to protect its business success.

Professional Liability

Among the first concerns a firm has about the brownfield marketplace is the impact that working on contaminated sites might have on their professional errors and omissions insurance. An informal survey of companies offering professional liability insurance found that virtually all of the companies include an exclusion for activities involving pollution and that these pollution exclusions are ambiguous and vague. In general, the pollution exclusions should not exclude the activities of the design professional engaged in handling hazardous materials either directly or indirectly. This same language is found in the insurance of engineering firms engaged in environmental engineering and site assessments. In fact, the fundamental nature of the design professional's tasks and interests are no different on the impacted site than on the nonbrownfield site.

The site design professional will perform an evaluation of the site and synthesize a design solution that satisfies the client and addresses the site constraints. In the course of the normal brownfield project, the design professional will not handle or produce hazardous materials or waste. Nor will the firm be involved in the management of the site or the off-site disposition of materials. If the firm includes employees or subcontractors engaged in the collection and analysis of samples, the amount of material involved in sampling is generally considered as de minimus amounts of material and not regulated in the same fashion as larger quantities. The purpose for which they are collected is for site characterization and not for disposal per se. Sample materials are transported to the laboratory for analysis and eventual disposal by the laboratory. Insurance brokers and providers should be contacted for an explanation of the pollution exclusion in their policies. In most cases a letter from the firm describing the scope of its activities in the brownfield marketplace serves two purposes: First, it allows the insurer to acknowledge that the activities are covered, and it gives the firm confidence as they perform their work. If the firm's insurer has a more stringent standard, the letter should prompt a discussion. The letter should clearly delineate the tasks the firm will perform and identify them as "design tasks." Second, the letter should also clarify the firm's view of its insurance status to the insurer; again, if the insurer has a different view, the letter should prompt a response.

Employees and subcontractors should be instructed to avoid directing operations on site and signing for the disposition of materials or wastes. Under no circumstances should the design firm become engaged in the management of cleanup contractors or the determination or arranging of the disposition of wastes or contaminated materials. The firm's status may change from design professional to that of an "arranger." In some cases the arranger has been found to be liable for the costs of accidents and poor practices associated with disposing of the contaminated materials or hazardous wastes. It is important for the firm to develop a clear polity on the limits of its activities on these sites. Clients are often looking for help to manage the contractors and details of these activities. The nature of the professional service firm may be to step in and help their client without understanding the risks associated with that decision. The line between professional consultant and responsible party may be crossed when the design professional begins to arrange for or direct the disposal of regulated materials. Firms considering an equity position in a project should explore how that might change their status.

Health and Safety

The *health and safety* (H&S) of personnel on a brownfield site is the responsibility of the site manager, whether that is a general contractor or an owner. *H&S plans* are the means of implementing and administering the minimum standards required by the Occupational Safety and Health Agency (OSHA) in *Safety and Health Industry Standards for General Industry and the Construction Industry*. The site manager is required to have materials and equipment inspected to be sure they are in compliance with OSHA and other applicable standards. Equipment is to be operated only by personnel that have been qualified by training or experience to do so. Each employee is to have been trained and instructed in the H&S regulations that apply to his or her work and to recognize and avoid unsafe conditions on the project site. All employees must have access to their personal medical records, including records of exposure to materials or contaminants.

In addition to training employees or subcontractors, the site manager must maintain site records of accidents that result in lost-time injuries or fatalities. As is true in all other workplaces, a copy of the OSHA poster must be posted on the site at all times, and workers have the right to see the OSHA rules upon request. Employees cannot be required to work under conditions that are either unsanitary, hazardous, or dangerous. OSHA also requires anyone working on RCRA or CERCLA sites or anyone designated to respond to hazardous materials incidents to have had the 40-hour training. On some sites or projects having OSHA trained design personnel may be required by the mitigation contractor in order to maintain compliance with the site H&S plan, but this is not typical on brownfield sites.

The H&S plan should be site specific in that it should address the specific conditions and risks associated with a given site. Special requirements for *personnel protective equipment* (PPE) such as respirators, dust masks, or disposable outer clothing should be addressed, including the availability of required PPE, the location of changing areas, and disposal practices. The determination of whether *hazardous waste operator* (Hazwopr) 40-hour training is necessary for workers should be made in the H&S plan. The name of the site safety officer and the location and phone number of local emergency services should be prominently displayed and contact numbers (phone and pager) listed. Although the site H&S plan is prepared for workers performing their duties on the site, design personnel visiting the site must comply with the site rules.

Though construction is clearly beyond the design phase of the brownfield project, site designers should consider construction activities such as staging and sequence as they prepare the site plans. Site designers should also be aware of the rights of workers and site personnel regarding exposure to contaminants and the need to follow health and safety plans.

Construction Workers

Although management of the construction personnel is not the function of design personnel and under most circumstances should be avoided, the responsibility to inform is a less clear standard. Under OSHA regulations and federal law, workers have a right to know about exposures and risks associated with the workplace. Brownfield sites may employ workers with various levels of knowledge and awareness about the risks to be found on a project site. Where workers certified with the 40-hour training have a greater awareness of the need for PPE and for methods of handling materials, untrained construction workers may have no appreciation for the importance of personal protection. Trained personnel have been taught to observe the site-specific instructions for personnel protection and the risks associated with exposures to hazardous or toxic materials. Workers that have not been trained may overreact to the risks involved or may underreact in the belief that what they cannot see will not hurt them. Although it may not be required, and the 40-hour course may not be necessary, a shorter, less intense version of hazardous materials training tailored to the site may be appropriate.

While it is clearly the responsibility of the site manager to instruct and supervise personnel, the site designer may assist in this process by the manner and completeness of the site plans. Construction plans should identify areas known to be of concern. Areas of contamination should be shown on the construction drawings. The staging of contaminated material should be specifically addressed so that clean areas are not contaminated and remediated areas are not contaminated again. Details for excavation in contaminated soils should address the staging and disposition of excavated material. The installation of materials or structures to be used for mitigation or remediation should be specific regarding their role. Design plans should include a statement of the materials and conditions known to be or suspected to be on a site. Professionals should decide whether they have a responsibility to inform site workers of hazards known to exist in the implementation of the site work.

The Design Professional and Staff

Landscape architects and site engineers may not be used to working on contaminated sites. In the early stages of a project, site visits and site evaluation may be underway before the environmental site assessment and characterization process is complete so that the character of risk and exposure is not known. Brownfield sites encompass the entire spectrum of real estate types; while some are indeed the hulking abandoned factory complex often envisioned as a brownfield, others are simply vacant lots perhaps with no environmental issues at all. Site design personnel must evaluate each site for its risks. It is uncommon for nothing at all to be known about a site, and in general, early information provides some indication to the anticipated site conditions and risks.

Prior to a site visit, the design professional should contact the environmental professional to discuss site conditions. Beyond risks from the presence of environmental contaminants, other risks may exist on the site from unsafe conditions such as a poor structural integrity, hidden-fall hazards, foot-puncture risks, confined-space risks, unstable storage piles, or fire hazards. In any case, it is a wise practice never to go to the unsecured site alone and never to take unnecessary risks.

The site design firm that does not include environmental services or brownfield services within its practice should prepare and train at least some of its staff to be familiar with the H&S requirements and practices used on such sites. The general contractor may require the design firm to submit its H&S plan as part of the requirements to work on the site. While it may not be required for the professional staff working on a redevelopment project to have the 40-hour safety course, a shortened 8- or 24-hour version may be appropriate, particularly for personnel that might be expected to be in the field.

The firm should consider drafting and adopting its own health and safety plan that will establish policies and procedures for protecting the health and safety of its employees during operations associated with site investigation and construction activities. Due to the unpredictable and hazardous nature of these operations, it is impossible to identify, evaluate, and control all possible hazards in a generic document. Strict adherence to the plan will reduce, not eliminate, the potential for injury. It should be made clear to employees that the firm cannot and does not guarantee the health and safety of on-site personnel, and it is the responsibility of field personnel to maintain an awareness while in the field, to observe safety protocols, and to report all potential hazards to the site manager and the firm's own project manager. The generic health and safety plan should address pertinent sections of 29 CFR 1910 and 29 CFR 1926 including procedures for accident prevention, personal protection, and emergency response. All affected employees should be trained and required to read the plan. Employees should be asked to confirm their training by signing an acknowledgment form.

The firm's plan can be developed in lieu of a site-specific health and safety plan. In the absence of a contractor-generated, site-specific health and safety plan, employees should be instructed to adhere to the methods and means described in the company plan. When a site-specific health and safety plan has been developed for a project, employees should be instructed to follow the more stringent plan.

Typical hazards associated with project sites include slip, fall, and trip hazards, hazardous materials, confined space, electrical shock, and risks to personnel from moving equipment. This plan includes programs for accident prevention, personal protection, and emergency response. The purpose of this plan is to ensure safe working conditions and to prevent health risks, environmental incidents, and exposures to hazardous materials during execution of site activities. The *accident prevention plan* is required to ensure that the employees are properly trained, appropriate personal equipment is provided, and safe operating procedures are followed. This section also includes management controls to ensure that the rules and regulations of the site health and safety plan are enforced. Although it is the responsibility of all individuals to work safely, responsible supervisory personnel should be clearly identified.

All employees should be given a general project overview and specific direction regarding their specific work tasks on site. An important part of this process includes information regarding site safety requirements. Specific project information should be provided to staff visiting the site by the project manager. Risks from potential contaminants that could be encountered, safety measures taken to avoid safety incidents and environmental releases, safety equipment availability and use, and emergency response should all be discussed. Some of the risks on brownfield sites may not be obvious construction site risks but rather the risks associated with unseen contamination.

Personal hygiene and the handling of work shoes and clothes worn on the site should be discussed. After on-site project work has been completed, all staff should be encouraged to practice good personal hygiene. This would include thorough washing of hands or other parts of the body that may have come in contact with contaminated materials, proper disposal or decontamination of coveralls, gloves, and equipment, and proper decontamination of respirators. When possible, all disposable personal protective equipment and disposable sampling equipment should be bagged or drummed and left at the site for proper disposal. In most cases staff will be working under Level D conditions, as shown in Table 7.1. This is the least stringent level of protection; however, it should not be confused with the absence of contamination. In areas where *permissible exposure limits* (PELs) are not exceeded for respiratory hazards, Level D PPE may be worn. Level D PPE may include a protecting coverall, safety shoes, gloves, hard hat, and safety glasses. As a precautionary measure, professional staff visiting brownfield sites should be encouraged to not wear the same boots home and should wash clothing soiled on the site separately. These steps will minimize the risk of bringing residues into the home. Such residues may remain in carpets and fabric for many years and represent an exposure risk to children who tend to play on floors.

In the event of an accident or an observed unsafe condition, employees should be instructed to report promptly to the project manager. Typically, the project manager will assume the responsibility of site safety officer for the firm. The project manager should be sufficiently trained and be experienced in site safety, environmental, and construction industry issues.

The used disposable PPE should be properly disposed of as part of the site cleanup. When it is not practical to leave the disposable PPE at the site, plastic bags containing the PPE should be returned to the firm for proper disposal.

Employees should be instructed to follow all of the safety and health practices in place on the site even though the

Table 7.1 Levels of Personal Protection

Levels of protection are described as the characteristics and equipment associated with various environmental conditions that might be found on brownfield sites. They are presented in decreasing levels of protection.

Level	Conditions	Required Equipment
Level A	Substances harmful to the skin Substances may be absorbed through skin Possible splash or emersion risks May involve confined space Low oxygen level or increased levels of toxic concentrations in air	Full face, positive-pressure supplied air Chemical-resistant clothing and gloves Chemical-resistant boots
Level B	Less skin protection required	Full-face, positive-pressure supplied air required Chemical-resistant clothing required Chemical-resistant gloves and shoes
Level C	Hazardous substance will not be absorbed through skin Adequate level of oxygen (>19.5%)	Full-face or half-mask respirator (NIOSH approved) Chemical-resistant clothing Chemical-resistant gloves
Level D	Minimal protection Low risk of splash or emersion Low risk of inhalation or contact	Coveralls Chemical-resistant shoes and gloves Hard hat

degree of risk or hazard seems slight. Violation of safety standards should be considered a serious breach of conduct. All staff should be equipped with, and wear as a minimum, approved steel-toe work boots and an approved hard hat. Prior to assignment to a project where wearing a respirator is required, a fit test and medical approval to wear a respirator is required.

In accordance with 29 CFR 1910.120, a medical surveillance program should be initiated for employees who meet the requirements stated. Under normal conditions it is unlikely that employees of the site design firm will be exposed to site conditions that require a medical monitoring program. The following employees would require a medical surveillance program:

1. All employees who are or may be exposed to hazardous substances or health hazards at or above the PEL for these substances, without regard to use of a respirator, for 30 days or more a year

2. All employees who wear a respirator for 30 days or more a year

3. HAZMAT site workers or emergency response employees as specified in 29 CFR 1910.120

Professional Practice

The design professional is charged with protecting the public health and safety, and landscape architects include a stewardship ethic among the basic tenets of the profession. Brownfield redevelopment in some ways offers a new dimension for these principles of professional practice. The redevelopment of brownfields serves communities by stabilizing potentially contaminated properties. Remediation or mitigation of contamination eliminates the pathways of exposure and health risks. Revitalized properties may employ more people or draw people to an area, improving the local economy. The redeveloped property may also serve to reinvigorate other property owners or at least remove a blemished property from the local landscape. The design of these improvements is an important undertaking, involving the protection of public health and safety, protection of the environment, a client's interests, and rights and the interests of the design professional.

The brownfield redevelopment is like any other site design project except with regard to contamination, which adds an unfamiliar facet to the professional's responsibilities. This is particularly true when the site design involves managing contamination in place. As mentioned in Chap. 3, the life of the design may not equal the life of the contamination. Design professionals may be faced with a new dilemma; how to balance their advocacy for their client and design for the protection of the public and the environment. Life cycle analysis may reveal that the future costs of maintenance or obsolescence are too great for a project to cover the costs of obsolescence at the end of a project's functional life. Site use limitations may be so significant that the permissible uses are incongruent with the neighborhood or have such low margins that the resources to fund future maintenance are unlikely. As new developers enter the brownfield marketplace, the financial model on which they based previous projects may not be applicable. While it is not the design professional's role to manage or even share knowledge of their client's business affairs, it would be consistent with sound professional practice to inform the client of these anticipated atypical project costs.

Design professionals are routinely asked for cost projections in the normal course of their responsibilities, and most approach such estimates cautiously. The courts have found that clients have a right to rely on the project cost estimates provided by a design professional. In most cases only construction estimates are requested; however, construction or initial costs that are to be included should also be discussed. In general, the costs of preconstruction remedial actions are not included in construction costs but could be part of an initial cost projection. When costing remedial actions, it is suggested that local unit costs be given along with an estimate of the number of units rather than a single lump-sum estimate. Volumes estimated in place may have significant expansion characteristics when excavated, particularly if wetted to keep dust down. For projects where the remedial action is completed before construction, the estimates of construction costs would include items similar to any development project. When estimating the costs associated with mitigation or engineering controls, there is a tendency to compare these activities to more familiar construction. For example, a capped site may be designed to serve as a parking lot, but the costs of that parking lot will be higher. Construction costs on such a site will be higher. Prior to submitting a construction estimate, the preparer should clearly establish what is to be considered and included.

The preparation of the initial cost or construction cost estimate will not reveal higher maintenance costs. Projects driven from an initial cost standpoint may presume operation and maintenance (O&M) costs based on previous experience that do not include the anticipated higher maintenance costs and shortened life cycle of pavements and vegetation on some brownfield sites. If these higher O&M costs were known, the economic consideration of the project might shift from initial costs to O&M costs.

The site design process should encourage early planning, and practitioners should be prepared to reach out to the environmental professionals working on the site. Being familiar with the ESA process and participating as the site character unfolds are important to the design professional's ability to lead the project. The environmental professional will tend to remain active in the project only as required for the assessment and remediation phases. It is the design professional that will be called upon to lead the project through the land planning process and many formal and informal meetings. It is important that the designer understand the character of the site well enough to articulate it to others as a matter of course. The site designer must also be open to new ideas and be prepared to solve new problems in the design. To do this, he or she must recognize and use the best principles of design and adopt a holistic point of view toward the site, the constraints, and the environment.

Brownfield redevelopment is a relatively new field of site development, and all practitioners are learning to some extent as they go. It is important that design professionals work only in areas where they are qualified. On its face, this may appear to preclude work on brownfield sites; in fact, there is little that is unique about brownfield sites except for the issues of contamination. While the site designer should be conversant with the language of the environmental professional, the site designer should not replace the environmental professional unless he or she has the requisite expertise. In this way the brownfield project is a collaboration between the professionals. The ability to discuss the project in the nomenclature of the environmental professional is important to the design professional in his or her role as the lead professional through the design and development stage. The environmental professional will provide the project with the expertise to remain consistent with professional practice regarding the remediation or mitigation procedures and compliance with laws, regulations, and permit conditions.

Ethics

Professional ethics are the personal responsibility of every professional. Landscape architects and engineers are licensed for the expressed purpose of protecting the public health and safety. By law, this is generally described as being in the form of protecting the public from the poor practices of unqualified designers, but as a matter of ethics, most professionals would agree that they perceive this as a duty to be expressed within the design. This is a duty that is discussed in terms of absolutes that are rarely found in practice. Brownfield projects often result in the use of strategies that acknowledge a risk, albeit a small one, to the public. In some projects workers are exposed to a higher risk than would be acceptable for the general public. These conditions are rarely expressed as or understood to be absolutes. Staff members may not be comfortable by what may be perceived as ambiguous or the lack of absolutes in the descriptions of brownfield risks.

Site design itself is, of course, rarely an exercise in absolutes. Designing grades, traffic patterns, or storm water facilities or the selection of paving material all include inherent, but familiar risks. It may be the unfamiliarity of the brownfield risks that is a concern to staff. Design firms are often unique mixes of talented people and are usually best managed in an environment of openness and trust. In such an environment managers must be sensitive to the dynamics of the group. On occasion some members of the firm will express concerns that managing contamination in place is not ethical, or is not consistent with protecting the public health and safety. These aspects of working on brownfield projects may be a change in the typical practice and perhaps should be discussed to elicit the feelings and attitudes about such work. This effort would also afford the project manager an opportunity to talk about the real risks associated with a particular site.

A properly managed and designed brownfield site is by definition an improved environmental condition. While in many cases this may involve leaving contamination in place, the decision to do so is based on sound risk-cost-benefit judgment. On sites where the contamination is very low or where there is no pathway to exposure, removal of the material and shipping it somewhere may present a greater risk than simply leaving it in place. In other cases, the cost of removal or aggressive treatment may be so high as to make the project unfeasible, in which case nothing is done and the site remains a potential source of exposure. Brownfield site strategies are sometimes an amalgamation of the best that can be done within the economics of a project, but they must always improve the environmental conditions of the site.

As in every project, the design professional must understand the parameters of the project. Particularly when dealing with the general public, there must be no misrepresentation of risk. It has become a practice on brownfield projects for firms to take a share of the risk by taking an equity role in the project. Every firm must make a judgment as to whether they can maintain the degree of objectivity required to protect the public health and safety and whether that objectivity would be questioned in the face of what could be seen as a conflict of interest.

Working with the Environmental Professional

It may be desirable for the design firm to add staff to perform the environmental assessment services in-house or to subcontract with a firm for these services. There are many ways of selecting an environmental professional to assist in the evaluation of a property or a site. The firm may have had previous experience with a firm or individual in the past, or perhaps a lender or client may suggest qualified firms. In the end, firsthand experience with an environmental professional may be the best recommendation available. In lieu of firsthand experience, however, there are some important considerations in selecting and evaluating an environmental consultant. If a firm expects to have a continuing need for the services of an environmental services firm, it may be possible to prequalify several firms. The quality and capabilities of firms providing environmental services fill a wide range, and not all firms are able to provide all services. While the prequalification process takes some time in the beginning, it enables a design firm to quickly and confidently choose the right firm with which to work. It also assures that in making price-based selections, the choice will be from among the most qualified firms and not merely the least expensive.

PREQUALIFICATION

The key in selecting a firm with which to work is to match their capabilities and productivity as closely as possible to the requirements of the project. Since there are many firms competing for work, it is often difficult to identify the best firm. Within a given firm, however, the individual environmental professionals should have had the education and experience necessary to undertake and complete the assignment for which they are considered. It is sometimes difficult to discern who is qualified because there are many different designations and types of environmental professionals in the marketplace.

A method designed to reduce the number of possible firms to a manageable number is the *prequalification process*. The prequalification process begins with identifying the types of services needed. Typically in development and rehabilitation, issues such as lead-based paint, asbestos, underground storage tanks, and soil contamination from previous uses of the property are anticipated problems. In demolition or renovation work, there might also be concerns about environmental and health issues during construction. While most environmental regulations are similar, there is some variability from state to state and even between local governments.

Once the general concerns are identified, *statements of qualifications and experience* (Q&E) are solicited from environmental firms. Solicitation can be advertised, or selected firms may be invited to submit their Q&E. The specific method of solicitation may be dictated by your organization. Table 7.2 is a list of typical items requested from environmental firms.

It is not necessary to rank firms as the best firm at this point; simply being qualified to do the work is enough. Each firm should be evaluated as either qualified or not qualified based on the Q&E materials. It is conceivable that all firms may be qualified to do the expected assignments, but it is likely that different firms will have unique strengths that recommend them for one assignment but not for another. For example, a firm with many years of experience with asbestos matters may have little or no experience with

Table 7.2   Typical Items Included in a Qualifications Review of Environmental Firms

A list of capabilities and services they provide
Résumés of the people who will perform these tasks, and the principles of the firm
A list of references, local references preferred
Sample reports or work products
A history of the firm
A description of similar projects undertaken by the firm, who in the firm was the project
   manager and who performed the work
A copy of the certificate of general liability, workman's compensation, and professional
   liability insurances
A list of projects completed in the last 5 years and the name of the project manager
A list of subcontractors used by the firm, including laboratories
Any previous experience with your organization
A copy of the firm's quality assurance plan (The quality assurance plan should outline
   the policies and practices employed by the firm to assure quality in your project.
   Typically these plans include sections on personnel training, the organization struc-
   ture, including identifying who is responsible for the final quality of the product,
   and the actions taken to be sure quality objectives are met.)
A profile of the firm's workforce training and certifications

underground storage tank issues. The final list of firms may include firms prequalified for different tasks; however, it may be more time-consuming to deal with many consultants and contractors on a given project. Once a firm is prequalified, proposals can be limited to the scope of work and price for a given project, and selections can be made from among the best qualified firms for the type of assignment. There are two general types of technical *requests for proposal* (RFPs). The first and most common need for an environmental professional involves the execution of well-defined tasks with limited scopes of work. These tasks include Phase I Environmental Site Assessments. Firms providing these services are usually able to provide pricing based on their experience. For this type of work, only a description of the property, the anticipated future use, and the required services are needed for the technical RFP.

The second type of RFP involves assignments that are more open-ended and more technically challenging. In these circumstances the more detail provided in the RFP, the more responsive the proposals will be. As listed in Table 7.3, the RFP should include a general description of the project including details of the existing conditions if available. It is often helpful to arrange a site visit for the environmental professionals prior to preparing their proposals. The specific outcome or deliverable that is expected should be identified in the RFP. The scope of work should break down the tasks and work elements to be performed by the EP. The assumptions that were made in determining the scope of work and the limitations should also be identified. The final work product should be stated in the scope (e.g., if the final work product is to be a report, is it to be in writing or in a presentation, and to whom is it to be addressed). The scope should also identify start and completion dates for the work. In some cases interim dates are also included. The date of the delivery of the final work product should be included. Specific staff people should be identified. It should be determined that the people evaluated to prequalify the firm are actually going to be assigned to perform or supervise the work. The design firm should always reserve the right to approve in advance any substitutions of staff on projects. Although specific contract language and conditions should be reviewed by an attorney, there are some general terms and conditions that should be understood. Contracts are the formal and binding agreement between the parties that describe the scope of work and the terms of each party's responsibilities and rights. The environmental professional's activities are limited to the scope of work described in the contract; sometimes the proposal is made part of the contract for these purposes. The cost for these services is also part of the contract.

The fee for performing the work can be based on either a *time and material basis,* a *fixed fee–lump sum* basis, or a combination of these. In the case of work performed on a

Table 7.3   Items for Open-Ended Request for Proposal

1. Location of the property
2. Character of buildings and structures (type of construction, age, general condition, previous use)
3. Past uses of the site
4. Past owners of the site
5. Anticipated future use
6. A summary of previous environmental work
7. Knowledge of special conditions or concerns on the site
8. Purpose of the work being requested
9. Objective of the assignment
10. Desired schedule

time and material basis, the environmental professional will provide an estimate of the expected fee but will bill for the actual time and material costs of completing the work. In some cases, the professional is asked for an upset or not-to-exceed figure to limit the possible fee. The project will be billed based on the time and materials spent on the job but will not exceed a given amount. When a fixed fee or lump sum fee is used, the professional and you agree that the tasks will be completed for a given fee regardless of the time spent by the professional. Each method has its advantages and disadvantages for both parties.

Under a lump sum contract, the environmental professional agrees to provide specific services for a fixed price. The price is not necessarily a reflection of the effort, time, or actual costs of the work. Lump sum work efforts usually requires a well-defined scope of work, with clear limits of work identified. The advantage of the lump sum contract is that the cost of the work is known; it will not exceed the lump sum agreed upon in the contract. The disadvantage of lump sum contracts for some types of environmental work lies in the character of the work itself. Environmental site assessments are a process of discovery, and therefore unexpected situations are often encountered that require additional work. In such cases the unpredictability of the work may require a step-by-step approach to the project. Depending on the scope of work, limitations and how the contract is set up, the lump sum method is often a disadvantage in this reiterative process.

The time and material contract allows for an estimate of the costs based on anticipated tasks. As the work effort is adjusted to the conditions discovered on site, subsequent estimates can be prepared. Invoices for time and material contracts include a breakdown as to the personnel, the rates, and hours spent on the job. The additional detail assists the project manager in managing the environmental professional.

Many contracts include an *indemnification clause* that simply says that the parties will indemnify, or reimburse each other, for costs arising from the acts of the other party. It is also referred to as a *hold harmless clause* where the parties agree not to be held liable for the damages arising out of the actions of others. There are a wide variety of indemnification provisions in contracts and the character of indemnification should be understood before being accepted. Most environmental professionals' contracts include a *limit of liability clause,* which states that the consultant will be held liable only to a figure that is equal to his or her fees on the project. Often the environmental professional will agree to remove that statement but usually, only in exchange for a higher fee.

MANAGING THE ENVIRONMENTAL PROFESSIONAL

The most common complaint heard about environmental professionals is that their clients do not understand the reports or that the reports are inconclusive. These complaints, however, are rarely expressed to the environmental professional directly. Much of the work of the environmental professional is technical and often it is prescribed by multiple regulations or laws that are intended to direct the methods and manner in which the work is performed. Just as often, the environmental professional is asked to project the meaning of limited information to a much larger site or concern. In these cases, the environmental professional must limit either the scope of the response or qualify the response by identifying the limitations of what is known or the range of assumptions. The qualifying statements often result in reports that cannot be understood by the client.

While the environmental professional has a duty to report the limitations of findings, the client is entitled to a clear understanding of what the known information may indicate. The ASTM Guidelines for Environmental Site Assessment and most other protocols call for the environmental professional to draw a clear conclusion as part of the site assessment. Buyers of environmental services should expect and insist upon a clear summary of findings and recommendations. Reports that do not provide understandable conclusions have little value. A vague report can be avoided by clearly identifying the goals and the specific questions that the environmental professional should answer. This can be done in the RFP; however, it is usually best to reiterate the objectives and expectations to the environmental professional in a start-up meeting. This level of detail will allow the environmental professional to focus his or her work on the question at hand. The environmental professional should be directed to answer those questions in the report. The environmental professional cannot make decisions for the designer; however, he or she can be expected to draw general conclusions and make recommendations based on his or her findings and experience.

The critical elements of a report are:

- A description of the objectives or purpose of the work

- A description of the actual work undertaken to answer those questions including the identification of sources of that information

- A summary of the information collected or reviewed for the report

- A summary of the laboratory analysis results
- Findings and conclusions
- Recommendations

The final arbiter of the successful client-consultant relationship is always the client. While quality and responsiveness should be expected, feedback to the consultant on project performance, both the areas of satisfaction and dissatisfaction, is also critical. The nature of brownfield sites should lead one to anticipate the unexpected. The discovery of new contamination, a previously unknown underground tank, or a myriad of other possibilities may be encountered during a project. A change order process should be discussed and agreed to at the outset of the contract. It is best if all changes in the scope of work are made in writing, always requiring the specific modifications to be itemized and the cost implications of each modification.

Areas of Opportunity

Brownfield redevelopment is one of many new opportunities for the site design practice. As society's recognition of the need to live sustainably increases, more opportunities can be anticipated. The challenge of defining the methods and materials of sustainable site design and development may be the most significant challenge faced by the design professions in the next 25 years. Already there are opportunities in finding solutions to the "undercrowding" issues faced by many cities. The flight to the suburbs and the shift from an urban industrial economy to a suburban service-information economy has left many cities with substantial numbers of empty houses, abandoned industrial districts, and block upon vacant block. Populations in many of these cities have declined steadily since the 1960s. Yet the infrastructure to support the larger population and industrial base still exists. There is growing recognition that the health of our environment and the health of our cities are inexorably correlated. Changes in public policy already on the horizon regarding storm water management, water quality, and "smart growth" can be expected to provide more opportunities in the areas of reducing the impacts of new development and encouraging the redevelopment or infill of developed areas. Finding ways to capitalize on the opportunities presented by the unanticipated open space and developable land in urban areas will be a significant facet in landscape architecture over the next 30 years.

Appendix A

EPA Region 3 Risk-Based Corrective Action Levels

Chemical	Tap Water, μg/L	Soil Industrial, mg/kg	Residential, mg/kg
Acetaldehyde	—	—	—
Acetochlor	730	41,000	1,600
Acetone	3,700	200,000	470
Acetonitrile	220	12,000	7,800
Acetophenone	0.042	200,000	1,600
Acrolein	0.042	41,000	0.14
Acrylamide	0.015	1.3	1.2
Acrylonitrile	0.12	11	8
Alachlor	0.84	72	12,000
Alar	5,500	310,000	12,000
Aldicarb	37	2,000	78
Aldicarb sulfone	37	2,000	78
Aldrin	0.0039	0.34	0.038
Aluminum	37,000	2,000,000	78
Aminodinitrotoluenes	2.2	120	4.7
4-aminopyridine	0.73	41	1.6
Ammonia	210	—	—
Aniline	1.9	1,000	1.1
Antimony	15	820	31
Antimony pentoxide	18	1,000	39
Antimony tetroxide	15	820	31
Antimony trioxide	15	820	31
Arsenic	0.045	3.8	0.43
Arsine	0.1	—	—

EPA Region 3 Risk-Based Corrective Action Levels (*Continued*)

Chemical	Tap Water, µg/L	Soil Industrial, mg/kg	Residential, mg/kg
Assure	330	18,000	700
Atrazine	0.3	26	2.9
Azobenzene	0.61	52	5.8
Barium	2,600	140,000	5,500
Baygon	150	8,200	3.1
Baythroid	910	51,000	2,000
Bentazon	1,100	61,000	2,300
Benzaldehyde	3,700	200,000	7,800
Benzene	0.36	200	22
Benzenethiol	0.061	20	0.78
Benzidine	0.00029	0.025	0.0028
Benzoic acid	150,000	8,200,000	310,000
Benzyl alcohol	11,000	610,000	23,000
Benzyl chloride	0.062	34	3.8
Beryllium	73	4,100	160
Biphenyl	300	100,000	3,900
Bis(2-chloroethyl)ether	0.061	5.2	0.58
Bis(2-chloroisopropyl)ether	0.26	82	9.1
**Bis(chloromethyl)ether	0.000048	0.026	0.0029
**Bis(2-ethylhexyl)phthalate	4.8	410	46
**Boron	3,300	180,000	7,000
Bromodichloromethane	0.17	92	10
**'Bromoethene	0.11	—	—
Bromoform	2.3	720	81
Bromomethane	8.5	2,900	110
Bromophos	30	10,000	390
1,3-butadiene	0.007		
1-butanol	3,700	200,000	7,800
Butylbenzylphthalate	7,300	410,000	16,000
Butylate	1,800	100,000	3,900
N-butylbenzene	61	20,000	780
Sec-butylbenzene	61	20,000	780
Tert-butylbenzene	61	20,000	780
Cadmium-water	18	1,000	39
Cadmium-food	37	2,000	78
Caprolactam	18,000	1,000,000	39,000
Carbaryl	3,700	200,000	7,800
Carbon disulfide	1,000	200,000	7,800
Carbon tetrachloride	0.16	44	4.9
Carbosulfan	370	20,000	780
Chloral	12	4,100	160
Chloranil	0.17	14	1.6
Chlordane	0.19	16	1.8
Chlorine	610	200,000	7,800

EPA Region 3 Risk-Based Corrective Action Levels (*Continued*)

Chemical	Tap Water, µg/L	Soil Industrial, mg/kg	Residential, mg/kg
Chlorine dioxide	0.42	—	—
Chloroacetic acid	73	4,100	160
4-chloroaniline	150	8,200	310
Chlorobenzene	35	41,000	16,000
Chlorobenzilate	0.25	21	2.4
P-chlorobenzoic acid	7,300	410,000	16,000
2-chloro-1,3-butadiene	14	41,000	1,600
1-chlorobutane	2,400	820,000	31,000
1-chloro-1,1-difluoroethane	100,000	—	—
Chlorodifluoromethane	100,000	—	—
Chloroethane	3.6	2,000	220
Chloroform	0.15	940	100
Chloromethane	1.5	440	49
4-chloro-2-methylaniline	0.12	9.9	1.1
Beta-chloronaphthalene	490	160,000	6,300
O-chloronitrobenzene	0.42	230	26
P-chloronitrobenzene	0.59	320	35
2-chlorophenol	180	10,000	390
2-chloropropane	210	—	—
O-chlorotoluene	120	41,000	1,600
Chlorpyrifos	110	6,100	230
Chlorpyrifos-methyl	370	20,000	780
**Chromium III	55,000	3,100,000	120,000
**Chromium VI	110	6,100	230
Cobalt	2,200	120,000	4,700
Coke oven emissions (coal tar)	0.0057	—	—
Copper	1,500	82,000	3,100
Crotonaldehyde	0.035	3	0.34
Cumene	660	200,000	7,800
Cyanide (free)	730	41,000	1,600
Calcium cyanide	1,500	82,000	3,100
Copper cyanide	180	10,000	3,900
Cyanazine	0.08	6.8	0.76
Cyanogen	240	82,000	3,100
Cyanogen bromide	3,300	180,000	7,000
Cyanogen chloride	1,800	100,000	3,900
Hydrogen cyanide	6.2	41,000	1,600
Potassium cyanide	1,800	100,000	3,900
Potassium silver cyanide	7,300	410,000	16,000
Silver cyanide	3,700	200,000	7,800
Sodium cyanide	1,500	82,000	3,100
Thiocyanate	3,700	200,000	7,800
Zinc cyanide	1,800	100,000	3,900
Cyclohexanone	180,000	10,000,000	390,000

EPA Region 3 Risk-Based Corrective Action Levels (*Continued*)

Chemical	Tap Water, μg/L	Soil Industrial, mg/kg	Residential, mg/kg
Cyhalothrin/karate	180	10,000	3,902
Cypermethrin	370	20,000	780
Dacthal	370	20,000	780
Dalapon	1,100	61,000	2,300
DDD	0.28	24	2.7
DDE	0.2	17	1.9
DDT	0.2	17	1.9
Diazinon	33	1,800	70
Dibenzofuran	24	8,200	310
1,4-dibromobenzene	61	20,000	780
Dibromochloromethane	0.13	68	7.6
1,2-dibromo-3-chloropropane	0.047	4.1	0.46
1,2-dibromoethane	0.00075	0.067	0.0075
Dibutylphthalate	3,700	200,000	7,800
Dicamba	1,100	61,000	2,300
1,2-dichlorobenzene	64	180,000	7,000
1,3-dichlorobenzene	14	61,000	2,330
1,4-dichlorobenzene	0.47	240	27
3,3'-dichlorobenzidine	0.15	13	1.4
1,4-dichloro-2-butene	0.0013	—	—
Dichlorodifluoromethane	350	410,000	16,000
1,1-dichloroethane	800	200,000	7,800
1,2-dichloroethane	0.12	63	7
1,1-dichloroethene	0.044	9.5	1.1
Cis-1,2-dichloroethene	61	20,000	780
Trans-1,2-dichloroethene	120	41,000	1,600
Total 1,2-dichloroethene	55	18,000	700
2,4-dichlorophenol	110	6,100	230
2,4-D	61	20,000	780
4-(2,4-dichlorophenoxy)butyric acid	290	16,000	630
1,2-dichloropropane	0.16	84	9.4
2,3-dichloropropanol	110	6,100	230
1,3-dichloropropene	0.077	32	3.5
Dichlorvos	0.23	20	2.2
Dicofol	0.15	13	1.5
Dicyclopentadiene	0.44	61,000	2,300
Dieldrin	0.0042	0.36	0.04
Diesel emissions	—	—	—
Diethylphthalate	29,000	1,600,000	63,000
Diethylene glycol, monobutyl ether			
Diethylene glycol, monoethyl ether	73,000	4,100,000	160,000
Di(2-ethylhexyl)adipate	56	4,800	530
Diethylstilbestrol	0.000014	0.0012	0.00014
Difenzoquat (avenge)	2,900	160,000	6,300

EPA Region 3 Risk-Based Corrective Action Levels (*Continued*)

Chemical	Tap Water, μg/L	Soil Industrial, mg/kg	Residential, mg/kg
1,1-difluoroethane	80,000	—	—
Diisopropyl methylphosphonate (DIMP)	2,900	160,000	6,300
3,3'-dimethoxybenzidine	4.8	410	46
Dimethylamine	—	—	—
2,4-dimethylaniline hydrochloride	0.12	9.9	1.1
2,4-dimethylaniline	0.089	7.6	0.85
N,N-dimethylaniline	73	4,100	160
3,3'-dimethylbenzidine	0.0073	0.62	0.069
1,1-dimethylhydrazine	0.026	2.2	0.25
1,2-dimethylhydrazine	0.0018	0.15	0.017
2,4-dimethylphenol	730	41,000	1,600
2,6-dimethylphenol	22	1,200	47
3,4-dimethylphenol	37	2,000	78
Dimethylphthalate	370,000	20,000,000	780,000
1,2-dinitrobenzene	15	820	31
1,3-dinitrobenzene	3.7	200	7.8
1,4-dinitrobenzene	15	820	3.1
4,6-dinitro-O-cyclohexyl phenol	73	4,100	160
4,6-dinitro-2-methylphenol	3.7	200	7.8
2,4-dinitrophenol	73	4,100	160
Dinitrotoluene mix	0.098	8.4	0.94
2,4-dinitrotoluene	73	4,100	160
2,6-dinitrotoluene	37	2,000	78
Dinoseb	6.1	2,000	78
Dioctylphthalate	730	41,000	1,600
1,4-dioxane	6.1	520	58
Diphenylamine	910	51,000	2,000
1,2-diphenylhydrazine	0.084	7.2	0.8
Diquat	80	4,500	170
Disulfoton	0.24	82	3.1
1,4-dithiane	370	20,000	780
Diuron	73	4,100	160
Endosulfan	220	12,000	470
Endrin	11	610	23
Epichlorohydrin	6.8	580	65
Ethion	18	1,000	39
2-ethoxyethanol	15,000	820,000	31,000
Ethyl acetate	5,500	1,800,000	70,000
Ethylbenzene	1,300	200,000	7,800
Ethylene diamine	730	41,000	1,600
Ethylene glycol	73,000	4,100,000	160,000
Ethylene glycol, monobutyl ether	—	—	—
Ethylene oxide	0.067	5.7	0.64
Ethylene thiourea	0.61	52	5.8

EPA Region 3 Risk-Based Corrective Action Levels (*Continued*)

Chemical	Tap Water, μg/L	Soil Industrial, mg/kg	Residential, mg/kg
Ethyl ether	1,200	410,000	16,000
Ethyl methacrylate	550	180,000	7,000
Fenamiphos	9.1	510	20
Fluometuron	470	27,000	1,000
Fluorine	2,200	120,000	4,700
Fomesafen	0.35	30	3.4
Fonofos	73	4,100	160
Formaldehyde	7,300	410,000	16,000
Formic acid	73,000	4,100,000	160,000
Furan	6.1	2,000	78
Furazolidone	0.018	1.5	0.17
Furfural	110	6,100	230
Glycidaldehyde	15	820	31
Glyphosate	3,700	200,000	7,800
Heptachlor	0.0023	1.3	0.14
Heptachlor epoxide	0.0012	0.63	0.07
Hexabromobenzene	73	4,100	160
Hexachlorobenzene	0.0066	3.6	0.4
Hexachlorobutadiene	0.14	73	8.2
Alpha-HCH	0.011	0.91	0.1
Beta-HCH	0.037	3.2	0.35
Gamma-HCH (LINDANE)	0.052	4.4	0.49
Technical HCH	0.037	3.2	0.35
Hexachlorocyclopentadiene	0.15	14,000	550
Hexachlorodibenzodioxin mix	0.000011	0.00092	0.0001
Hexachloroethane	0.75	410	46
Hexachlorophene	11	610	23
1,6-hexamethylene diisocyanate	—	—	—
Hexane	350	120,000	4,700
2-hexanone	1,500	82,000	3,100
Hexazinone	1,200	67,000	2,600
HMX	1,800	100,000	3,900
Hydrazine	0.022	1.9	2.1
Hydrogen chloride	—	—	—
Hydrogen sulfide	110	6,100	230
Hydroquinone	1,500	82,000	3,100
Iron	11,000	610,000	23,000
Isobutanol	1,800	610,000	23,000
Isophorone	70	6,000	670
Isopropalin	550	31,000	1,200
Isopropyl methyl phosphonic acid	3,700	200,000	7,800
Tetraethyllead	0.00061	0.2	0.0078
Lithium	730	41,000	1,600
Malathion	730	41,000	1,600

EPA Region 3 Risk-Based Corrective Action Levels (*Continued*)

Chemical	Tap Water, μg/L	Soil Industrial, mg/kg	Residential, mg/kg
Maleic anhydride	3,700	200,000	7,800
Manganese-nonfood	730	41,000	1,600
Manganese-food	5,100	290,000	11,000
Mephosfolan	3.3	180	7
Mepiquat chloride	1,100	61,000	2,300
Mercuric chloride	11	610	23
Mercury (inorganic)	—	—	—
Methylmercury	3.7	200	7.8
Methacrylonitrile	1	200	7.8
Methanol	18,000	1,000,000	39,000
Methidathion	37	2,000	78,000
Methoxychlor	180	10,000	390
Methyl acetate	6,100	2,000,000	78,000
Methyl acrylate	180	61,000	2,300
2-methylaniline	0.28	24	2.7
4-(2-methyl-4-chlorophenoxy) butyric acid	370	20,000	780
2-methyl-4-chlorophenoxyacetic acid (MCPA)	18	1,000	39
2-(2-methyl-4-chlorophenoxy)propionic acid (MCPP)	37	2,000	78
Methylcyclohexane	6,300	—	—
Methylene bromide	61	20,000	780
Methylene chloride	4.1	760	85
4,4′-methylene bis(2-chloroaniline)	0.52	44	4.9
4,4′-methylene bis(N,N′-dimethyl)aniline	1.5	120	14
4,4′-methylenediphenyl isocyanate	—	—	—
Methyl ethyl ketone (2-butanone)	1,900	1,200,000	47,000
Methyl hydrazine	0.061	5.2	0.58
Methyl isobutyl ketone (4-methyl-2-pentanone)	2,900	160,000	6,300
Methyl methacrylate	1,400	2,900,000	110,000
2-methyl-5-nitroaniline	2	170	19
Methyl parathion	9.1	510	20
2-methylphenol	1,800	100,000	3,900
3-methylphenol	1,800	100,000	3,900
4-methylphenol	180	10,000	390
Methylstyrene mix	55	12,000	470
Alpha-methylstyrene	430	140,000	5,500
Methyl tert-butyl ether	6,300	—	—
Metolachlor (dual)	5,500	310,000	12,000
Mirex	1.2	410	16
Molybdenum	180	10,000	390
Monochloramine	3,700	200,000	7,800

EPA Region 3 Risk-Based Corrective Action Levels (*Continued*)

Chemical	Tap Water, μg/L	Soil Industrial, mg/kg	Residential, mg/kg
Naled	73	4,100	160
Nickel refinery dust	—	—	—
Nickel	730	41,000	1,600
Nitrate	58,000	3,300,000	130,000
Nitric oxide	610	200,000	7,800
Nitrite	3,700	200,000	7,800
2-nitroaniline	—	—	—
**Nitrobenzene	3.5	1,000	39
Nitrofurantoin	2,600	140,000	5,500
Nitrofurazone	0.045	3.8	0.43
Nitrogen dioxide	6,100	2,000,000	78,000
**Nitroglycerin	4.8	410	46
4-nitrophenol	290	16,000	630
**2-nitropropane	0.0013	—	—
N-nitroso-di-n-butylamine	0.012	1.1	0.12
N-nitrosodiethanolamine	0.024	2	0.23
N-nitrosodiethylamine	0.00045	0.038	0.0043
N-nitrosodimethylamine	0.0013	0.11	0.013
N-nitrosodiphenylamine	14	1,200	130
N-nitrosodipropylamine	0.0096	0.82	0.091
N-nitroso-n-ethylurea	0.00048	0.041	0.0046
N-nitroso-n-methylethylamine	0.003	0.26	0.029
N-nitrosopyrrolidine	0.032	2.7	0.3
M-nitrotoluene	120	41,000	1,600
O-nitrotoluene	61	20,000	780
P-nitrotoluene	61	20,000	780
**Nustar	2.6	1,400	55
Oryzalin	1,800	100,000	3,900
Oxadiazon	180	10,000	390
Oxamyl	910	51,000	2,000
Oxyfluorfen	110	6,100	230
Paraquat dichloride	160	9,200	350
Parathion	220	12,000	470
Pentachlorobenzene	4.9	1,600	63
Pentachloronitrobenzene	0.041	22	2.5
Pentachlorophenol	0.56	48	5.3
Permethrin	1,800	100,000	3,900
Phenol	22,000	1,200,000	47,000
M-phenylenediamine	220	12,000	470
O-phenylenediamine	1.4	120	14
P-phenylenediamine	6,900	390,000	15,000
2-phenylphenol	35	3,000	340
Phosphine	11	610	23
Phosphoric acid	—	—	—

EPA Region 3 Risk-Based Corrective Action Levels (*Continued*)

Chemical	Tap Water, μg/L	Soil Industrial, mg/kg	Residential, mg/kg
Phosphorus (white)	0.73	41	1.6
P-phthalic acid	37,000	2,000,000	78,000
Phthalic anhydride	73,000	4,100,000	160,000
Polybrominated biphenyls	0.0075	0.64	0.072
Polychlorinated biphenyls	0.033	2.9	0.32
Aroclor-1016	0.96	82	5.5
Aroclor-1221	0.033	2.9	0.32
Aroclor-1232	0.033	2.9	0.32
Aroclor-1242	0.033	2.9	0.32
Aroclor-1248	0.033	2.9	0.32
Aroclor-1254	0.033	2.9	0.32
Aroclor-1260	0.033	2.9	0.32
Polychlorinated terphenyls	0.015	1.3	0.14
Polynuclear aromatic hydrocarbons			
Acenaphthene	2,200	120,000	4,770
Anthracene	11,000	610,000	23,000
Benz[a]anthracene	0.092	7.8	0.87
Benzo[b]fluoranthene	0.092	7.8	0.87
Benzo[k]fluoranthene	0.92	78	8.7
Benzo[a]pyrene	0.0092	0.78	0.087
Carbazole	3.3	290	32
Chrysene	9.2	780	87
Dibenz[a,h]anthracene	0.0092	0.78	0.087
**Dibenzofuran	24	8,200	310
Fluoranthen	1,500	82,000	3,100
Fluorene	1,500	82,000	3,100
Indeno[1,2,3-C,d]pyrene	0.092	7.8	0.87
**2-methylnaphthalene	120	41,000	1,600
**Naphthalene	730	41,000	1,600
Pyrene	1,100	61,000	2,300
Prometon	550	31,000	1,200
Prometryn	150	8,200	310
Propachlor	470	27,000	1,000
Propanil	180	10,000	390
Propargite	730	41,000	1,600
N-propylbenzene	61	20,000	780
Propylene glycol	730,000	41,000,000	1,600,000
Propylene glycol, monoethyl ether	26,000	1,400,000	55,000
Propylene glycol, monomethyl ether	26,000	1,400,000	55,000
Pursuit	9,100	510,000	20,000
Pyridine	37	2,000	78
Quinoline	0.0056	0.48	0.053
RDX	0.61	52	5.8
Resmethrin	1,100	61,000	2,300

EPA Region 3 Risk-Based Corrective Action Levels (*Continued*)

Chemical	Tap Water, μg/L	Soil Industrial, mg/kg	Residential, mg/kg
**Ronnel	300	100,000	390
Rotenone	150	8,200	310
Selenious acid	180	10,000	390
Selenium	180	10,000	390
Silver	180	10,000	390
Simazine	0.56	48	5.3
Sodium azide	150	8,200	310
Sodium diethyldithiocarbamate	0.25	21	2.4
Strontium, stable	22,000	1,200,000	47,000
Strychnine	11	610	23
Styrene	1,600	410,000	16,000
2,3,7,8-tetrachlorodibenzodioxin	0.00000045	0.000038	0.0000043
1,2,4,5-tetrachlorobenzene	1.8	610	23
1,1,1,2-tetrachloroethane	0.41	220	25
**1,1,2,2-tetrachloroethane	0.053	29	3.2
Tetrachloroethene	1.1	110	12
2,3,4,6-tetrachlorophenol	1,100	61,000	2,300
P,a,a,a-tetrachlorotoluene	0.00053	0.29	0.032
1,1,1,2-tetrafluoroethane	170,000	—	—
Tetryl	370	20,000	780
Thallic oxide	2.6	140	5.5
Thallium	2.6	140	5.5
Thallium acetate	3.3	180	7
Thallium carbonate	2.9	160	6.3
Thallium chloride	2.9	160	6.3
Thallium nitrate	3.3	180	7
Thallium sulfate (2:1)	2.9	160	6.3
Thiobencarb	370	20,000	780
Tin	22,000	1,200,000	47,000
Titanium	150,000	8,200,000	310,000
Titanium dioxide	150,000	8,200,000	310,000
Toluene	750	410,000	16,000
Toluene-2,4-diamine	0.021	1.8	0.2
Toluene-2,5-diamine	22,000	1,200,000	47,000
Toluene-2,6-diamine	7,300	410,000	16,000
P-toluidine	0.35	30	3.4
**Toxaphene	0.0096	5.2	0.58
1,2,4-tribromobenzene	30	10,000	390
Tributyltin oxide	11	610	23
2,4,6-trichloroaniline	2	170	19
1,2,4-trichlorobenzene	190	20,000	780
1,1,1-trichloroethane	540	41,000	1,600
1,1,2-trichloroethane	0.19	100	11
Trichloroethene	1.6	520	58

EPA Region 3 Risk-Based Corrective Action Levels (*Continued*)

Chemical	Tap Water, μg/L	Soil Industrial, mg/kg	Residential, mg/kg
Trichlorofluoromethane	1,300	610,000	23,000
2,4,5-trichlorophenol	3,700	200,000	7,800
2,4,6-trichlorophenol	6.1	520	58
2,4,5-T	370	20,000	780
2-(2,4,5-trichlorophenoxy)propionic acid	290	16,000	630
1,1,2-trichloropropane	30	10,000	390
1,2,3-trichloropropane	0.0015	0.82	0.091
1,2,3-trichloropropene	30	10,000	390
1,1,2-trichloro-1,2,2-trifluoroethane	59,000	61,000,000	2,300,000
1,2,4-trimethylbenzene	12	100,000	3,900
1,3,5-trimethylbenzene	12	100,000	3,900
Trimethyl phosphate	1.8	150	17
1,3,5-trinitrobenzene	1,100	61,000	2,300
2,4,6-trinitrotoluene	2.2	190	21
Uranium (soluble salts)	110	6,100	230
Vanadium	260	14,000	550
Vanadium pentoxide	330	18,000	700
Vanadium sulfate	730	41,000	1,600
Vinclozolin	910	51,000	2,000
Vinyl acetate	410	2,000,000	78,000
Vinyl chloride	0.019	3	0.34
Warfarin	11	610	23
M-xylene	12,000	4,100,000	160,000
O-xylene	12,000	4,100,000	160,000
P-xylene	—	—	—
Xylenes	12,000	4,100,000	160,000
Zinc	11,000	610,000	23,000
Zinc phosphide	11	610	23
Zineb	1,800	100,000	3,900

SOURCE: Adapted from EPA Region 3 Risk-Based Concentrations Table.

Glossary

Americans with Disabilities Act (ADA)   Federal law enacted to protect disabled persons from discrimination in the workplace and public facilities. Title III of the Americans with Disabilities Act (ADA) requires that public buildings meet minimum standards and make reasonable accommodations for disabled persons.

aluminum   Aluminum is a naturally occurring metal. As soil pH decreases, aluminum ions present in the soil become more available, and aluminum toxicity to plants increases and may restrict root growth. Aluminum tolerance may be important in plants selected for a site with a low pH soil.

ASTM   The American Society of Testing and Materials is a standard development organization made up of volunteer members that develop technical standards through a consensus development process. Copies of the ASTM Standard Guides may be purchased from the ASTM. The ASTM is located at 100 Barr Harbor Drive, West Conshohocken, PA 19428-2959. They can be reached at (610) 832-9500. Publications can be ordered from (610) 832-9585 or on the Web at www.astm.org.

Agency for Toxic Substances and Disease Registry (ATSDR)   The ATSDR is an agency of the U.S. Department of Health and Human Services that maintains a database of

259

information on various toxic materials. Visit the *HazDat Database* or ToxFAQs pages on their Web site for information on many toxic materials: http://atsdr1.atsdr.cdc.gov.

Atterberg limits The Atterberg limits describe the variations in different soils that are a function of grain-size distribution, clay mineralogy, and organic content. Included are the liquid limit and plastic limit. The difference between the liquid limit and plastic limit is called the *plasticity index.*

benthic life Organisms that live at the bottom of streams, rivers, and lakes.

bioavailability The availability or accessibility of a chemical to an organism.

bioremediation The practice of introducing microorganism with known abilities to fix or metabolize pollutants. Also refers to the practices of adding nutrients and altering environmental conditions to promote vigor and growth in naturally occurring microorganisms.

brownfields Underutilized or abandoned properties with known or perceived environmental contamination usually associated with past industrial or waste disposal activities.

carcinogen A cancer causing substance.

cation exchange capacity (CEC) Describes ability of a soil to absorb exchangeable cations and is a measure of a soil's ability to convey nutrients to plant roots.

CERCLIS The Comprehensive Environmental Responsibility Compensation and Liability System; a list of sites suspected to have environmental contamination. Each site is investigated and ranked. The sites with the highest scores (the worst sites) are placed on the National Priority List.

chlorofluorocarbon (CFC) Inert, nontoxic chemicals used in refrigeration and air conditioning equipment, solvents, and propellants in aerosol dispensers. CFCs are persistent in the environment and act to destroy ozone in the upper atmosphere. The manufacture and distribution of CFCs was ended in the United States and other developed countries by the Montreal Accord.

coefficient of roughness (*n*) The factor representing the degree of friction between a surface and moving water.

due diligence The effort made prior to purchasing or leasing a property to investigate the conditions on a site or in a building. The measure of effort is that it be consistent with good commercial and customary practice. This has come to mean a Phase I ESA.

electromagnetic exploration (EM) Several techniques that use electromagnetic conductivity to locate buried items.

EPA The U.S. Environmental Protection Agency, the department of the federal government charged with the oversight and development of environmental regulations and programs in the United States. The EPA also oversees important research and public information and education activities. A wide variety of important programs, helpful information, and links to other environmental sites are found on the EPA's Web site http://www.epa.gov. For information on state agencies, regulations, or regulatory programs, go to the laws and regulations page and look under state programs.

Emergency Response Notification System (ERNS) A database of reported releases and spills of oil and hazardous substances.

ex situ Off site.

field duplicate An extra or duplicate sample taken for the purposes of quality control. Both samples are submitted for analysis with a different identification number. Analytical results are compared to each other for consistency.

ground-penetrating radar Down-looking radar used to identify subsurface structures and anomalies.

hazardous materials Materials defined as having a hazard by various regulations administered by the U.S. Environmental Protection Agency and the U.S. Department of Transportation. Hazardous materials are not necessarily wastes and may include products such as pesticides, cleaning agents, and water treatment chemicals.

hazardous waste Waste materials as defined by the Resource Conservation and Recovery Act, including materials that are defined as being corrosive, reactive, ignitable, and toxic, as well as materials specifically listed in the act.

Hantavirus   A virus found in rodent feces. Under dry conditions where cleanup activities may result in airborne dusts, the hantavirus may be breathed by unprotected workers. Site investigators should be aware of the risks of hanta in dry, dusty conditions associated with buildings. Care should be taken to minimize dusts, provide respiratory protection to workers and to contain all dusts.

hydrochloroflourocarbons   Substitutes for CFCs that cause less ozone damage.

innocent landowner   An innocent landowner is a person that can demonstrate that he or she acquired a property through no fault of his or her own (inheritance), in an action to secure a loan or that he or she had no knowledge or reason to know of contamination after completing research with due diligence prior to purchase.

hydraulic conductivity (K)   The measure of the permeability or infiltration rate of a soil. Hydraulic conductivity varies widely as a function of soil type and the degree of saturation.

hydrostatic testing.   Describes a number of different tests in which a vessel is pressurized and observed to identify any pressure drops that could indicate a leak.

in situ   In place or as is.

infiltration   The rate at which a liquid will travel through a porous solid or matrix of solid particles.

laboratory blanks   Laboratory-grade samples that are of known concentration that are tested with field samples to verify accuracy of equipment.

lead-based paint   Lead was used as an ingredient in paint until 1978. Lead is highly toxic and poses a health threat, especially to children. Workers should avoid breathing dusts or fumes. Workers are covered under OSHA, and contractors should comply with all requirements of 29 CFR 1926.62. Food and cosmetics should not be stored or used in work areas.

letter of no further action   A letter offered under some voluntary cleanup programs and brownfield programs that serves to notify owners that an agency contemplates no further remedial or enforcement actions. Such letters tend to be specific and subject to reopeners.

life cycle analysis   A process of evaluating all anticipated costs over the life of a project or a decision. Historically, life cycle analyses have not considered environmental externalities as part of the costs of a project.

liquid limit   The moisture content at which a soil tends to flow and lose its shape.

material safety data sheet (MSDS)   A summary of the characteristics of a material. The OSHA hazard communication standard requires an MSDS to include the material's common and chemical name, hazardous ingredients, carcinogenic ingredients, the physical and chemical hazards, and the health hazards as well as exposure limits, precautions, and safety equipment, first-aid procedures, and cleanup procedures.

matrix spike   A field sample that is spiked with a known quantity of a target analyte. The spike amount is subtracted later to determine an accurate concentration.

maximum contaminant level (MCL)   The maximum contaminant levels are established under the primary drinking water standards of the Clean Water Act and are the enforceable quantitative allowable concentrations of chemicals in regulated drinking water supplies.

minimum search distance   The approximate distance from a subject site that a database search would encompass. These distances are approximate and may be modified at the discretion of the environmental professional based on the relative density and character of a site.

mitigation   Actions taken to reduce or eliminate the affect of a contaminant such as capping a site or restricting certain uses.

National Priority List (NPL)   Established by CERCLA, the NPL is made up of over 1,200 sites from the CERCLIS list. These are the sites that scored the highest and are among the sites with the greatest hazards and risks.

National Environmental Policy Act (NEPA)   The NEPA was signed into law in 1970. The act establishes the basic environmental policy approach for federal projects.

no further remedial action proposed (NFRAP)   Under the Common Sense Initiative, the EPA purged more than 25,000 sites from the CERCLIS list by declaring them as NFRAP sites.

Occupational Safety and Health Administration (OSHA)   The federal agency charged with regulating working conditions and practices for the purpose of protecting worker health and safety in the United States. For more information, visit the OSHA home page at www.osha.org. The Web site offers search capabilities for various standards and regulatory programs.

permeability   The rate at which water will drain from a soil.

pesticides   A group of materials including herbicides, rodenticides, fungicides, nematocides, and pesticides. The toxicity and persistence of these materials vary. Many are included among the priority pollutants.

Phase I Environmental Site Assessment (ESA)   There are a number of different Phase I Environmental Site Assessment (ESA) protocols which have been developed. Some lenders have an in-house protocol or format, and different professional organizations have created recommended formats, but the most common protocol used is the American Society for Testing and Materials (ASTM) Standard Guide for Phase I Environmental Site Assessments E-1527. These guidelines are periodically updated to reflect changes in the professional practices associated with ESAs. There are other ASTM guides that may be used to guide the conduct of an assessment and the evaluation of the work.

Phase II Environmental Site Assessment   A site assessment undertaken to identify the character and extent of suspected contamination. Phase II site assessments involve the collection of samples for analysis and often require several rounds of testing before they are complete.

plastic limit   The moisture content at which a soil deforms.

plasticity index The numerical difference between the liquid limit and plastic limit; the range in which a soil will behave as a plastic material (i.e., will maintain its shape).

polychlorinated biphenyl (PCB) A regulated hazardous chemical substance used in a wide variety of products and materials including dielectric fluid in transformers, capacitors, and light ballasts. PCBs are among the priority pollutants. For more information, visit the ATSDR Web site and search for PCB on the ToxFAQs: http://atsdr1.atsdr.cdc.gov.

polycyclic aromatic hydrocarbon (PAH) A group of more than 100 chemicals that are formed from incomplete combustion and degradation of organic molecules. PAHs are believed to be carcinogens. PAHs are among the priority pollutants.

porosity The amount of pore space in a soil. It is related to particle grain size and consolidation.

potable water Water that is safe for consumption in eating, drinking, and cooking.

practically reviewable Information that is in a form that does not require extraordinary analysis in order to identify facts that are relevant to a property.

phytoremediation The use of plants to reduce or alter contamination in soils.

priority pollutants The priority pollutants are a list of pollutants given in the Clean Water Act regulations and used as a screening tool in general environmental sampling.

radon A colorless, odorless, naturally occurring radioactive gas byproduct of the decomposition of uranium. Found in varying degrees nearly everywhere. Radon tends to collect into higher concentrations in basements and crawlspaces. The EPA has established guidelines for responding to radon gas concentrations of greater than 4.0 picocuries per liter of air. Radon mitigation involves either isolation from the source of radon or ventilation. The EPA has published several mitigation guidebooks for homeowners and developers. For more information, visit the ATSDR Web site and search for Radon on the ToxFAQs page and on the *HazDat Database:* http://atsdr1.atsdr.cdc.gov. Also visit the EPA Web site at www.epa.gov.

rational method A storm water modeling technique first developed in Rochester, New York, based on using uniform rainfall intensity in a watershed, measuring the time of travel from the furthest point in the watershed to the point of discharge, to determine a peak flow for a design storm event.

recognized environmental condition The presence or likelihood of a hazardous substance or petroleum on a property under conditions that indicate a release or threat of a release to the environment. Includes conditions that might be in compliance with the law but generally does not include small or de minimis quantities, such as retail-size quantities.

remediation Any process that is undertaken to remove, clean up, or chemically change contamination into a non-toxic form.

reopeners The conditions placed on a release from liability that allow the state to rescind the liability release should these conditions not be met. Generally reopeners include a fraudulent application or documentation, actions by an applicant that exacerbate the contamination, or failure to meet cleanup objectives or maintenance agreements.

Resource Conservation and Recovery Act (RCRA) The federal law that defines hazardous waste and establishes the permitting and management process for the generation, transportation, treatment, and disposal of hazardous waste.

Resource Conservation and Recovery Information System (RCRIS) A federal database that contains information on hazardous waste generators, transporters, treatment, and disposal facilities.

responsible person (RP) A landowner or an operator of a facility is considered responsible for the environmental conditions found on a property regardless of whether the landowner or operator caused the condition.

risk-based corrective action Project objectives based on managing or reducing risk rather than simply working to a fixed cleanup concentration. Risks to human health and the environment are both considered.

sediment loading   The amount of sediment carried by a stream. The capacity to carry sediment is exponentially correlated with stream volume and velocity so that, as a stream volume doubles, the ability to convey a sediment load increases four times.

semivolatile organic compounds (SVOC)   A broad category of chemicals with a wide range of toxicity factors. SVOCs are among the priority pollutants.

soil strength   A soil's resistance to deformation or failure. Soil strength is a function of the friction between soil particles.

stakeholder   Any person or organization with an interest in a project or in the outcomes of a project.

Superfund   The popular name applied to the Comprehensive Environmental Responsibility, Compensation and Liability Act (CERCLA).

underground storage tank (UST)   When more than 10 percent of a vessel or a tank is underground, it is considered an underground storage tank, but this does not include tanks that are freestanding in basements. After December 23, 1998, all tanks must have met federal standards for corrosion protection and spill protection. There are exceptions including allowances for heating oil tanks that are used for residential purposes.

vitrification   A number of different processes, all of which accomplish solidifying or vitrifying the soil into a monolithic, impermeable mass. The vitrification process reduces impermeability and binds contaminants into the mass. Vitrification can be accomplished by adding materials such as clays or portland cement. It can also be accomplished by electrically heating the soil until the organic portions burn off and the inorganic portions melt.

volatile organic compound (VOC)   Artificial or naturally occurring organic compounds associated with petroleum products and byproducts. Many VOCs are among the priority pollutants.

voluntary cleanup program (VCP)   Voluntary cleanup programs are state initiatives created to encourage private investment into the redevelopment of brownfield sites. VCPs usually provide financial assistance or incentives, remove or reduce the liability of purchasers, and provide some predictable cleanup standards.

References

Chapter 1

Brown, Kenneth A., and Matthew W. Ward. 1997. *Building a Brownfield Partnership from the Ground Up: Local Government Views on the Value and Promise of National Brownfields Initiatives.* National Association of Local Government Environmental Officials.

Orloff, Neil, and George Brooks. 1980. *The National Environmental Policy Act: Cases and Materials.* Bureau of National Affairs. Washington, D.C.

Rogoff, Marc. 1997. "Status of State Brownfield Programs: A Comparison of Enabling Legislation." *Remediation Management,* 2nd quarter, vol. 3, no. 2.

Chapter 2

ATSDR. 1997. *ATSDR/EPA Priority Pollutants for 1997,* atsdr1.atsdr.cdc.gov.

ASTM. E-1527-97, Practice for Environmental Site Assessments: Phase I Environmental Site Assessment Process. *1998 Book of Standards, Section 11, Water and Environmental Technology,* vol. 11.04.

U.S. EPA. 1998. *Risk Based Concentration Table.* EPA Region 3. www.epa.gov/reg3hwmd/risk/riskmenu/htm.

Chapter 3

Arditi, David A., and Hany M. Messiha. 1996. "Life-Cycle Costing in Municipal Construction Projects." *Journal of Infrastructure Systems*. March 1996, vol. 2 no. 1.

McDowell, Alexander Scott. 1998. *Case Studies in Natural Attenuation*. Presented at 30th Mid-Atlantic Industrial and Hazardous Waste Conference, Philadelphia, July.

Myers, Tommy, and Ning Tang. 1998. *Natural Attenuation of Dioxins in Exposed Dredged Materials*. Presented at 30th Mid-Atlantic Industrial and Hazardous Waste Conference, Philadelphia, July.

Ott, Wayne R., and John W. Roberts. 1998. "Everyday Exposure to Toxic Pollutants." *Scientific American*. February.

Russ, Thomas. 1987. "Radon Risk Assessment and Mitigation Objectives." *Proceedings of the 1987 Speciality Conference on Environmental Engineering*. American Society of Civil Engineers. Orlando, Florida, July.

U.S. EPA. 1997. Office of Underground Storage Tanks. http://www.epa.gov/swerust/cat/natatt.htm.

U.S. EPA. 1997. Office of Solid Waste and Emergency Response. http://www.epa.gov/OUST/directiv/9200_417.htm.

Whitman, Ira. 1997. "Engineering the Remediation of Brownfield Sites," *Environmental Management*. April.

Chapter 4

Aron, Gert, and Charles McIntyre. 1990. *Permeability of Gabions Used as Outlet Control Structures in the Design of Detention Basins*. Pennsylvania State University.

Barfield, B. J., R. C. Warner, and C. T. Haan. 1987. *Applied Hydrology and Sedimentology for Disturbed Areas*. Oklahoma Technical Press. Stillwater.

Brewer, David, and Charles P. Alter. 1988. *The Complete Manual of Land Planning*. Prentice-Hall, Englewood Cliffs, New Jersey.

Center for Watershed Protection. 1996. *Watershed Protection Techniques, 1995–1996*. Baltimore.

Federal Register, vol. 60, no. 151, Monday, August 7, 1995. Rules and Regulations, p. 40230.

Dodson, Roy. 1996. "Computing Peak Flow: Which Method Is Most Rational?" *Civil Engineering News*. January.

Ferguson, Bruce, and Thomas Debo. 1990. *On-Site Stormwater Management: Applications for Landscape and Engineering*. Van Nostrand Reinhold, New York.

Jarrett, A. R., and J. R. Hoover. 1979. *Runoff and Erosion Reduction Via Drainage and Increased Infiltration*. Office of Water Research and Technology, National Technical Information Service PBBO-111917.

King County Environmental Division (Oregon). 1993. Best Management Practices for Golf Course Development and Operation.

Oregon Department of Environmental Quality. 1998. Storm Water Management Guidelines.

Pitt, Robert. 1996. "New Critical Source Area Controls in the SLAMM Stormwater Quality Model." Presented at Assessing the Cumulative Impacts of Watershed Development on Aquatic Ecosystems and Water Quality Conference, March.

Sloat, Mark S., and Hwang, Ralph B. 1989. "Sensitivity Study of Detention Basins in Urbanized Watershed." *Journal of Urban Planning and Development*. American Society of Civil Engineers, vol. 115, no. 3.

Tourbier, J. Toby, and Richard Westmacott. 1989. "Looking Good: The Use of Natural Methods to Control Urban Runoff." *Urban Land,* April.

Chapter 5

Brown, D., C. L. Hallman, J. Skogerbee, K. Eskern, and R. Price. 1986. *Reclamation and Vegetative Restoration of Problem Soils and Disturbed Lands*. Noyes Data Corp., Park Ridge, New Jersey.

Craul, P. J., and J. C. Patterson. 1991. *The Urban Soil As a Rooting Medium*. Global Releaf. American Forestry Association.

Darmer, Gerhard, edited by Norman L. Dietrich. 1992. *Landscape and Surface Mining—Ecological Guidelines for Reclamation*. Van Nostrand Reinhold, New York.

Goldman, S. J., K. Jackson, and T. A. Bursetynsky. 1986. *Erosion and Sediment Control Handbook*. McGraw-Hill, New York.

Perry, T. O. 1991. *Conditioning for Plant Growth*. Global Releaf. American Forestry Association. 1992.

Rogoshewski, P., H. Bryson, and K. Wagner. 1983. *Remedion Action Technology for Waste Disposal Sites*. Noyes Data Corp., Park Ridge, New Jersey.

Urban, James R. 1989. "Evaluation of Tree Planting Practices in the Urban Environment." *Proceedings of the Fourth Urban Forestry Conference*, St. Louis, Missouri, October.

Urban, James. 1991. Presentation at the 1991 annual meeting of the American Society of Landscape Architects, Kansas City, Missouri, November.

Zion, Robert L. 1968. *Trees for Architecture and the Landscape*. Van Nostrand Reinhold, New York.

Chapter 6

Brown, D., R. Hallman, C. Lee, J. Skogerbee, K. Eskern, R. Price, N. Page, M. Claz, R. Kort, and H. Hopkins. 1986. *Reclamation and Vegetative Restoration of Problem Soils and Disturbed Lands*. Noyes Data Corp. Park Ridge, New Jersey.

Goldman, S. J., K. Jackson, and T. A. Bursetynsky. 1986. *Erosion and Sediment Control Handbook*. McGraw-Hill, New York.

Perry, T. O. *Conditioning for Plant Growth*. Global Releaf. American Forestry Association.

Index

DISK WARRANTY

This software is protected by both United States copyright law and international copyright treaty provision. You must treat this software just like a book, except that you may copy it into a computer in order to be used and you may make archival copies of the software for the sole purpose of backing up our software and protecting your investment from loss.

By saying "just like a book," McGraw-Hill means, for example, that this software may be used by any number of people and may be freely moved from one computer location to another, so long as there is no possibility of its being used at one location or on one computer while it also is being used at another. Just as a book cannot be read by two different people in two different places at the same time, neither can the software be used by two different people in two different places at the same time (unless, of course, McGraw-Hill's copyright is being violated).

LIMITED WARRANTY

McGraw-Hill takes great care to provide you with top-quality software, thoroughly checked to prevent virus infections. McGraw-Hill warrants the physical diskette(s) contained herein to be free of defects in materials and workmanship for a period of sixty days from the purchase date. If McGraw-Hill receives written notification within the warranty period of defects in materials or workmanship, and such notification is determined by McGraw-Hill to be correct, McGraw-Hill will replace the defective diskette(s). Send requests to:

McGraw-Hill, Inc.
Customer Services
P.O. Box 545
Blacklick, OH 43004-0545

The entire and exclusive liability and remedy for breach of this Limited Warranty shall be limited to replacement of defective diskette(s) and shall not include or extend to any claim for or right to cover any other damages, including but not limited to, loss of profit, data, or use of the software, or special, incidental, or consequential damages or other similar claims, even if McGraw-Hill has been specifically advised of the possibility of such damages. In no event will McGraw-Hill's liability for any damages to you or any other person ever exceed the lower of suggested list price or actual price paid for the license to use the software, regardless of any form of the claim.

McGRAW-HILL, INC. SPECIFICALLY DISCLAIMS ALL OTHER WARRANTIES, EXPRESS OR IMPLIED, INCLUDING, BUT NOT LIMITED TO, ANY IMPLIED WARRANTY OF MERCHANTABILITY OR FITNESS FOR A PARTICULAR PURPOSE.

Specifically, McGraw-Hill makes no representation or warranty that the software is fit for any particular purpose and any implied warranty of merchantability is limited to the sixty-day duration of the Limited Warranty covering the physical diskette(s) only (and not the software) and is otherwise expressly and specifically disclaimed.

This limited warranty gives you specific legal rights; you may have others which may vary from state to state. Some states do not allow the exclusion of incidental or consequential damages, or the limitation on how long an implied warranty lasts, so some of the above may not apply to you.